GREENH*the*OUSE
gardener

ANNE SWITHINBANK

GREENHOUSE *the*
gardener

Photographs by
JOHN SWITHINBANK

FRANCES LINCOLN

Frances Lincoln Ltd
4 Torriano Mews
Torriano Avenue
London NW5 2RZ
www.franceslincoln.com

Acknowledgments

First, I would like to thank the publishers, Frances Lincoln, for allowing us
so much time for growing the plants, taking their photographs and writing
this book. In particular, editor Anne Askwith and designer Caroline de Souza
have been a fabulous team to work with, concentrating on every detail and
never flinching when alterations were suggested.

Although the majority of the photographs were taken at our garden in
East Devon, John did have to travel for some of them. Thanks go to the
following for allowing us access to their plants: RBG Kew, RHS Wisley,
West Dean Gardens in Sussex (especially for greenhouse crops),
Heligan (particularly for the photograph on page 101),
Reads of Norfolk (especially for citrus), South West
carnivorous plants and close neighbour Dennis Hunt,
who collects pelargoniums.

PAGE 1 Tomato seedlings ready for pricking out
PAGES 2–3 Multi-coloured *Cuphea hirtella*
THIS PAGE Fan-trained nectarine

CONTENTS

INTRODUCTION

If you are new to growing plants under glass, you are about to start down one of the most exciting, rewarding and therapeutic pathways gardening has to offer. Plants develop fast in the comfortable atmosphere of a greenhouse and in just one growing season you can fill your greenhouse with a jungle-like profusion of growth.

A greenhouse condenses all the dramas of the garden outside and presents them to you in close-up and at eye level. Seedlings push their way through compost, bulbs burst into growth and buds pop open right under your nose. You don't need to crouch low to admire your plants and inhale their perfume and there are new surprises every day as the processes of growing, flowering and resting unfold.

Ripening tomatoes and lengthening cucumbers rub shoulders with the shiny purple paddles of aeoniums and crisp, pine-scented foliage of pelargoniums. Toothed, succulent *Aloe vera* leaves make strong lines against blue-green dianthus and sage plants destined for the garden. Constant scene changes are wrought as plants pass through the greenhouse in their different stages of growth.

I hope this book will introduce you to these pleasures, inspire you to try growing new plants and help you make the most of your greenhouse.

The fabulously spotted and easy-to-grow *Tigridia pavonia*

The bright pink flowers of *Ixia* 'Mabel' open in summer

This book is aimed at anyone with a tiny lean-to or porch-like structure, the smallest 1.8m/6ft x 1.2m/4ft house or a larger greenhouse like my 5.2m/17ft x 3m/10ft one. Even the smallest glass space has huge potential, so if you have one and you're not already using it, store those old bikes and broken deckchairs in a shed and start growing plants. Only the lucky few will be able to heat their greenhouses to a minimum of 10°C/50°F or more during winter, so I concentrate here on what can be achieved where every effort is made to exclude frost, but there is little more heating than that. I will also show that there's even a lot you can do in a greenhouse with no resort to artificial heat at all: you can use it to give winter protection to pot-grown hardy and borderline hardy evergreens in windy areas where their foliage could easily be damaged or the plants blown over outdoors, enjoy spring bulbs and then fill it with annuals and crops during summer. The greenhouse is also a propagation unit and can become the nucleus of the whole garden.

There are so many plants to try growing in a greenhouse. Crops that struggle to yield fruit in the outdoor garden will surprise you with their generosity and abundance under glass. For some, produce will always take priority, and I notice friends who use their greenhouses exclusively for tomatoes, cucumbers, aubergines, basil and other tender crops looking at my ornamentals as if to say, 'Why is she bothering to grow them?' But to me it makes sense to use the extra warmth and protection provided by the greenhouse in as many ways as possible, and the opportunities it provides for growing flowering plants are impossible to resist.

We all like a challenge, and in gardening this means attempting to grow plants not really suited to our climate. This is not a new pastime: there were wooden plant houses and orangeries in sixteenth-century Europe. Glass roofs were not popular until the end of the eighteenth century, when standing exotic, half-hardy or tender plants outside in large containers during summer and then having an army of gardeners heave them into heated orangeries for winter became all the rage. Today on a much smaller scale many of us are still as ambitious, and a greenhouse enables us to enjoy potted bananas, cannas, olive trees, citrus and birds of paradise and the like outdoors in summer and then haul them inside during autumn in order to shield them from wet, cold weather until it is safe to put them back out the following spring.

Collections of tender bulbous plants such as pineapple bulb (*Eucomis comosa*) and *Zantedeschia elliottiana*, which need winter protection from both frost and long periods of saturation during rainy periods, are best stored inside a frost-free greenhouse during winter, while dormant in their pots, until growth resumes in spring.

A greenhouse is also a place to overwinter a wide range of tender perennials such as pelargoniums, fuchsias, argyranthemums and gazanias to use the following year as bedding plants. These are pruned back, lifted, potted and brought in during autumn, though some gardeners prefer to overwinter them as rooted cuttings to save space.

My own ornamental plant collection is the result of eclectic taste, curiosity and inability to turn down gifts from other gardeners. Sometimes, when I visit those who specialize in, say, pelargoniums, South African bulbs or cacti

and succulents, I seriously wish I could be as disciplined. Some of my permanent collection has been with me for as long as twenty years, though I might have replaced the original plants with cuttings or offsets from the same stock. I love every plant as if it is a friend and I look forward to their flowering periods as familiar markers in the year. I raise other plants annually simply because I like the look of the flower in a seed catalogue. Now and again I'll let an old friend go, and use the space to grow something new.

What I love most about greenhouse gardening is the day-to-day routine of care. I can't wait to slide the door open in the morning and take in that unique earthy, slightly perfumed, humid smell. Anyone with a caring side to their nature will love the daily rhythm of checking the plants' needs such as watering and ventilation. You can put off outdoor jobs like mowing, weeding and planting, but your greenhouse plants can't wait. We are all bombarded with urgent tasks, but own a greenhouse and you have a cast-iron excuse to disappear to it through the dewy morning garden, coffee mug in hand. Another joy of owning a greenhouse is being able to work in it when the sky is grey and rain is lashing down, or on a raw, windy day. You can still be in the garden then and enjoy as much light as possible, sheltered from the worst of the elements.

STARTING UP

1

Even though I'm passionate about greenhouse gardening, it was two years after moving to our new house and garden before we acquired a greenhouse and put it up. Until then my plants and I had to make do with a bright office and small glass porch, because the large sloping site offered no obvious place for a greenhouse to go. Eventually, as plans took shape in my head, I could see exactly where the greenhouse would sit and even how its traditional shape would look. All we had to do then was clear masses of old hedging, level some ground and find a structure we could afford. Dream a little to work out what you really want and you'll end up with a well-designed space to be really proud of. The practicalities of setting up a greenhouse are important, and although it's all about vents, heaters and hardware, kitting out your glass space will be good fun.

Sweet pea seedlings thrust their way towards the light

SETTING UP YOUR GREENHOUSE

Style

When I started to plan my current greenhouse, I looked at brochures and was spoilt for choice. I knew exactly where I wanted to put it and that I wanted a classic straight-sided, free-standing wooden greenhouse up to 6m/20ft x 3m/10ft. Aluminium is all very well, but if the greenhouse is to be a focal point in the garden and from the house, I'm afraid there's no contest: looks will win over practicalities every time with me. I'd rather have to weather-treat wood every so often than have low-maintenance aluminium.

A lean-to greenhouse is great if you have a wall to lean it against, because the vertical supplied by the wall offers many opportunities for training fruit or ornamental climbers. Solid brickwork also means better heat retention.

Curvilinear and Dutch light type houses (those whose sides slope outwards at the base) let in more light than a conventional, straight-sided house, but to my mind the former looks too commercial and the latter is great for growing crops but not so practical for runs of staging for ornamentals. I was also sold on having a brick base to raise my greenhouse off the ground, because brick not only looks good but helps insulate plants against frosts hovering at ground level.

Eventually, a second-hand greenhouse came up for sale, measuring just over 5.2m/17ft long and 3m/10ft wide. Wooden, and with upright sides to sit on a low brick wall, it was just what I was after. The structure itself cost very little and I'd already collected some beautiful old bricks. Most of my money went on paying builders to take it down and put it up again, but anyone with the time and inclination for DIY would stand to make good savings by buying a second-hand greenhouse and re-erecting it themselves.

Siting

Even if you are not handy enough to put a greenhouse up, taking a precise interest in the materials used and the exact positioning can make a big difference to its visual appeal as well as its effectiveness. My biggest input in the build lay in plotting exactly where it was to go in the corner of the kitchen garden. Two hours with measuring tape and pegs meant that I was able to look from the kitchen window right through the doorway of the greenhouse to the back wall. In an ideal world, you should find somewhere for your greenhouse that is sheltered from frost and wind, yet away from buildings or trees that might cast shade or drop leaves and even branches. Light should be able to penetrate the glass all winter long, even when the sun is low in the sky. It is generally held that the ridge of a greenhouse should run from east to west, so that one long side always faces the sun and the ridge casts less shade on the plants. However carefully you try to meet all the criteria of good siting, though, there will probably be one that won't work for you, so be prepared to make a calculated compromise.

Siting my current greenhouse was difficult, because living a mile from the sea we have a windy garden, and with river valleys on two sides it can be frosty too. I wanted the greenhouse to be in the fenced kitchen garden and luckily it was able to nestle in a corner with conifers and shrubs behind it, which provide shelter from frost and north wind without casting shade. The structure lies out of the wind and although the ridge runs north-east to south-west, this alignment keeps the wind out of the vents and the sun shines mainly into one side throughout the year. Fortunately, the distribution of light is ideal for the plants I grow.

A newly installed greenhouse may look stark at first, but with imaginative planting it will settle into the garden within a year

LEFT A mixture of hard materials makes an attractive entranceway
RIGHT The late-summer display is damped down and well ventilated

Water and electricity

When deciding on a site, you need also to take into account sources of water and electricity, if you want to use it. A supply of mains water is always handy, even if you store rain water in butts for general use. I have a tap fixed just outside the greenhouse, because that way the hosepipe won't take up valuable indoor space. But an indoor tap has the advantage that it will not need lagging against frost. Electricity means that you can have a light and sockets for propagators and heaters.

Planning a greenhouse in a garden undergoing renovation is easier than in an established one because you can dig a trench out from the house, or wherever your electricity and water originate. The pipes and cables for these can easily be buried underground without disturbing paths, lawn and borders. Needless to say, installing water and electricity has to be done in a proper and safe way without overloading the system and is usually a job for professionals. Make a note of where the cables and pipes lie underground and keep this with copies of your house deeds; this way the information can easily be passed on to any future owners – besides which, unless the services run under a path or along an obvious route, you will quickly forget where they are and may need a reminder before tackling other jobs.

Beds, borders and paths

Some kind of site preparation will always be necessary for a greenhouse, even if it is just making an area flat, ready to take a base that comes with a kit. At this stage, you need to plan whether to have a solid concrete floor or a concrete floor with beds.

Sometimes all that is needed is a plinth for the sides to stand on and a few slabs to make a pathway up the middle. A soil bed under the staging provides plenty of planting opportunities and creates humidity. It is better than concrete, because like the plants, it retains and evaporates water, helping the interior stay cooler in the heat of a summer's day. Soil also means that plants can root themselves into the bed, where they will romp away and need less care. The disadvantage of a soil floor is that you have to grovel about on hands and knees weeding and planting.

A concrete floor can be damped down regularly (see page 179) and provides a solid base on which to stand large plants in pots, where they will drain well and worms won't be able to burrow their way up into the compost. I opted for a concrete floor with a bed at the far end of my greenhouse, but I often wish I'd left a bed for crops all the way down the sunniest side as well.

Height, doors and vents

When ordering a new greenhouse, don't just accept what you are offered. Often the manufacturer can be flexible enough to add extra vents in the roof and sides. In general, a greenhouse should have ridge ventilation equivalent to 20 per cent of the ground area. That means for a 1.8m x 2.5m/6 x 8ft greenhouse three average-sized vents; for a 2.5 x 3m/8 x 10ft greenhouse four vents; for a 3 x 3.7m/10 x 12ft greenhouse six vents. If the model you like does not come with side vents, ask if several louvre-type panes can be supplied to replace some of the side and even end panes. Louvres are good for letting in air while protecting against wind and rain. Adequate side – and therefore lower – ventilation is important because cooler air enters, heats up, rises and escapes through the top vents.

One would think that automatic vent openers would be the ideal solution for the problem of ventilation, but

I've never got on with the things. They don't seem to open soon enough for me, especially in winter, and whatever setting I put them on, I always have a random urge to override the system. But I am lucky and work from home, which enables me to check the greenhouse and make adjustments according to the weather. For those out at work all day, automatic vent openers are a great bonus, but you will need to watch to make sure that they are working properly.

If ordering a greenhouse without seeing and experiencing an actual model, pay particular attention to the height inside. If all you can afford or accommodate is a tiny 1.8m/6ft x 1.2m/4ft greenhouse, you will still have lots of fun; for two years, this was all I had to play with and I really enjoyed my small glass space. But I'm only 1.6m/5ft 3in tall and could at least stand up in it. Think too about doorways. In a larger greenhouse, it's really handy to be able to fit a wheelbarrow through the entrance. Folk restricted to wheelchairs can enjoy greenhouse gardening, but the door will need to be wide enough and the entranceway smooth.

Shading

Shading the glass is essential for the well-being of plants inside and helps keep temperatures down during summer as well as protecting delicate leaves from scorching. Although there are cheap, temporary arrangements for providing shading (see page 179), this subject deserves some thought in the planning stages.

The ideal shading for a greenhouse is provided by old-fashioned slatted blinds, fixed on a roll to the outside of the roof. They look great and deflect heat before it enters the glass, and you have the option of letting the shading down on really hot, scorching days and rolling it back up (usually on a pulley system) when dull weather means that you want as much light as possible to enter. I think these types of shading are too heavy for light-hungry crops like tomatoes and physalis but ideal for decorative plants.

There are cheaper options involving narrow, cane-like material and a range of interior blinds. Most greenhouse gardeners, though, opt for pinning up their own shading or painting it on the outside (see page 179).

A removable shelf helps accommodate young plants in spring

Staging

When ordering a new greenhouse, you will have the option of buying staging at the same time. I think slatted staging is great, because it allows you to grow plants of different sizes and types needing completely different watering regimes cheek by jowl: excess water simply drips away and falls to the floor. Some staging consists of solid metal sheets, with slightly dished areas designed to make water stand, and these are ideal to take capillary matting or horticultural-quality sand (see page 178). However, if you have slatted staging you can stand metal trays on top of it or not according to what you are growing.

Before buying manufactured staging, it is worth working out whether you can make your own or have it made just as cheaply. If you can, the advantage is that you might be able to make it better looking and sturdier; and you can have it made to precisely your own specifications of height, width and depth. I have a movable shelf to add during busy periods. When my greenhouse is in peak production for three months during spring I need staging along both long sides. So I'm about to design two sections of wooden staging that are hinged so that I can fold them away and store them when I clear the way for growing bags for tomatoes. If you make your own staging, use treated timber and it won't rot away in the damp.

LEFT Seeds and cuttings snug in a heated propagating case
MIDDLE Clay pots filled with bulbs, ferns and winter flowers
RIGHT Wooden pressers create a smooth, flat surface for seeds

Heaters

If you want to grow a wide range of frost-tender plants, heating is a necessity. Having bought your greenhouse, therefore, your next big purchase will be a heater to see these plants through winter. I like thermostatically controlled electric fan heaters because they are neat, controllable and don't cause any condensation; in fact, they are good for air circulation. But not all greenhouses have the luxury of an electricity supply, and even if yours does, what do you do if there's a power cut or your heater suddenly packs up? The best plan is to have a cheap paraffin heater and keep some fuel handy during winter in case you need it. Paraffin heaters are usually basic contraptions with no thermostatic control and they need regular maintenance to keep the fuel topped up and the wick trimmed to reduce fumes.

These heaters also increase humidity, which is best avoided during winter. Opening a vent to give a tiny crack of air is often advisable to avoid fumes and keep the air moving. Bottled gas heaters are an option, but there's the danger that the gas bottle might run out at a critical moment. A switchover valve allows a second bottle to take over when the first runs out. Again, a small degree of ventilation is advisable to combat condensation and the build-up of fumes.

Basic kit

THERMOMETER A maximum-minimum thermometer is a crucial item. Without this, you will have no idea how low temperatures dropped during the night. You will also need it to monitor high day temperatures during summer.

PROPAGATING CASE A thermostatically controlled, heated propagating case will enable you to make early sowings and will help some cuttings to root quickly.

POTTING BENCH OR TIDY This is essential to hold compost and for working on. It needs to be movable, so that you can stand it on a small temporary table in or outside the greenhouse. I sometimes work on a wooden board on the staging, but when this is needed for plants to stand on, I revert to a plastic potting tidy that stores away under the staging when not in use. Whatever you use, make sure that it is at the right height to prevent backache.

HAND BRUSHES You'll need these to sweep up compost and debris on the staging. I use old wooden shoe-polishing brushes because they are both useful and attractive. A soft broom for cleaning glass and a hard-bristled broom for sweeping the floor, plus a dustpan and brush, will help you keep the greenhouse clean inside.

WASTE BINS Keep two buckets on the go, one for organic waste to put on the compost heap and the other for plastic rubbish.

POTS AND CONTAINERS A good variety of pots will cater for all eventualities, so collect all sizes from 8cm/3in upwards, including the half pots so useful for seed sowing, where width rather then depth is required – and

LEFT Watering cans are indispensable items of kit
MIDDLE Keep a variety of canes and twiggy sticks handy as supports
RIGHT Collect frames and obelisks for climbers such as jasmine in pots

using these will save on compost. Collect both plastic and clay. Large plastic pots are especially useful for crops. Plants seem to grow equally well in clay and plastic pots, but clay look better, even if they are more cumbersome to carry around. If anyone offers you the chance to forage for old clay pots in a neglected garden, grab it; otherwise, gradually build up a collection of new ones. They soon weather and look superb. Keep a few hanging baskets, which are ideal for trailing plants and fill that empty space in the ridge of the greenhouse. Trays and crates are useful too, for collecting batches of plants in small pots and transporting them around, for instance when hardening off.

POTTING COMPOST should be used fresh, so don't keep too much in stock. A bag each of John Innes No. 2 (a basic loam-based potting compost), soil-less multi-purpose potting compost, and grit or sharp sand, and a small pack of fine vermiculite should meet most of your needs (see also page 26).

PRESSERS For seed sowing, a variety of wooden pressers (pieces of wood with flat surfaces) in round and rectangular shapes are great for producing the smooth, flat surface you need.

A TRUG Keep a small trug or something similar filled with labels, a lead pencil, a slender dibber (I use a slim plant cane sharpened to a blunt point) for planting seedlings and cuttings, rust-proof secateurs, the pressers, and garden string and raffia. Don't store seed packets in the greenhouse, because it will be too damp.

STAKES AND SUPPORTS A variety of plant stakes and supports are vital. Keep flexible wire, split canes, bamboo canes, twiggy sticks and metal obelisk-type structures made to fix into pots for climbing plants.

WATERING CANS Ideally you should have a collection of three: one small 2 litre/3½ pint type fitted with a very fine rose (sprinkler) for seedlings and small plants, and two larger 7–10 litre/1½–2 gallon cans.

KNIFE A straight-bladed pocket knife for taking cuttings is essential. Mine lives in my pocket permanently, along with a small polythene bag in which to keep cuttings fresh. To keep that knife razor sharp, you'll also need a sharpening block and some oil. Most straight-bladed knives have a sharp edge on only one side, so push this in one direction along the oiled stone, and afterwards make one push on the other side to remove any burrs.

SPRAYER You'll need a small graduated pressure sprayer for applying chemicals, even if you only use horticultural soft soap. Use an old sprayer for shading paint.

LABELS Label pots of seeds and cuttings, as you're likely to forget what's in them. Include the date of sowing or striking for reference and where they came from, in case you want to reorder from the same supplier.

RAISING PLANTS FROM SEED

Although buying ready-germinated seedlings, plantlets and mature plants saves time, you can't beat raising your own plants from seed. Apart from the challenge and satisfaction, there are other advantages to be had from doing so. Large numbers of plants are usually cheaper if grown from seed, but the overwhelming plus is choice, whether it is a tomato cultivar, a single colour of antirrhinum or an unusual tender plant.

The biology of seeds

Seeds are fascinating objects containing everything necessary to create a new plant. All this potential life is held dormant inside a tough outer seed coat until the right conditions trigger germination. Seeds can survive harsh conditions far more effectively than their parents and in many cases are a means not just of procreation but also of surviving drought and freezing cold winters. Although seeds vary considerably from one plant species to another, most seeds that the greenhouse gardener is likely to encounter will respond to one basic logical method of germination.

In order for a seed to break dormancy and start the process of germination, the contents need water, and this has to enter through the seed coat. Stored food then becomes available to provide energy for the embryo plant to grow. So by sowing the seed into good moist seed compost and providing an optimum temperature, you will enable germination to take place. When this happens, first the root of the new plant pushes down into the compost and begins to take in both water and minerals, and then the new shoot grows upwards towards the light.

Predictably, there are complications, especially where seeds are influenced by so-called germination inhibitors or have especially hard coats. These are usually measures the plant has evolved to make sure that it will germinate only when conditions are absolutely safe for the seedling to grow in. There are ways to breach these defences and allow water to enter, so that the process of germination can start. Usually, a soaking in water washes away chemical inhibitors and softens the seed coat. Seeds armed with extra-thick coats often respond to being nicked carefully – without damaging the layers beneath – with a knife or rubbed with sandpaper, to let in water. Some – the seeds of *Strelitzia reginae*, for example – even respond to the extreme of having boiling water poured on them.

Storage

Seeds must be kept cool and dry to remain fresh and viable, so as soon as I buy packets or they arrive through the post, I store them away in old biscuit tins, sometimes with one of those little silica-filled packets that come with new handbags to absorb dampness. Keep the tin in the house, somewhere cool and dry.

Germination

Successful germination depends more than anything else on common sense. Deciding where to put the seeds to germinate is crucial and depends on the type of plant and time of year. Most seeds arrive with instructions as to what temperature is ideal for germination. Many, including bedding and greenhouse display plants, need warmth to germinate (15–22°C/60–72°F). They may also need a late-winter or early-spring sowing to give them the time they need to grow and flower during the coming growing season. A heated propagating case will be the best place for seeds, especially in an otherwise barely heated greenhouse, but if you cover the sown seed with polythene or glass to keep the moisture in, you could place them in a warm room indoors to germinate instead. The same goes for sowings of tomatoes, melons, cucumbers and other tender crop plants.

HOW TO SOW

Although seeds and their requirements vary, there is a basic sowing method that is suitable for bedding plants and most other tender plants raised in the greenhouse.

1 Fill a container with seed compost (see page 26), pushing down lightly with a presser to achieve a smooth surface. If you don't have a presser, use the base of a pot. To fill cells with compost, pour it over the top and push it down lightly into all the cells before brushing away the excess with your hand.

2 I then water the compost, using a fine rose on the can, to make sure that the surface is moist. Use tap water for seeds and seedlings, as rain water collected in a butt might be infected with disease spores.

3 Sow seed thinly over the prepared compost surface of pots and trays; or if you are using cells make a small depression with your finger in each cell of compost and put one or a small sprinkle of seeds in each depression, depending on type.

4 I take a handful of compost, avoiding lumps, and sprinkle it lightly over the surface to cover the seed by no more than its own depth. Some gardeners find it easier to use a sieve for this. Some tiny seed does not need covering at all. Press lightly again, to bring the seed into contact with the moist compost.

5 I give large seeds another light sprinkling of water, but leave small seeds alone. Some gardeners like to do all their watering from below, by standing the sown container in a pan of water for a while. Always label the seeds with their name and the date they were sown.

LEFT Germinated seedlings at the right stage for pricking out
RIGHT Pricking out grid fashion is a useful, space-saving method

As the sun rises in the sky and it grows hotter, you will need to shade a propagating case to prevent the seeds and seedlings inside from cooking. A simple way to do this is to spread some fleece, newspaper or even thin brown paper over the top and weigh it down. Towards summer, you may need to turn the case off altogether but continue to use it, shaded from sun.

Later in the spring and during summer, seeds will germinate in the natural warmth of the greenhouse without needing a propagating case. This is the time to sow seeds not expected to perform within a tight timeframe, including herbaceous plants and some biennials (such as honesty and foxgloves), as well as a wide range of decorative plants, cacti and succulents. Seeds should not dry out, so cover with polythene or glass and shade from harsh sun. Large seeds like those of French and runner bean will be protected by their covering of compost and will stay moist without further protection.

After germination, remove pots of seedlings from a propagating case promptly, or alternatively take off the glass or polythene. It is important that seedlings develop in good light and, usually, at cool temperatures. This stops them from becoming etiolated (long and drawn) and making too much soft growth. Avoid overwatering, especially early in the year, as this, along with bad ventilation and overcrowding, will encourage damping off disease (see page 183).

Pricking out

When the seedlings are large enough to handle, prick them out into pots or individual cells, filled with a multi-purpose compost. Alternatively, prick them out into seed trays, having first planned a grid across the surface of the compost. In an average, full-sized tray I might put 7 seedlings across the top and 5 down the side, or if they are small, 8 along the top and 6 down the side; in a half tray, 5 along the top and 4 down the side would be normal.

Transfer the seedlings one at a time, holding each by a leaf to save damaging the delicate stem. Generally, choose the healthiest and strongest, unless you are attempting to select a good colour range from a seed packet containing mixed colours (see below). Dig a hole in the compost with your dibber, put the root in and firm the seedling gently. Implausibly, tall, lanky seedlings can be planted deeper, right up to their leaves, without incurring any harm. Water the seedlings in straight away, using a fine rose (sprinkler) on the can.

When pricking out seedlings during early spring, choose a warm morning and bring the compost and water into the greenhouse to warm up first. The seedlings can then settle into their new compost and excess water will drain away before the cold of the night.

Label everything, all the time. You might think that you'll remember what you've sown or pricked out, but believe me, you won't. As I said earlier, I always include the date of sowing and the source of seed, in case I want to reorder from the same company.

Colour mixtures

Pricking out seedlings destined to yield flowers or foliage in a mixture of colours requires a different technique to that for single-colour types. The normal method of selecting the strongest, healthiest seedlings from the pot might mean you inadvertently select only one of the colours from a mix. It is important to work systematically through a patch of seedlings and take small, pale seedlings as well as dark, stronger-looking ones. This ensures that you end up with the colour mix intended by the seedsman and not just that produced by the healthiest seedlings.

Avoiding pricking out

There are ways to avoid the delicate task of pricking out, by sowing directly into cells or small pots. Exactly how this is done depends on the type, size and expense of the seed. With experience, each gardener will evolve the best method for them and their plants. I sow expensive seeds one per cell or pot, especially where there are only a few in a packet. I want every single one to survive and will sacrifice the odd cell of compost where any fail to germinate. On the other hand, I'll save space by sowing cheap, plentiful seed two or three to a pot or cell. After germination, the weakest are removed, leaving only one per unit. Most plants will fare better without the competition of close neighbours, but for a quick crop of basil, for instance, a small mass of seedlings can be allowed to grow up together like those sold in supermarkets.

Golden rules for seed sowing

GET THE TIMING RIGHT This is important for most plants, for several reasons. After germination, young seedlings and plants need to benefit from the best growing conditions. For instance, you would not want vulnerable seedlings of tender plants germinating in the middle of winter during periods of low temperatures and miserable light. Some plants are grown to a timetable that fits the seasons and use of space. Bedding must reach an ideal stage for planting out in late spring. Tender and hardy crops need maximum growing time in order to crop during summer. A large number of plants, whether destined to spend winter outdoors or under glass, need to establish in their pots before conditions turn colder and darker.

SPACE Avoid overcrowding at all stages, from spacing seeds over the compost surface (you don't have to sow every seed in the packet), to pricking out or thinning as necessary. Having potted up a batch of plants, set them close together to start with, but move them apart so their leaves are not quite touching as they grow.

HARDEN OFF The hardening-off process is essential for all plants raised under glass but destined to finish up in the garden. The transition from a warm, frost-, rain-

TOP LEFT Sowing straight into individual cells neatly sidesteps pricking out
TOP RIGHT After germination, zinnias are thinned to one seedling per cell
ABOVE Pricking out one tomato seedling per pot is just right

and wind-free environment to the outdoors needs to be managed carefully so as to let plants toughen up properly before their roots are disturbed by planting. When frost is no longer likely, stand plants outdoors, but be ready to bring them back in or wrap with fleece if frost is threatened. After a week, they should be ready for planting.

TAKING CUTTINGS

TOP Having cut under a node, remove the bottom leaves
ABOVE LEFT Insert the cuttings into gritty compost
ABOVE RIGHT Pot rooted cuttings for plenty of the perennial *Lamium orvala*

An important way of increasing plants both inside and outside the greenhouse is by taking cuttings. A similar method can be used for a wide range of ornamental greenhouse plants, hardy herbaceous perennials and shrubs. Each plant probably has an optimum time of year for cuttings to root, but I tend to be guided by what I see. After a while, you develop an eye for good material and see likely shoots on the plants waving to you like flags.

The biology of cuttings

When we take a cutting, we are exploiting a plant's natural tendency to produce adventitious roots from a damaged stem or, sometimes, leaf or leaf stalk. These roots are most likely to develop from the cambium, a layer of cells involved in the thickening of stems, and are encouraged by auxins (plant hormones). The cambium is most active at the nodes of a stem (thickened areas where leaves and buds sit), which explains why many cuttings are made by trimming just under this area. Needless to say, a stem without roots is vulnerable and prone to losing water through its leaves. This is why we sometimes have to reduce the leaf area of a cutting by removing leaves or cutting large ones in half; we also keep cuttings out of full sun and cover them with plastic or polythene to create a close, humid environment.

Taking spring stem cuttings

In spring, plants inside the greenhouse wake up and start making new growth. This is often a signal to prune tender perennial plants such as pelargonium, fuchsia, plumbago and tibouchina. Sometimes the shoots you prune away look as though they'd make healthy cuttings, but more often it is the soft re-growth after pruning that makes the best material. These are softwood cuttings and root quickly. Short lengths of new shoots can often be pulled away from the parent plant with a small heel of older wood attached and these make ideal cuttings.

Outside, herbaceous plants are sending up new shoots and these, too, root fast and well. We usually think of bulking up our herbaceous perennials by dividing them, but a box of basal cuttings – basal shoots turned into cuttings and inserted into a tray or pot of gritty cuttings compost – is far more productive. Again, if you are careful, you can peel these shoots from the crown of the plant in such a way as to bring a small section of older wood away too. This saves cutting into the soft stems. The type of herbaceous perennials I am always bulking up by taking cuttings includes border geraniums, centaurea and *Lamium orvala*.

Shrubs such as hydrangea and buddleja also root well from spring cuttings.

HOW TO TAKE STEM CUTTINGS

You can take cuttings of slightly softer material in spring, or harder (riper) stems in summer. using the same basic method.

1 Gather together all you'll need and then take the cuttings from the plant, here a New Zealand Christmas tree (*Metrosideros kermadecensis* 'Variegata'). Either peel away short stems with a 'heel' of older wood attached (as shown) or cut away the stems you want.

2 Using a sharp knife, tidy up any long snags from heel cuttings. Trim others to length by cutting just beneath a node (this is the area where leaves join the stem). Most cuttings are best made short, 5–10cm/2–4in long.

3 Further prepare the cutting by removing the lower leaves, leaving a clear stem at the base. Nip out soft growing tips to prevent wilting. If dealing with cuttings of a large-leaved plant, cut the leaves in half to reduce moisture loss.

4 Insert into a pot or tray of moist, gritty compost. Most root better and faster if dipped into hormone rooting compound first, but some don't (such as figs and pelargoniums). Cuttings tend to root better around the edge of the pot and most prefer being slightly crowded.

5 Water the cuttings in gently, with a rose (sprinkler) on the can. Use tap water rather than butt water, as the latter may contain disease spores. Label and place the pot in a shaded propagating case, or inside a loosely knotted polythene bag out of full sun.

Rooted cuttings of shrubby *Phlomis lanata* ready for potting

Taking summer stem cuttings

During mid- to late summer the young stems on shrubby plants begin to toughen up and this is the best time to take semi-hardwood or semi-ripe cuttings from a wide range of plants, both indoor and out. These will have slightly tougher bases but may have soft tips, which are vulnerable and often best pinched out to avoid wilting and moisture loss. Again, it is often possible to pull away from the main stem side shoots of an optimum 8–10cm/3–4in length, furnished with small heels of last year's wood attached.

Towards the end of summer, take cuttings of tender perennials to keep in the greenhouse over winter as young plants. Many of these are used as bedding plants outside in the summer, and taking cuttings saves having to lift, pot and accommodate a lot of large old stock plants.

The best compost for rooting cuttings is 50:50 soil-less multi-purpose compost and grit or sharp sand. If you can't find good grit, then fine perlite or vermiculite (both inert materials) will do instead. I find that for most plants, hormone rooting compound helps both the speed and quality of rooting, as long as the product you use is fresh.

Aftercare

Make sure that cuttings are well rooted before removing the polythene or taking them from the propagating case. Try to resist the temptation to pull the shoot to see if there is resistance from the hoped-for roots. The best way to test for rooting is to watch for fresh growth on the top, though some cuttings make this without having grown roots. Another way is to gently upturn the pot and tap the ball of compost out of the pot, to see if roots are pushing to the edge. When they are, stand the pot of cuttings on the staging for a week or more to accustom them to ordinary growing conditions. Then pot them separately, though not in the middle of winter.

Unless a plant is naturally free-branching, or you are training a standard by growing a long trunk-like stem, most shoot tip cuttings will need pinching out. After the cutting has settled into its new pot for a few days, pinch out the growing tip between thumb and forefinger. This stimulates side shoots to develop, making the plant bushier. You can continue to pinch out the side shoots if you want, to gain an even bushier plant with, potentially, more flowers.

Cuttings rooted and potted in spring must be hardened off thoroughly before being planted out.

Other ways of propagating

Although most plants can be propagated by stem cuttings, for some plants a different method is better.

ROOT CUTTINGS are a useful way of increasing herbaceous plants with fleshy roots such as eryngiums, Oriental poppies (*Papaver*), phlox, anemone, drum-headed primula (*Primula denticulata*) and perennial mulleins (*Verbascum*).

The best time to take root cuttings is during a plant's dormant season, usually from autumn to late winter. Lift the plant, cut it back, shake the roots and wash them in a bucket of water. Select a root of average thickness and cut it off close to the crown. Remove any fibrous side roots and trim to about 5cm/2in long by cutting the top straight and the bottom at an angle. It is best to plant these cuttings upright, so it is important to know top from bottom. Fill a pot with good potting compost; then dibble the cutting in until the top is just visible. Cover with grit, water in and leave on the staging to develop thin, fibrous roots. The rest of the parent plant can be replanted.

With shrubs such as tree poppy (*Romneya coulteri*) or clerodendron, it is best to excavate one or two roots without disturbing the parent. Nurserymen prepare plants for lots of quality root cuttings by lifting a plant during one dormant season, cutting its roots back (though not using these) and replanting. By the next dormant season the plant will have produced a whole rash of fresh, almost identical roots for cuttings.

LEAF CUTTINGS are specific to certain types of plant. They are likely to be used in the greenhouse for streptocarpus, and in warmer conservatories and in the house for rhizomatous begonias (such as *B. rex*, *B. manicata* and *B. bowerae*) and peperomias. The only plants in my cool greenhouse from which I regularly take leaf cuttings are Cape primrose (*Streptocarpus*). Simply throw away the midrib and insert each long leaf section, cut veins down, into a tray of cuttings compost. Water in and place in a polythene bag out of full sun to root.

PLANTLETS are produced by many plants, including indoor hen-and-chicken fern (*Asplenium bulbiferum*) and outdoor soft shield fern (*Polystichum setiferum*). When any plant produces a replica of itself, the propagation method is fairly obvious. Let that replica reach a reasonable size, and then pull it or cut it away from the parent, push the base into cuttings compost and encourage it to form its own roots. Many plantlets start making roots before this stage. You can also hedge your bets by introducing the plantlet to a pot before severing it from the parent. In the case of ferns, you can cut off a whole plantlet-laden frond and lay it over the surface of a tray of compost.

OFFSETS, where a plantlet develops on a stem below or above ground, are also rather obvious propagation material. Cactus, bromeliads and houseleeks (*Sempervivum*) are amongst the plants that produce them. Wait until the offset has reached a good size before carefully removing it. Sometimes you can do this without

Taking streptocarpus leaf cuttings is easy

disturbing the parent; in other cases you will have to lift the plant or remove it from its pot and cut away the offset with a knife. Some offsets come away with their own roots, but if they don't, treat them as a stem cutting, keeping them humid and lightly shaded until roots have formed.

DIVISION is another obvious propagation method, used for a wide range of greenhouse stalwarts including *Clivia miniata*, African lily (*Agapanthus*) and bird of paradise (*Strelitzia reginae*). Once a clump of several crowns has formed, remove the whole lot from the pot and divide them up. Sometimes you can do this with your hands, but more often you'll need to use a knife, secateurs, trowel, two forks or even a half-moon edging iron. You can divide until you have separated every crown, but it is often best to keep two or more together so that each new 'plant' created is larger and nearer flowering size. Don't be put off dividing up or splitting a mature clump of growth because a plant is said to 'flower better pot bound': there comes a time when large, congested clumps benefit from being split and re-potted. As long as the crowns or portions of growth are large and fairly mature, they should continue to bloom the following year.

POTTING ON

Potting composts

Potting composts have nothing to do with the garden and kitchen waste made to rot down on a compost heap. Some gardeners do sieve the latter to use as an ingredient in their own, ingenious home-made potting composts, but garden compost can carry pests, diseases, worms and weed seeds, so on the whole it is best used as a soil conditioner for the garden rather than for greenhouse plants.

There are two sorts of compost on the market. Loam-based John Innes types consist of seven parts loam, three parts peat and two parts of grit, plus a base fertilizer and lime. For years this was the standard mix. These types are available as a seed compost and three different strengths of potting compost. John Innes No. 1 holds the least fertilizer and is for young plants; No. 2 holds a moderate amount of fertilizer and is general purpose; and John Innes No. 3 is rich in fertilizer and serves hungry plants such as chrysanthemums and fuchsias.

Soil-less potting composts contain no loam and are based either on peat or, if they are peat free, coir fibre, finely chopped bark or other fibrous material. Sand, grit, perlite or vermiculite are mixed in to improve drainage and they usually have fertilizer added to bring them to the same sort of strength as a John Innes No. 2. Having experimented with composts over the years, I've concluded that for my plants a 50:50 mix of John Innes No. 2 and a good soil-less compost is just right. I keep bags of both type in stock all the time.

I also buy grit or sharp sand and vermiculite (a light, inert material). For South African bulbs, cacti and succulents, I add grit to the mix at about three parts compost to one of grit. For plants such as streptocarpus, I add vermiculite at the same rate. To make a gritty cuttings compost, I mix 50:50 soil-less compost and grit. There are ready-made composts sold for specific plants, but the only one I bother with is one for orchids based on bark, coarse peat, perlite, foam and charcoal.

Store potting compost in a covered area where rain cannot soak it. Should you open a bag and find that the contents are saturated, spread them out to dry somewhat before use. Cover unused compost on the potting bench to keep it moist. If it dries out, always mix water into it before use.

Potting on

When a plant has filled its pot with roots it has probably exhausted the supply of fertilizer in the compost (usually after six weeks) and will rely totally on liquid feeding for its nutrition. Although feeding compensates for lack of food, there comes a time when roots of a potted plant are so congested they can no longer take up enough water and food for continued growth. The logical next step is to pot the plant into a slightly larger pot with some new compost around its roots.

Short-lived plants need to grow quickly if they are to fulfil their potential of leaf and flower before they die. As soon as one of these – a salpiglossis, coleus or celosia, for instance – has filled its small, 9cm/3½in pot with roots, move it on to a 13cm/5in pot, which will probably be its final one. Longer-lived plants such as bird of paradise and ginger lilies need potting on every year as youngsters, so that they can reach flowering size as soon as possible. Once they reach the biggest pot you can accommodate, leave them to bulk up for several years until growth and flowering potential start to deteriorate.

Sometimes there are arguments against potting on, for instance when you don't want a plant to grow much larger because you lack space, or when it has reached the final pot size in keeping with the scale of its growth. If this is the case, keep the plant healthy for as long as possible with a combination of liquid feeding and top

HOW TO POT ON

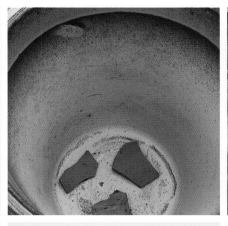

Potting on plants at the right time helps them reach their full potential. This one, *Ampelopsis brevipedunculata* var. *maximowiczii* 'Elegans', doubled its size within two months.

1 Find a new pot a couple of sizes larger than the old one (see page 26), make sure that it is clean, and if the pot is clay crock the base by setting broken pot shards bridge fashion over the hole, so that soil cannot fall out, but water can escape, and put some compost in to cover the crock. Plastic pots don't need crocking.

2 Upend the plant and tap the rim on a hard surface to loosen the roots. Slide them out, and check them for problems such as root mealy bug. If the plant is very pot bound, tease a few roots away from the mass.

3 Put some compost in the base of the pot and stand the plant on it. Add or remove compost underneath until the rootball is at the correct height, with the top a couple of centimetres from the rim, so there is a watering gap at the top. Straighten a wonky plant by tilting the rootball in the pot.

4 Once you are satisfied with the position of the rootball and plant, feed compost around the sides, firming it gently with your fingers rather than thumbs. When all is tidy, make sure that the watering gap is adequate and that there are no mountains of compost around the stem. A final tap will level the compost.

5 Water the plant in well, using a watering can fitted with a rose. Wait until the compost surface begins to dry out before watering again.

LEFT Before top dressing, tickle up and remove surface compost
RIGHT This olive will benefit from the fresh potting compost added
OPPOSITE Potting on or top dressing keeps a collection in good condition

large enough to fit a finger width around the outside of the roots. Slow-growing plants will not want to be moved into too large a container, because their roots will be surrounded by a lot of wet compost and won't be able to breathe properly. Fast-growing plants could probably manage a larger pot because they have the vigour to fill it quickly. Try to use clean pots, or at least brush out the old compost. This helps avoid pests and diseases and also stops the roots sticking too much to the pot sides. I prefer clay pots, mainly for aesthetic reasons. Their porous nature helps roots breathe better and is helpful when plants are overwintering at low temperatures. But thirsty plants such as maidenhair ferns do better in plastic because the clay seems to suck the moisture away from their fine feeding roots.

Potting on is usually carried out during spring and summer while growth is active rather than dormant. Roots should be moist – neither dry nor saturated. If you have just pruned a plant, leave it until shoots have sprouted before potting on. If a plant needs pruning, pot it on first, let new roots grow into the compost and prune it about a month afterwards.

Top dressing

When plants have reached their final pot size and won't be potted on again, you can help them by adding fresh potting compost to the top of the pot. This is usually best done in spring and it is possible only when the original compost has eroded, leaving a gap. You can try to dig out or tickle up the top surface of the old compost, but if you do so, avoid damaging too many roots. Sometimes there is a deep gap in the top anyway, where watering has forced compost away or the compost has broken down over a long period. Simply fill the gap with fresh potting compost. You can mix in some slow-release fertilizer for greater benefit. Some plants almost heave themselves out of the pot by producing masses of fleshy roots and these are virtually impossible to top dress.

dressing, but take steps to replace tired specimens with new plants raised from seed or cuttings.

Although it is usually obvious when a plant needs re-potting, you can check by turning the pot upside down, while supporting the plant and compost underneath with one hand. Gently tap the pot rim sharply against a firm surface and the roots should slide from their pot like a sand castle from its bucket. You'll probably be amazed at the root growth you see. Make a quick assessment before sliding the rootball back in. When the roots begin to reach the outside of the compost and start netting to create a web of roots, it is time to pot on.

The next pot size for a plant will usually be at least 5cm/2in wider than the original and should be just

RAISING FLOWERS FOR THE GARDEN

2

With the warm, protected environment of the greenhouse at your disposal, it makes sense to grow in it a wide range of flowering plants for the garden. Growing bedding plants and herbaceous perennials from seed, shrubs from cuttings and dazzling canna and dahlia plants brought on from rhizomes (underground stems) and tubers is satisfying and can save you money. Young plants are easy to care for under glass, where they are not so much at the mercy of weather and slugs. So make full use of your greenhouse in spring by filling it with young plants. Most will be hardened off and planted out by late spring, leaving the way clear for tender greenhouse crops such as tomatoes and cucumbers. Batches of seedlings and rooted cuttings can be just as attractive and fascinating as mature flowering plants and you can incorporate them into the display. Best of all, you will enjoy your garden plants twice as much having raised them yourself.

The stunning pink daisies of the herbaceous perennial *Echinacea purpurea* 'Magnus'

BEDDING PLANTS FROM SEED

Most plants used for bedding are half-hardy annuals and tender perennials capable of growing to flowering size within one year and filling your garden with colour all summer. Some start flowering almost as soon as they are planted out in late spring and early summer and will carry on until the first frost of autumn kills them off. Some gardeners like to fill whole areas with bedding plants, creating patterns and almost painting their beds and borders with them. Others use them to fill gaps in mixed borders, sometimes leaving a few holes on purpose for some stately tobacco plants or a patch of brightly coloured antirrhinums. Tall bedding plants make great cut flowers and suit a kitchen garden. I now leave most of a long border free for a flamboyant mixture of tender or half-hardy plants chosen especially to give maximum colour between high summer and autumn.

There are times when quick vertical growth is needed to screen an ugly wall or fence, or help colonize a newly planted pergola while hardy, permanent climbers are putting down roots and establishing a framework. Fast-moving annual climbers raised from seed in the greenhouse are perfect for these situations: by summer, they'll be smothered in flowers or fruit. As with bedding plants, these climbers are a mixture of half-hardy annuals and tender perennials needing an early start under glass.

How to grow bedding plants

The seeds of bedding plants are sown from late winter to late spring. If you are sowing many different types, it will pay to stagger the sowings, so as to allow for space in the propagating case as well as avoiding masses of pricking out in the same week.

TOP The tobacco plant *Nicotiana alata* is valued for its evening fragrance
BOTTOM I use *Zinnia* Oklahoma Series to brighten up the kitchen garden

Half-hardy annuals will germinate best in warm temperatures of 15–22°C/60–72°F). Start with small seeds that need a longer growing period, such as *Begonia semperflorens* and antirrhinums. Zonal pelargoniums also need plenty of time to reach a good size by late spring. By mid-spring, sow petunias, nicotiana and other seeds of moderate size and growth speed. Finish with fast-growing, large-seeded types like French and African marigolds, tithonia (Mexican sunflower), cleome (spider flower), cosmos and morning glory (*Ipomoea*) towards late spring.

When the greenhouse is bursting at the seams in late spring, start hardening plants off, prior to planting out – but in colder areas don't rush this. If you got your timings wrong and find that some plants are now rather too big for their seed trays or cells, there will be a danger of them suffering while waiting to be planted. One option is to pot each plant, so that the roots have fresh compost and a little extra space to tide them over for another three or four weeks. This may mean extra work, but you'll have some super plants at the end of it. Alternatively, give well-established plants a weekly liquid feed (see page 179) to keep them healthy.

Once the plants are hardened off and ready to plant, choose a calm day, avoiding conditions of harsh sun and drying wind. Prepare the planting area by weeding, loosening the soil with a fork, and digging in well-rotted garden compost or other soil conditioner and some general-purpose fertilizer. Set the plants out where you want them to go, using an average spacing of 20cm/8in apart, and plant using a trowel. Always water plants in well after planting and go back after dark with a torch to check on slug activity.

TOP Ipomoea seedlings are almost as beautiful as the flowers that come later
BOTTOM Home-grown bedding plants ready for hardening off and planting out

EASY BEDDING PLANTS

PLANT

Ageratum houstonianum
Timeless Series, mixed
Floss flower
H 50cm/20in S 30cm/12in

Antirrhinum majus
'Brighton Rock'
Snapdragon
H 45cm/18in S 30cm/12in

DESCRIPTION

Floss flowers have been raised from the annual Mexican species *Ageratum houstonianum*. I've always loved the soft effect of the fuzzy blue, pink, lilac and white panicles, each consisting of around forty small flowerheads, but most types are too short for my liking. This taller mixture can be grown for cutting as well as filling gaps in the garden, where the branching stems are sturdy enough to withstand wind and weather. Use the plants informally, where groups can mingle their colours together. They look particularly good against *Stachys byzantina* and other plants with silvery foliage. Those who like to make patterns with their plants will find the shorter, bushier cultivars at 15–20cm/6–8in useful. Butterflies love floss flowers and will visit them for their nectar.

Snapdragons, in the foxglove family (*Scrophulariaceae*) are fabulous early-season bedding plants, though they tend not to last right into the autumn, sometimes going past their best by late summer. Alternatively, plant tall antirrhinums in rows among crops in the kitchen garden and use them for cutting. Most bedding types are hybrids of *A. majus*, originally from south-west Europe and the Mediterranean. Among the many varieties, the madly striped and spotted 'Brighton Rock' is my favourite. I also enjoy those with bicoloured flowers, such as deep crimson and white 'Night and Day', also 45cm/18in high. Then again, the fancy double 'Madame Butterfly' is hard to resist, with its jewel-like colours of white, yellow, red and pink on plants 60–90cm/24–36in high.

HOW TO GROW

Sow into shallow pots during early spring, and then place in a propagating case at a cosy 18°C/65°F. Prick out seedlings into trays or cells and grow on. Progress will be slow to start with, but the small plants soon gain speed as temperatures rise.

Sow the tiny seeds during late winter and early spring, sprinkling them thinly on to prepared moist compost in a half pot or small tray. Germinate in a warm propagating case at 16–18°C/61–65°F. Once up, the seedlings are able to survive surprisingly low temperatures. Sometimes I prick them out closely in a tray and then pot them separately into 9cm/3½in pots before hardening them off. But to save the fiddle of potting, you can prick the seedlings out thirty-five or forty-eight to a tray. They don't seem to mind being pulled apart when you plant them out and will grow away quickly in well-cultivated soil.

Cerinthe major
'Purpurascens'
Honeywort
H 60cm/24in S 30cm/12in

Cleome hassleriana
'Colour Fountain'
Spider flower
H 1.2–1.5m/4–5ft S 75cm/30in

Heliotropium arborescens
'Marine'
Cherry pie
H 45cm/18in S 30cm/12in

Relatively new to the scene, this metallic-looking perennial from the borage family (*Boraginaceae*), with its origins in the Mediterranean, will sometimes survive winter but is much better raised fresh each year. From the encouragingly large, robust-looking seeds, plants quickly grow and branch, with spoon-shaped, blue-green leaves that are sometimes spotted. The stem tips soon curve over, and the closely spaced slatey purple-blue bracts give way to downward-pointing, tubular purple flowers at the tips. The combined shape and colour is most attractive and honeyworts associate well with other flowers. Plant in groups or intermingle with other plants.

The showy and resilient South American spider flower from the caper family (*Capparaceae*) loves a long hot summer. Given a good, well-nourished soil, early-summer plantings will romp away into magnificent plants. This colour mixture yields four-petalled flowers of white and various shades of pink and mauve, opening over a long period from buds at the ends of branching stems. The leaves, made up of five to seven leaflets, have an exotic look too. They excel themselves towards the end of summer and into autumn by producing more and more blooms until the first frosts. I add plants into gaps and spaces in the kitchen garden, where, along with sunflowers, they create jungle-like masses of growth.

Fragrant bedding plants always score points with me, and the fruity, cherry-pie scent of heliotrope blooms can be mouth-watering. I like to see them in containers, clustered together in the sun, so that their coiled bunches of rich purple flowers give off maximum perfume. Butterflies find these nectar-rich plants enchanting too. This selection of Peruvian *Heliotropium arborescens* yields dark-leaved plants 38cm/15in high. They have a shrubby habit of growth, and their handsome foliage and heads of rich, deep purple flowers combine to create a distinctive air. Heliotropes grow relatively slowly, coming into flower during midsummer and continuing until the first frosts.

Most seeds germinate, so sow singly one per cell during spring and place in a warm but well-ventilated and shaded propagating case at around 16°C/60°F, so as not to cook the seed. These are hardy plants, so once they've filled their cells with roots, harden them off and plant them out whenever they are ready. Seeds are readily produced at the end of the season and you can either collect them and store them until spring, or let them self-seed, though they have a knack of coming up like weeds everywhere except where they are most needed.

Cleomes love warmth and I sometimes think it pays to delay their sowing until late spring. I sow them into a pot kept at 18°C/65°F and prick them out into individual 9cm/3½in pots. Natural warmth then ensures even growth and development without too much of a check. Keep plants growing until they are well established before hardening them off and planting them out, because small plants with indifferent root systems often falter if exposed to a sudden spell of cold wet weather. Although potentially drought tolerant, spider flowers perform best when their roots are treated to generous soakings of water during drought.

Sow in late winter or early spring in temperatures of 15–18°C/60–65°F. I sow into shallow pots, and then prick the seedlings out into small cells rather than pots because the young plants don't like too much cold wet compost around their roots. They can be potted on later and planted out as established plants in early summer. Seedlings may yield plants of variable quality, but in the autumn you can lift the best and pot them. Overwinter them in a frost-free place, prune in spring by two-thirds if the plants become leggy and use the shoot tips as cuttings (see page 22). There are other named varieties not available as seed that you can buy as plants.

EASY BEDDING PLANTS

PLANT

Nicotiana sylvestris
Tobacco plant

H 1.5m/5ft S 75cm/30in

Rudbeckia hirta
Cherokee Sunset Group
Black-eyed Susan or coneflower
H 60–75cm/24–30in S 30cm/12in

DESCRIPTION

The Argentinian queen of the tobacco plants, a member of the potato family (*Solanaceae*), is a stately number guaranteed to grace your borders or make a summer hedge of bright green foliage and white, night-scented flowers. These elegant blooms flare out like trumpets from long tubes and give their best performance at dusk. There are other kinds of tobacco plants to try. If you want to grow the most scented tobacco plant, you need seed of *Nicotiana alata* (see page 32). The plants reach 90cm/3ft and the white flowers open wide in the evening. For unusual colour, seek out the floriferous *N.* 'Lime Green' at 60cm/2ft or small-flowered *N. langsdorffii*, capable of reaching 1.5m/5ft and ideal for containers.

Rudbeckias belong to the daisy family (*Asteraceae*). Those grown as bedding plants have a longer flowering period than their more perennial cousins, producing masses of blooms from midsummer onwards. The display keeps going strong well into autumn, when their yellow, golden and russet shades seem to be just what is needed. Even if they are not to form part of your main display, it is worth raising a dozen or so really good plants and growing them on in pots, outdoors, ready to fill gaps that appear during the summer. Most bedding plant types are raised from *Rudbeckia hirta*, a biennial or short-lived perennial from the central USA. Single 'Marmalade' and double 'Goldilocks' are reliable, gold-flowering sorts reaching 60cm/2ft, but I like 'Cherokee Sunset' for its height and showy mixture of double and semi-double flowerheads in shades of golden yellow, orange, mahogany and bronze. The rather bristly stems are thick and strong.

HOW TO GROW

I sow the seeds thinly in early spring in a small pot and germinate at 18°C/65°F, and let the seedlings reach a healthy size before pricking out one per pot. As the plants are generally placed towards the back of a border, let them grow to a good size so that they can compete with other plants. Once they have filled their pots, keep in the warmth of the greenhouse and feed weekly. After hardening off, plant into well-nourished soil. Keep well watered and outwit slugs.

These are relatively large-seeded plants, so you can leave sowing them until late spring. I usually sow mine into small cells, germinating them in the propagating case at 15–18°C/60–65°F and then potting them on later.

Tagetes patula
'Scotch Prize'
French marigold
H 75cm/30in S 25cm/10in

Tithonia rotundifolia
'Torch'
Mexican sunflower
H 1.2m/4ft S 75cm/30in

Zinnia
'Zebra'
H 60cm/24in S 30cm/12in

Marigolds – from the daisy family (*Asteraceae*) – are not only popular bedding plants but invaluable in the greenhouse for repelling whitefly. Some may say this is an old wives' tale, but tall marigolds dotted in between tomatoes, aubergines and peppers have worked for me. They won't clear an established infestation, but introduced before the whitefly appear they seem to keep them away. This yellow and rich red-striped single-flowered variety dates from 1829 and was a great favourite with Victorian florists and gardeners. I love it too. Its long-stemmed flowers are good for cutting and, either indoors or out, are popular with bees. For a shorter alternative, try compact 'Boy-o-boy' at 15cm/6in, a mixture with first-class colours. The unusual 'Vanilla' at 35cm/14in bears large cream-coloured flowerheads, a sophisticated change from the usual cheerful yellow and orange.

The fabulous Mexican sunflower – from the daisy family (*Asteraceae*) – resembles a giant orange zinnia and will quickly fill large gaps in borders, making a great addition where hot colours predominate. Flowering starts in mid- to late summer and will continue with great profusion until the first frosts. Branching stems of large soft leaves produce generous quantities of orange flowers held on stems long enough for cutting. Smaller and larger types are available. Tithonias are great teamed with dahlias, but don't underestimate their size.

Fabulously showy, the zinnia tribe – from the daisy family (*Asteraceae*) and originating in Mexico, the USA and South America – will produce single or double flowers all summer. This distinctive old variety dates from the 1890s and produces astonishing double flowers whose petals are of one colour striped with another. Some of the pink and cream or red and cream sorts put me in mind of old-fashioned deckchair canvas, while the red on yellow are particularly wacky and full of character. Hunt the seed down in a catalogue, as you are unlikely to find striped zinnias in a garden centre – a good reason for raising your own. There are dwarf zinnias as short as 25cm/10in and taller kinds like the Oklahoma Series (see page 32) up to 90cm/3ft. The latter is ideal for cutting, and worth raising in good numbers if you are to be sure of enjoying the full colour range of scarlet, pink, salmon, yellow and white.

Marigolds germinate best at 21°C/70°F and grow rapidly, so for outdoor use sow them in mid- to late spring, or else they will go past their best while waiting to be planted out. I usually sow the large seed into half pots or trays and prick out the seedlings into individual pots. But you could sow into individual cells to save time.

Mexican sunflower grows fast from seed and flourishes in warmth, so I delay sowing until late spring, setting two seeds to each cell of compost. Germinate in a propagating case at 15–18°C/60–65°F, remove as soon as seedlings appear and thin to one per cell. When the plants have filled their cells with roots, pot on in 8–10cm/3–4in pots and harden off when there is no more danger of frost. Alternatively, sow into a pot and prick seedlings out into individual 9cm/3½in pots.

Zinnia seedlings resent disturbance and so it is best to bypass the pricking-out stage by sowing seed two per cell, germinating at 15–18°C/60–65°F and thinning down to one later. You can harden off the plants and plant them out straight from the cells, or you can buy time by potting them on. All zinnias branch well once they are planted out and thriving.

ANNUAL CLIMBERS

PLANT

Cucurbita pepo subsp. ovifera
Gourds

H and S 3.7m/12ft

Eccremocarpus scaber
Chilean glory vine

H 3m/10ft

DESCRIPTION

One summer, we needed an easy stop-gap for a long expanse of bare fence destined for permanent planting the following autumn, and ornamental gourds provided a humorous quick fix. These tender plants in the cucumber family (*Cucurbitaceae*) are straightforward to grow, romping away with reaching stems and curling tendrils. Their large yellow flowers can be up to 15cm/6in across, are lightly perfumed and attract many bees. The fruits are yellow, striped or warty and can be picked, dried and preserved as ornaments.

This dainty evergreen climber hoists itself aloft by coiling tendrils around its support. Although commonly grown as an annual, this Chilean native from the catalpa family (*Bignoniaceae*) is truly a perennial. The leaves are attractively divided into leaflets and make a lush backdrop, from late spring to autumn, for the branched stems of tubular flowers in fiery colours. The typical shade is orange-red, but seed mixtures such as 'Carnival Time' will yield red, pink and yellow too.

HOW TO GROW

Starting plants under glass gives more control over their germination and a head start on slugs, snails and other mechanical damage. Most of the seeds germinate, so I usually sow one per 9cm/3½in pot, setting the seed on edge to prevent rotting. Mid-spring sowings placed in a heated propagator at 18–21°C/65–70°F will yield plants large enough for planting out during late spring. Or you can sow in late spring and leave the seeds on the staging with no extra heat to germinate. Initially the stems will need tying in to a fence or other support, and then they will grip it with their tendrils. If there are no wires or individual pales for attachment, tie string to the base of each plant, wind it about the stems and secure it higher up. Once the plants have started to climb, further stems will clamber up each other. Frost will kill the vines and roots, which are easy to clear away in autumn.

For maximum growing time and the earliest display of flowers, sow during late winter or early spring. An ideal germination temperature is around 15°C/60°F, so take care not to cook seedlings in a warm propagating case. Sow into a pot, cover it with polythene and place in the ambient warmth of a room indoors to germinate, but bring it back into the cool brightness of the greenhouse as soon as the seedlings are up. You could plant three to a 45cm/18in wide pot for the patio or grow it in pots for the greenhouse. Fix an ornamental obelisk or some canes into the pot for support.

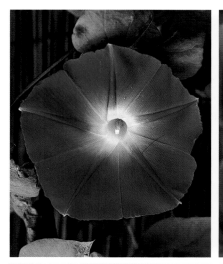

Ipomoea tricolor
'Heavenly Blue'
Morning glory
H and S 3.7m/12ft

The fabulous tropical morning glories we grow from seed each spring are cultivars of South American *Ipomoea tricolor* and *I. nil*. These tender perennials are benign members of the bindweed family (*Convolvulaceae*) and with their thin, heart-shaped leaves and saucer-shaped flowers 8cm/3in across make stunning late-summer colour whether intermingling with shrubs or clothing a fence. 'Heavenly Blue' is a classic among ipomoeas, but try too 'Crimson Rambler' or 'Black Knight'.

Unless your greenhouse is very warm, I would delay sowing until late spring or even early summer, when natural warmth is guaranteed. Set the seeds in a generous half pot and place it inside a heated propagating case at around 18°C/65°F until the beautiful seedlings have emerged. They will grow rapidly in summer warmth, whereas earlier sowings tend to produce sickly plants that struggle to survive cold nights. Prick each seedling out into its own pot and they will grow rapidly. After hardening them off, plant them into well-nourished soil. When they are growing well, apply a liquid feed and attach strings for them to climb. Unlike their pernicious relatives, the bindweeds, they are killed off by the cold, roots and all.

Lathyrus odoratus
Sweet pea 'Wiltshire Ripple'

H and S 2.2m/7ft

With their frilly-petalled, fragrant flowers, Spencer sweet peas (in the *Papilionaceae* family) are everybody's favourite, and there are many types to choose from. They have their origins in Italy. Grow them against a row of canes or up a fence or wigwam of rustic sticks and they'll look as good in the kitchen garden as in borders. Do also try the un-'improved' species, sometimes sold as 'Matucana' or 'Cupani'. While 'Cupani' is shorter than usual, 'Matucana' is full height. Both have simple blue and purple flowers that are are highly fragrant.

I always start my sweet peas off under glass. I know that the best plants can be enjoyed from an autumn sowing, but an early-spring sowing is easier, because you don't have plants sitting around all winter. I fill a number of 9cm/3½in pots with a 50:50 mix of John Innes No. 2 and a soil-less compost. I sow five seeds per pot and leave the pots on the staging for the seeds to germinate in natural temperatures. I don't usually bother to pinch out their growing tips, unless a delay in planting out has resulted in straggly growth. When they are big enough, I stand the young plants outside to harden off before planting them out against tepees of canes or bean sticks driven into good soil in a circle with their tops drawn together over the centre. I might separate the plants, but if there are plenty and I'm in a hurry, I often end up planting whole potfuls together. Feed regularly and tie stems in to canes.

Tropaeolum peregrinum
Canary creeper

H and S 1.8–3m/6–10ft

This tender, vigorous Peruvian annual is closely related to the humble nasturtium in the family *Tropaeolaceae*. The dainty plants are adept twiners, whose fringed, bright yellow flowers stand out well against lobed, grey-green leaves. With spurs and two large fringed upper petals, the flowers resemble little yellow birds. Sown in mid-spring and planted out in late spring in good soil, plants romp away, sending shoots in all directions.

The optimum germination temperature is around 15°C/60°F, so make sure that the seeds don't cook in a propagating case. Sow individually into cells of seed compost, and then pot on after germination. Provide young plants with canes or they will tangle themselves up with their neighbours. Watch out for blackfly, as they are as susceptible as their common cousins, though I tend to find that if I turn a blind eye to these pests, garden predators and parasites eventually see them off. One year I planted them with gourds and sweet peas against a tepee in the kitchen garden. The plants were left to fight it out between themselves and the canary creepers gave a good account of themselves. The onset of winter withers the stems and roots, but seedlings often arise in spring if the soil is undisturbed.

QUICK-GROWING BIENNIALS AND PERENNIALS FROM SEED

ABOVE The native foxglove is easy to raise from seed
OPPOSITE Freshly pricked-out hollyhock seedlings to bloom next summer

Biennials and perennials are the hardy stalwarts of the flower garden and most are easy to raise from seed, but it helps to learn first how they behave. Biennials grow from seed one year, remain green during winter and flower the following spring or summer, after which most will die off after setting seed. They include stalwarts such as honesty, hollyhock, sweet rocket, sweet William, clary sage and foxglove. Many are efficient self-seeders and will be self-perpetuating once introduced. As a group, they are particularly good at bringing colour to the garden in late spring and early summer.

Biennials should be sown after mid-spring and before midsummer, because sowing earlier can confuse plants into flowering prematurely in their first growing season, before they have reached full size. Sowing too late means that plants will not be large enough to come through winter unscathed and those that do may not reach their full potential.

A temperature range of 15–18°C/60–65°F suits most biennials. This is best provided by placing sown pots on the staging or in a lightly shaded and ventilated, unheated propagating case to help keep them moist without cooking. After they have been hardened off, I usually set the young plants out straight into their flowering positions. They make a lot of growth in autumn and again in spring.

Herbaceous perennials are non-woody plants whose growth dies back in winter but returns in spring, year after year. Some will flower during their first year from seed, and suit the current vogue for low-maintenance, prairie-style planting. Some of these tough plants are best sown in autumn and left in an unheated greenhouse or outside to feel the cold, which helps break their dormancy. Others are sown in spring and happy to germinate quickly at warmer temperatures.

Raising these plants from seed makes it easier and cheaper to create generous drifts of them or repeat plants such as honesty and sweet rocket in groups around the garden.

BIENNIALS AND PERENNIALS

PLANT

Agastache scrophulariifolia
Purple giant hyssop

H 1.5m/5ft S 30cm/12in

Aquilegia 'Virginia'
Columbine

H 90cm/3ft S 45cm/18in

DESCRIPTION

The understated North American purple giant hyssop from the mint family (*Lamiaceae*, formerly *Labiatae*) is a herbaceous perennial that, like others of its tribe, is rapidly growing in popularity. Seeds virtually jump up out of their compost and plants grow quickly, sending up stout stems of nettle-like leaves, which in this case are topped by long soft spikes of soft pink bracts during late summer. Ideal for wildlife-friendly gardens, they are attractive to bees and butterflies, dying gracefully during autumn, when they are often visited by seed-eating birds such as goldfinches. Anise hyssop (*Agastache foeniculum*) is aniseed-scented with violet calyces and blue flowers. Mexican hyssop (*A. mexicana*) is bushier, with aromatic leaves and purple flower spikes. A. rugosa 'Golden Jubilee' is a shorter plant at 60cm/2ft, grown for its golden foliage. Of similar height, A. 'Apache Sunset' has larger, apricot-orange flowers and fine foliage.

Columbines are perennial cottage garden favourites from the buttercup family (*Ranunculaceae*), originating from across a wide sweep of the northern hemisphere. They are a promiscuous bunch, and if you start with a few seed strains — you might select from plants already in your garden — and add them to your borders, the plants will cross-pollinate and seed themselves around, and within a few years you will have a colony of lovely aquilegias unique to your garden. I have yet to come across a columbine flower I don't like; one cannot help but be pleased with the results. You could start with short-spurred *Aquilegia* Biedermeier Group, a long-spurred type such as 'Bluebird' or golden-leaved Vervaeneana Group, then stand back and see what happens. If you wish to steer your plants in a particular direction, rogue out the colours or heights you don't like by pulling plants up as soon as they reveal their flowers, before their pollen can be added to the mix.

HOW TO GROW

To achieve flowering in the first year from seed, sow during early spring in a heated propagating case. But I think better plants come from a more leisurely sowing in early summer, germinated in natural warmth of 13–18°C/55–65°F. Sow into half pots, and then prick out the enthusiastic seedlings into individual cells or pots. When the plants throw up one long stem, pinch it back by removing the growing tip with finger and thumb to encourage a bushier shape.

Seed germinates easily from a spring sowing at 15–18°C/60–65°F and the plants will bloom in their second year from seed. Sow generously in a half tray and prick the seedlings out, grid fashion, into a box before planting out.

Digitalis purpurea
Foxglove

H 90–120cm/3–4ft S 30–60cm/1–2ft

Echinacea purpurea
'Magnus'
Purple coneflower

H 1.2m/4ft S 45cm/18in

Hesperis matronalis
Sweet rocket, dame's violet

H 60–90cm/2–3ft S 45cm/18in

The common, native foxglove (in the family *Scrophulariaceae*) is grown as a biennial, although it behaves like a short-lived perennial. A rosette of soft leaves builds up during the first summer, overwinters and then a stem rises up to bloom in the early summer of the second year. Tall, one-sided spikes of buds open from the bottom upwards, each tubular flower being pink or white, and intricately spotted inside. It liberally produces and scatters seed. There are various improved strains such as the Gloxinioides Group, plants of which bear rather open flowers in a wider range of colours including salmon pink and creamy yellow, all beautifully spotted inside. There are also other species of *Digitalis* to try. After flowering, a plant is weakened and although it might produce offsets and bloom again, it will have lost its initial vigour.

Large, pink daisies with central dark brown and orange cones make the perennial purple cone flower one of the finest border plants. In the *Asteraceae* family, it originates from the North American prairie and looks great planted in generous swathes, along with other similar perennials and grasses. These plants are not the easiest to divide and can resent root disturbance, so raising a large number from seed and establishing them as young plants is an excellent way of achieving the desired effect of massed plantings. On good soil the stout stems of *Echinacea purpurea* 'Magnus' bear flowerheads up to 13cm/5in across, yet there is rarely the need for staking. Plants from a spring or summer sowing should flower in their second year, and from the third year onwards these fabulous daisies will really hit their stride.

Best described as a biennial or short-lived perennial, this fabulous plant from the cabbage family (*Brassicaceae*, formerly *Cruciferae*) will light up your garden during early summer. I like to plant it liberally throughout several borders, so that when it flowers the borders are united by the common thread of its luminous white, lilac or purple flowers. These are fragrant and show up particularly well at dusk, making them an ideal choice for busy workers who enjoy their gardens in the evening. Insects find them attractive too. Well-grown plants branch well, producing masses of bloom before attractive, longish, pink-tinged seed pods. Sweet rocket is an efficient self-seeder.

Sow seeds during late spring, scattering them thinly in a seed tray and setting them to germinate in natural warmth on the greenhouse staging. Prick the seedlings out into trays or individual pots, grow them on and then harden them off. As soon as the plants are large enough, transplant them to their permanent positions so that they can put down as much root as possible during the growing season.

The seeds can easily cook in a heated propagating case and are best germinated in a cooler temperature of around 13°C/55°F. Sow into a shallow pot during spring and prick the seedlings out into pots.

Sow into a wide pot or small seed tray during late spring and set the seeds to germinate on the staging in natural temperatures. Germination is usually very good. Prick out the desired number of seedlings into individual 9cm/3½cm pots, let them grow on, then harden them off and plant them out. Alternatively, set two seeds per cell of compost and after germination pull out the weakest, grow the rest on and plant them out.

BIENNIALS AND PERENNIALS

PLANT

Knautia macedonica

H 60–75cm/24–30in S 45cm/18in

Lunaria annua
Honesty

H 1m/39in S 30cm/12in

DESCRIPTION

The maroon, pincushion-style flowers of the Balkan knautia (in the scabious family, *Dipsacaceae*) appear over a long period, are a trendy deep colour and attract plenty of insects to the garden. The flowers are similar in structure to those of their cousin the scabious. The foliage makes a splendid, weed-smothering mass and the flowers are held well above it, on stems strong enough to stay upright with no staking. All these attributes are guaranteed to make this knautia a reliable herbaceous perennial.

For semi-wild areas of the garden, a haze of purple honesty is hard to beat. Originating from south-east Europe, this biennial plant belongs to the cabbage family (*Brassicaceae*, formerly *Cruciferae*) and often escapes from gardens and appears wild. Happy to grow in partial shade as well as full sun, it makes rosettes of lush foliage during the first summer and flowers during the following late spring. The show of purple or sometimes white flowers is strong, and followed by fabulous flat, translucent seed pods, providing a long season of interest. Even in winter, these flat 'pennies', as they're often called, still look good, having turned a papery silver-white. Once introduced to a garden, honesty usually self-seeds successfully but never invasively. It is an ideal plant to colonize hedge bottoms.

HOW TO GROW

Seed germinates readily as long as it is not overheated in a warm propagating case. Sow into a pot, cover with a sprinkling of grit and leave to germinate on the greenhouse staging or in a cold frame. I have enjoyed some of my best results from an autumn sowing, left to stand in an unheated greenhouse all winter. Some seeds germinated within a few weeks and the rest came up in spring. The plants will wait until their second or even third year to begin flowering, but are long-lived and eminently gardenworthy.

Sow during late spring or early summer, into a small tray, and then prick out seedlings into cells or small pots. Alternatively sow straight into cells and pot on from those. The seeds will germinate readily on the greenhouse staging in natural temperatures, as long as they are kept moist. Once thriving, the plants can continue growing outside until their roots have filled their pots and they are ready to be planted out during late summer and autumn.

Lupinus Russell hybrids
Lupin

H 90cm/3ft S 75cm/30in

Monarda 'Lambada'
Bergamot, Oswego tea,
bee balm

H 60–90cm/2–3ft S 45cm/18in

Papaver orientale
'Coral Reef'
Oriental poppy

H 75cm/30in S 75cm/30in

Although the showiest lupins (herbaceous perennials in the pea family, *Papilionaceae*) are named varieties propagated by cuttings and division so that they are exactly the same as their parent, some good plants can be grown from seed. Lupin breeders seeking to emulate the work of experts such as George Russell look for large, colourful blooms produced close together on the stem, so that no stem is visible. The older, bottom-most flowers should not fade before the top ones have all opened and the plants should be reliably perennial. To achieve this kind of perfection, plants producing undesirable flowers are pulled up so that only the best pollinate each other. Seed produced in this way should yield gardenworthy plants. Watching your lupins flower for the first time is exciting. They can be white, yellow, purple, pink, red, orange or combinations of these.

North American members of the mint family (*Lamiaceae*, formerly *Labiatae*) bergamots are aromatic herbaceous perennials whose pink or red flowers are borne in tiered whorls at the top of the stems during the latter part of summer. It is usual to buy named varieties, but seeds are reliable too and from a spring sowing will bloom in their first summer. I like 'Lambada' for the subtle effect of its pink flowers and pink-tinged, almost silvery bracts that light up the top of the plant. The narrow leaves smell like sage. I've recently planted a dozen in dappled shade where the soil is moist in summer and well drained in winter. For wilder parts of the garden, they have a natural-looking appeal.

Oriental poppies (in the family *Papaveraceae*), whose origins are in the Caucasus, Turkey and Iran, are the flamboyant stars of many an early-summer border. The best moment is when the bristly, rounded buds split, revealing the delicate silky petals inside. It's hard to imagine that so much could be folded up inside so small a bud. In this case, the 13cm/5in wide flowers are coral pink with black centres. After the petals have fallen, an attractively shaped velvet-topped seed pod is left behind. The hairy leaves can be a little wayward, but if after flowering you cut the old ones back, shorter, newer leaves will re-grow and lie low all summer. Once established, these are long-lasting perennial plants capable of building up into large clumps usefully able to tolerate dry soil.

The large seeds germinate easily, when sown into cells or trays during spring in natural greenhouse temperatures of 10–15°C/ 50–60°F, but you can speed this process up by rubbing the seeds gently between two layers of sandpaper to break the seed coat and help water enter faster. Pot the young plants up as they grow. Plant them out, ideally into well-cultivated, slightly acid soil, and enjoy their first-year flowers.

The seeds are simplicity itself to germinate, and the seedlings of bergamot soon emerge in the 15°C/60°F warmth of a heated propagator in spring. The seeds will germinate equally well, though more slowly, without extra heat. As soon as the seedlings are up, stand the pot on the staging and let them grow a little before pricking them out into individual cells or pots. When they have filled their pots with roots, harden them off and plant them out either into nursery rows or in their final position.

Sowings made in autumn seem to be just as successful as those made during spring, but in either case I find the plants take two or three years before flowering profusely. Sow into a wide shallow pot, sprinkle fine grit over the seeds to cover them and germinate on the greenhouse staging at 10–21°C/50–70°F. Allow the seedlings to reach 2.5cm/1in high before separating them into pots of their own. Grow them on in a nursery bed before transplanting to a permanent position in spring.

STARTING DAHLIAS
FROM TUBERS

Dahlia 'David Howard' bears neat orange blooms against bronze foliage

Dahlias (*Asteraceae*, formerly *Compositae*) first reached Europe from Mexico in 1789, brought by travellers who assumed that they would become crop plants for their tubers. These proved unpalatable, but people eventually realized the ornamental value of the flowers. Bobbing in and out of fashion over the years, dahlias are currently the darlings of the late border, widely grown for their magnificent blooms produced over a long period. Historically, dahlias used to be grown together in dedicated beds, but these days we are more likely to mix them in with other plants, choosing their colours and shapes to blend or contrast with other flowers and foliage. Dahlias make excellent cut flowers and no kitchen garden or cutting border should be without them. Although not normally grown for greenhouse display, the tubers are often encouraged into growth under glass early during spring, so that cuttings can be made of their new shoots.

These are perennial plants, reaching 30cm–1.8m/12in–6ft in height, dying back to tubers after the first frosts of autumn. In milder areas the tubers can be left in the ground during winter, under a duvet of mulch, but there is always the danger of unusually cold weather or excessive waterlogging killing them off. If you leave them in the ground, mark the position of the tubers clearly, as it is all too easy to unearth them while cultivating the border. Dahlias also grow well in containers. In colder areas, or to be on the safe side, lift the dahlia tubers in autumn after frost has blackened the foliage and store them in trays or shallow boxes of almost dry compost in a cool, frost-free place until spring. The tops of the tubers should remain uncovered; the compost is there only to prevent shrivelling.

Forcing tubers under glass

Forcing stored or newly bought tubers into growth during spring is easy and brings the plants into flower earlier than if they were planted later into the ground – or left in from previous years. You can simply pot the tubers, so that they can be planted out in late spring as well-developed plants. But the shoots from tubers make good cuttings, capable of giving as good a performance in one season as the parent. So this method, yielding quick results, is ideal for bulking up your stock.

Find a seed tray large enough to take the tuber, or save one of the plastic trays supermarkets use to display vegetables, and make small holes in the base for drainage. Cover the base with soil-less potting compost, place the tuber on top, and then cover the fingers of the tuber, leaving the stem exposed. Label with the cultivar name and date, and water in using a rose on the end of the can. Place the tray in a heated propagating case to coax the tuber into growth; or place it inside a loosely knotted polythene bag and stand it in the warmth of the house until temperatures have risen naturally inside the greenhouse.

When the shoots are well grown and the greenhouse is warmer, move the tray out on to the staging and take cuttings by slicing through the stem of a shoot just above a leaf, removing shoots 8cm/3in long. Trim just under a leaf, remove the bottom leaves and insert the cuttings several to a 9cm/3½in pot in cuttings compost (50:50 soil-less compost and grit). Water them in and return the tray to a shaded propagating case, or cover with polythene and stand it in a warm place out of full sun. Alternatively, try rooting your cuttings in pots of rooting gel as described on the packet. The original tuber will make new shoots and should be potted up properly after these have sprouted.

When the cuttings have rooted, pot them separately into 9cm/3½in pots and when their roots have filled these, pot on into 13cm/5in pots. After a while, harden these and the mother plant off and, ultimately, plant them out into well-cultivated soil in late spring. Once established, the plants will need staking and regular watering and feeding to give of their best.

Pinching, stopping and disbudding

Having mastered the art of raising dahlias from cuttings, you can manipulate their growth by pinching out the growing tips to make them branch. Whether and how much you decide to do this depends on what you want from your plant. Having allowed the cutting to settle in its new pot, let it grow until it has made three pairs of leaves, then nip out the growing tip protruding beyond the third pair. This will encourage side shoots to grow and bush out. Harden the plant off and plant it out. The leading shoots can be pinched again to encourage even more shoots and flowers for garden display and cutting. But if you want a large-flowered dahlia to make the biggest, prize-winning blooms possible, one stop during its growing season may be sufficient.

TOP Buds burst from the tuber when it's safe in the propagating case
BOTTOM Shoots are taken as cuttings to yield late colour the same year

Larger tubers will often push up a forest of shoots in spring and if you are looking for quality rather than quantity, it is wise to thin these down to five per plant early in their development.

To encourage large flowers on long stems, you need to disbud your plants. Each main stem will carry one terminal (topmost) bud with two smaller buds below. If you remove the smaller buds, all the energy will rush into the terminal bud and create one large flower.

CANNAS

Canna 'King Midas'

Indian shots or cannas (from the *Cannaceae* family) continue to grow in popularity as plants that add flamboyance to outdoor borders, particularly towards the end of summer. Cultivars such as bronze-leaved, orange-flowered 'Wyoming' and yellow-flowered 'King Midas' are the stalwarts of many a 'hot' border of red, flame and gold. Combining well with dahlias, crocosmias and Mexican sunflowers, cannas add colour with their lush foliage as well as their exotic blooms. The plants we grow are hybrids that reach anything from 60cm/2ft to 2.2m/7ft high, created by a long history of cross-breeding between species originally from Asia and tropical North and South America.

I like to grow a few plants exclusively for display in the greenhouse, for which a favourite is *Canna* 'Panache' (see page 107). But most gardeners use the greenhouse to provide a frost-free winter home for their plants – cannas are of borderline hardiness – or to bring them on during spring to create larger specimens to be planted out when all danger of frost has passed.

Forcing cannas under glass

Cannas left in the ground outside during winter are relatively slow to come back into growth and unlikely to flower much before late summer and autumn. A cold spring followed by an indifferent summer can mean that sometimes plants are only just beginning to flower when the onset of autumn forces them to die back again.

These are compelling reasons to lift cannas carefully in spring, divide the rhizomes if necessary, pot them up and bring them under frost-free glass to make early growth. Your time and effort will be repaid by having fresh plants in full leaf to harden off and plant out in late spring. These will grow fast, produce better foliage and flower earlier than those left in the ground.

Bring the whole plant on to the potting bench, knock some soil away from the roots and take a good look at the rhizomes. Don't split them up into tiny sections, but aim instead for clumps suitable for pots of 25–30cm/10–12in diameter, with enough room for your fingers to push compost around the outside of the roots. Young plants may not need splitting at all. Larger ones can be divided by half and then into quarters. Look for healthy buds and shoots on the rhizomes, and then use a knife or secateurs to cut through thick rhizomes, leaving buds on each portion. Remove all dead leaves and old flower stalks, pot the sections separately, water them in and stand the pots on the floor or staging.

Aftercare

Wait until the compost surface dries out before watering again to make sure that air gets to the roots. New foliage is vulnerable to strong sunshine, so apply light shading to glass (see pages 15 and 179) where appropriate. In an unheated greenhouse, forcing will be slower than in a heated one and you must keep an ear to the weather forecast. When late frosts are expected, drape a double layer of horticultural fleece over the plants, or move them temporarily to a warmer shed or porch. As spring merges into early summer, harden plants off and, when there is no longer any danger of frost, plant them out in well-nourished soil.

Buying new cannas

The most reliable purchase is a potted plant bought during summer while actively growing. It will be flowering well by late summer or autumn and can be potted on for greenhouse display or planted out into good soil to perform outdoors. Some canna stock is infected with virus, so buying plants offers the chance to look for healthy growth and avoid any with streaked or splotched foliage.

A cheaper type of plant material is available during early spring, when packets containing short lengths of canna rhizome can be bought in garden centres or by mail order. Pot these as soon as possible, setting the rhizome horizontally in a shallow pot of good compost. Although it would seem likely that shoots should sprout fastest in a heated propagating case, my experience shows they are likely to 'cook' and rot away. Keeping them on a warm windowsill or on the greenhouse staging are better ways of coaxing them into growth.

TOP To divide and pot up a canna, first carefully fork it up in spring
BOTTOM On the bench, cut through rhizomes to divide the clump

RAISING VEGETABLES AND HERBS FOR THE GARDEN

3

I find it much easier to feed my family healthy quantities of fresh vegetables, fruits and salads when they are literally on my doorstep and I don't have to keep remembering to shop for them. And early in the year, when the soil is cold and wet, I love to get ahead by sowing and growing crop plants for the kitchen garden under cover. While the soil is warming up outside I can watch my young plants developing, and when planted out they create an instant vegetable patch.

Newly potted purple sage raised from cuttings

EARLY STARTS

It is true that most of the crops gardeners want to grow in their kitchen gardens and allotments can be sown direct into the soil. In many ways this is good practice, because seedlings germinated *in situ* save time and equipment, and in theory establish better as they are not subject to root restriction or disturbance.

In reality, however, early starts are often thwarted by rotten weather and wet, sticky soil. Yet with the likes of onions, shallots and garlic it is important to give them as long a growing season as possible. Also, where summers are relatively short, we need to squeeze the cropping of tender crops such as courgettes, sweetcorn and pumpkins between the last frosts of spring and the first of autumn. Sowing under glass and planting out decent-sized specimens when temperatures are warm gives us a head start. The plants will romp away and soon be yielding. Larger plants are also less likely to be decimated by slugs, whose nocturnal grazings are capable of annihilating newly germinated seedlings.

Direct outdoor sowings are wasteful and imprecise, because you have to sow plenty of seed into drills to be sure of adequate germination. Later, when you thin out young plants to the correct spacings, with few exceptions the thinnings are wasted. Indoor sowings are more controlled as you can prick out every seedling and grow it on to make a plant, which is an important consideration if you've invested in expensive F_1 seed.

Indoor sowings and plantings are useful for space management too. In tiny plots, the turnaround of crops is fast and you might need to sow in a bed where a previous crop is still finishing off. By using the greenhouse for the initial stages of sowing and raising young plants, you can gain a month or more of much-needed time. If you want your kitchen garden to be decorative as well as productive, it also enables you to constantly plug gaps with sizeable plants.

There are two golden rules for growing plants for the kitchen garden. One is hardening off (see page 21).

Plants raised under glass will be softer than their direct-sown counterparts, so it is vital to accustom them to colder temperatures, wind and weather before the next shock of having their roots disturbed. The soft leaves will be a temptation to slugs and rabbits, so make sure when hardening off that you protect them from both. The other golden rule is rotation.

Rotation

When you plant out vegetable plants, you must pay attention to crop rotation. This is the principle of making sure that you do not grow plants from the same family of vegetables in the same patch of soil year after year. Rotation helps to avoid the build-up of pests and diseases and also helps the gardener to make the best use of the different fertility levels in the soil.

Most gardeners use a three-year rotation, by allocating compatible groups of vegetables to three areas. These groups are legumes (peas and beans) and plants from the onion family; root crops, including plants from the carrot and potato families; and plants from the brassica (cabbage) family. Every year, each group rotates to the adjacent area, and the soil is prepared in each area according to what is to be grown in it that year. This means that in one section in the first year there will be legumes and onions. Their soil receives plenty of manure but no fertilizer. These are followed the next year by brassicas – cabbages, sprouts, kales and so on. They get some manure, fertilizer and lime – but never put lime and manure on the soil together. Then in the third year come the root crops such as carrots and potatoes. They need no manure or lime, but some fertilizer.

I divide my plot into four, because I allocate a sizeable area to pumpkins, which I slot into the sequence after the legumes. You can slip in catch crops (quick-growing crops) like salads anywhere there's room.

What vegetables to grow

Not all vegetables are suitable for an early start in the greenhouse and though it is great to experiment, root crops like parsnips, swedes and most carrot varieties won't take kindly to being restricted in pots and then transplanted. Here are some crops that do respond to being started off under glass, roughly in their order of sowing.

Onions

The first sowings of the year should be onions, as they benefit from a long growing season. Regardless of when they are sown, there comes a point in summer when the plants start to turn yellow and the bulbs won't grow any larger. That is the moment to fork them up, loosen their roots and leave them on the soil to ripen in the sun. After a couple of weeks, gather the onion crop and dry them further by laying the bulbs on a rack or crate in the sun and moving them under cover during rain. This way, their skins harden enough to store through winter.

During winter and early spring, fill small pots with seed compost and sow the small, black seeds evenly over the surface. They will germinate without any extra heat, but you can speed up the process by placing them in a propagating case at 10–15°C/50–60°F. Narrow, grassy seedlings emerge and should be pricked out when the second leaf is at what I call the 'elbow' stage – that is, poking out sideways. I prick lots of them out into 15–17cm/6–7in pots, spacing the seedlings about 2.5cm/1in apart. Leave them to grow on the staging in a cool temperature (an unheated or frost-free greenhouse is ideal) until they are about 15cm/6in tall. By this point, the soil outside will be greatly improved and you can separate the individuals and plant in their rows, 13cm/5in apart. Where space is an issue, try setting three to a station, with 8cm/3in between the plants and 20cm/8in between the clumps. Make sure that they go in at the right depth, with the base of the bulb about 1cm/½in below the surface.

Plants of the early summer cabbage 'Marshall's Kingspi' are given a good start under glass

Leeks

A valuable winter crop, leeks also need a long growing season. Make a late-winter sowing and germinate at 13°C/55°F. Having pricked out the seedlings 4cm/1½in apart into a larger pot, let the young leeks reach pencil thickness and 15–20cm/6–8in high, without staying under glass too long or suffering from the stress of being restricted in their pot. They should be fresh and green, with good root systems but not competing for space and nutrients. Aim to plant during spring, dropping each into the bottom of a hole 5cm/2in wide, 15cm/6in deep and 15cm/6in apart, made using a dibber. Do not firm them in, but water them so that the water washes soil around the roots. Like onions, leeks can be planted three per station to save space. Early varieties will be ready by late autumn, but leeks are hardy and stand well in the soil all winter.

FROM LEFT TO RIGHT Lettuce 'Little Gem' seedlings at the right stage for pricking out; now filling their pots, young plants of lettuce 'Sangria' are ready for hardening off; lettuce 'Little Gem' plants are ready for planting out and have a head start on the slugs

Lettuces

Cut-and-come-again lettuce types are grown close together because they don't need room to heart up and are therefore best sown in drills straight into the ground. But it is worth giving lettuces that are to grow to maturity outside an early start under cover. Lettuce can also be grown inside the greenhouse during winter (see page 64).

Great discipline is required for lettuce sowings, because the job is never finished. For the longest cropping, sow a pinch of seed every two to three weeks from spring to late summer. Scatter the seed thinly over the surface of a 9cm/3½in pot, cover it lightly with compost and set it in a propagating case to germinate. The temperature must not be too high, as seeds are inhibited from germinating above 21°C/70°F. Prick the seedlings out into cells or small pots and grow on in a cool, well-ventilated greenhouse. After hardening off, plant them out about 23cm/9in apart. Don't grow too many at once and vary the variety so that you don't get bored with the same one. You could sow two different kinds in the same session – perhaps a red-leaved butterhead type such as 'Sangria' with a dense cos such as 'Little Gem' – to yield at the same time. I find that iceberg types do better early in the season, because they tend to cook in the heat of summer. In late summer and autumn sow hardy lettuce varieties to stand during winter and produce early crops in spring. They may need cloche protection in colder regions.

Celeriac

Sow celeriac in spring as it needs a long growing season. Germinate it at 18°C/65°F and prick the seedlings out without delay into individual pots or cells. Plant out the young plants in late spring 30cm/12in apart in rows 35cm/14in apart. Make sure that they don't go short of water, clean the tops of old leaves as they die back and crop from autumn onwards.

Artichokes

The seeds of globe artichoke germinate readily at 15°C/60°F in spring, yielding plump, attractive silvery seedlings full of vigour and raring to go. When propagator space is at a premium, sow into a small pot, remove the seedlings when germinated, let them develop and then transfer them to individual pots or cells to grow on. If you have plenty of space, save time by sowing one seed directly to each cell in a pack. Move on to a slightly larger pot later. These will be large plants and unless you are mad about artichokes, a few will be plenty. The mound of silvery leaves is attractive enough to use out in the garden as a foil to brightly coloured flowers.

Sweetcorn

By spring, temperatures in the greenhouse are warm enough for sweetcorn to germinate on the staging. Fill a pack of cells with seed compost, pressing lightly and brushing excess compost away. Sow one seed per cell by making a small hole with your fingertip and burying the seed by its own depth. In no time, pointed, bright green seedlings will be thrusting their way through and the young plants will soon be ready to harden off. If their bed is ready, plant them out as youngsters 8–10cm/3–4in high. You can buy extra time by potting them on in the greenhouse to become larger, more

FROM LEFT TO RIGHT Artichokes are easy to raise from seed, as the silvery seedlings of 'Vert Globe' prove; a batch of sturdy young sweetcorn 'Applause' ready for hardening off and planting out; pumpkin seeds are sown edgeways to avoid rotting

established plants maybe 20cm/8in tall. Sweetcorn needs warmth to grow and in colder areas, beware of making too early a start. It is not frost hardy and if you take a gamble with an early planting, put out good-sized plants and stand by to cover them with horticultural fleece should a late frost be forecast. I usually make my first sowing in mid-spring and a further sowing in late spring or early summer. For good pollination, plant out in grid formation with 30cm/12in between each plant, or go for a more informal approach and create a square planting area: tread a diagonal path from one corner to another, and then set the plants out randomly but roughly 30cm/12in apart on each side before planting.

Cucurbits

Marrows, courgettes, cucumbers, squashes and pumpkins are related and those that are destined to be grown outdoors receive the same basic treatment. These plants are not frost hardy, so timing is crucial in order to plant them out during late spring and early summer. I sow into 9cm/3½in pots, setting two seeds to each pot, positioning them on edge as that way they are said to be less prone to rotting than if laid flat. After germination, remove the weakest. If sowing an expensive variety with few seeds per packet, sow one seed per cell to save wasting any. Should the plants fill their pots while the weather is still cold outside, pot them on into 13cm/5in pots so as to hold them under glass for longer. Outdoor ridge type cucumbers such as 'Marketmore 70' or 'Burpless Tasty Green' can be planted against a climbing frame to save space. For marrows, courgettes and pumpkins, I put a bucketful of manure and garden compost on the soil and fork it in, creating a small mound. I make a flat dent in the top and plant into this.

For giant pumpkins, you need the earliest start possible. Grow a large plant under glass and move it outside earlier than normal, creating a polythene or glass cover to shield it from wind and weather. Established early and kept as warm as possible, with luck the plant will flower and set fruit early, for a longer growing season.

Brassicas

All brassicas are prone to clubroot, a debilitating disease which once in your soil will remain there for twenty years. Make a rule always to grow your plants in soil-less compost and never buy or accept as gifts from other gardeners plants raised in garden soil or loam. That way you will protect your soil from possible infection. There is a succession of brassicas to grow throughout the year and with all of them I sow into pots first, and then prick the seedlings out into small pots or cells. You can save space by setting three or five seedlings per pot, as these tough little plants don't mind being pulled apart later. Brassica seedlings are prone to legginess, but you can sink the seedlings up to their leaves in compost to rectify the situation.

My favourites are the winter brassicas raised from spring sowings, because they crop at a time of year when there is little other fresh green stuff around. Careful planning ensures a succession, with an early-spring sowing of Brussels sprouts to crop from autumn through winter, a spring sowing of Savoy cabbages for winter and a spring sowing of kales for winter and early spring. A late-spring sowing of sprouting broccoli and winter cauliflower will yield in early spring. The edible parts develop when there are no caterpillars around.

BEANS

Full of starchy reserves, large bean seeds germinate with speed and enthusiasm. To have them erupting through the compost surface right under your nose on the greenhouse staging is exciting stuff. The three main types of bean regularly grown in our kitchen gardens can all be started under glass.

Broad beans

The first sowings of the season will be of the hardier broad bean. Varieties like 'Aquadulce Claudia' and 'Reina Blanca' are sown straight into the soil in late autumn, but can also be started in late winter under glass. To save space I sow these beans into a deep seed tray, setting them 5cm/2in apart grid fashion. But germination is so reliable that you could set them one per small pot or cell. When they have grown to 5–10cm/2–4in high, harden them off and plant them outside. Shake the seedlings from their box and gently prise their roots apart. I generally set mine in staggered double rows with 20–23cm/8–9in between the plants and 30cm/12in between the rows. I leave a slightly wider gap before the next double row to leave room for picking.

French beans

French beans are slightly hardier than runner beans, but they will not germinate or grow well if the soil temperature is under 10°C/50°F. When spring is cold and wet, an indoor sowing buys valuable time. I grow dwarf French beans such as 'Delinel', which has quite a meaty texture, and 'Pongo', a succulent type with narrower pods. Using somewhat shallow 15cm/6in pots, I space the seeds out 4cm/1½in apart over the

TOP Broad bean seedlings, grid fashion in a tray
BOTTOM LEFT A damp, cool day is best for setting out young plants
BOTTOM RIGHT Each young plant is firmed into the soil

surface of multi-purpose compost and then bury each by its own depth with my finger. At this time of year, the staging is usually full, so I stand the bean seeds on the floor in a crate to germinate. In spring greenhouse temperatures, the seedlings are up within two weeks and ready to harden off after another two. I plant them in double staggered rows in late spring, with 10–13cm/4–5in between the plants. A second sowing of French beans made in high summer will crop before the weather turns cold and wet in autumn. Of course there are climbing French beans too, but I tend to favour runner beans for climbing.

Runner beans

The most obvious advantage to raising runner beans under glass is being able to plant them against their supports, exactly where you want. Sow the beans about a month before you want to plant them out, timing the planting to avoid the last, late frost as they are not hardy. Don't fall into the trap of being too early with runners, as they will only sulk in cold soil, and early batches sometimes experience a bad set because the flowers open during cold weather when pollinating insects are scarce and pollination itself slowed down by chilly nights. My sowing method is similar to that for French beans, except I choose slightly deeper pots. I set the seeds 5cm/2in apart over the surface, water them in and leave inside the greenhouse to germinate. When the young plants reach about 10cm/4in high, you can harden them off and plant them out. Meanwhile, you can be getting on with fixing rows or tepees of canes or hazel poles to support the plants.

TOP LEFT Runner bean seeds are spaced evenly over the compost surface
TOP RIGHT Within a couple of weeks, the seedlings come thrusting through the compost
BOTTOM At this stage, runner bean plants are ready for planting out

SHALLOTS AND GARLIC

Bulbs of garlic 'Solent Wight' are broken into cloves for potting

Shallots and garlic are started from bulbs and cloves rather than from seed. They benefit from an early start because, like onions, their growing period extends only to high summer and when weather conditions decree, their leaves start to turn yellow and they will make no more growth. You can then loosen the crops from the soil, lift them and leave them to dry off in the sun before storing.

Garlic

Theoretically, the best time to start garlic is during autumn, because direct planting them then ensures that the roots are established before the growing season begins in earnest. Reliable varieties such as 'Solent Wight' are bred for a mild, damp climate rather than a drier Mediterranean one and usually do well even on heavier soils. The cloves are often planted into ridges, in an attempt to keep the young roots drier during wet winters.

If you don't manage an autumn planting through lack of time to prepare soil or bad weather conditions, I can vouch for late-winter plantings made under glass. This is always a pleasant job, usually carried out against a backdrop of fragrant early-spring bulbs such as hyacinths and narcissus. No extra heat is needed and the potted cloves stand on the staging until they have made good growth and conditions have improved outside.

Shallots

Shallots are like small, mild-flavoured onions, but they grow differently. Bought as small single bulbs to plant out in late winter, these single bulbs proliferate in the soil and form a clump. So at harvest time, a cluster of seven to ten bulbs are produced where one was planted.

The growing method is similar to that for garlic, except that the small bulbs are already single and ready to be planted in their pots. Again, make a small hole for each bulb and firm it in with the neck just above the surface. A cluster of leaves sprout and the plants should be hardened off and planted out as for garlic. Stand a few pots in the kitchen early in the year and in the warm they will sprout tasty leaves, ready to be snipped off and chopped as a fresh, tasty garnish in the same way as chives.

Storage and use

After harvesting, break the shallots into individual bulbs and keep both these and whole garlic cloves dry and frost free with good air circulation for use through winter. You can set aside small proportion of each crop to use as stock for potting up during the next winter.

HOW TO GROW GARLIC

Young garlic plants will have an excellent start under glass and as long as you plant individual cloves in late winter, the bulbs will be of good quality by midsummer.

1 On the workbench, break the garlic bulb carefully into individual cloves and fill a corresponding number of 9cm/3½in pots with good potting compost.

2 Using a finger as a dibber, plant each clove into the middle of a pot, firming it in gently, so that its tip is just above the compost.

3 Water the cloves in, stand the pots on the staging and let the cloves sprout into young plants. When the plants are well grown, but before they become pot bound, harden them off and then plant them out into double rows. I space them 15cm/6in apart, with 30cm/12in between the rows.

cost to buy one decent-sized, ready-grown specimen. As well as sowing seed, you can raise herbs from cuttings, which is a useful method when you already have plants to use as stock or need to bulk up named varieties of sage, lavender, thyme, marjoram or rosemary that will not come true from seed.

Herbs from seed

BASIL (*Ocimum*) is probably the odd man out because this tender herb likes warmth and prefers to stay under glass permanently. I sometimes sow it into a pot, and then prick out three seedlings per small pot to grow on. Or I might sow several seeds to each cell of compost in a block. To do this, make a flattish dent in the surface of each cell with a finger, sprinkle the seed in and gently cover it. After germination, pot the lot on as one. Use the plants quickly and you'll have eaten them before they start competing with one another. One year I pricked seedlings out 5cm/2in apart over the surface of a wide, shallow bowl and made a miniature basil garden. Always make sure that the container is well drained, use good compost and water in the morning, because a combination of wet roots and cooler nights spells disaster for basil. There are many varieties to try, all with subtly different flavours. Large-leaved 'Siam Queen', and lime, cinnamon, Greek and purple-leaved basils are a few examples. They are so easy to use, raw or cooked.

TOP LEFT Basil 'Red Rubin' was sown three seeds to a pot
TOP RIGHT One pinch of seed per cell gives rise to clusters of basil seedlings
BOTTOM Grow clusters of basil seedlings together for a quick crop

A quick peep at any seed catalogue reveals a mouth-watering range of herbs that are easy to raise from seed. Anyone setting up a herb garden or, like me, attempting to line the paths of a kitchen garden with a tapestry of useful and aromatic plants can save a fortune by growing large numbers of plants for less than it would

THYME (*Thymus vulgaris*) To grow plenty of common thyme, sow a pot or small tray with seed, germinate it in a propagating case at 15°C/60°F, or on the greenhouse staging, and then prick the seedlings out either grid fashion in a large tray, or individually to small cells. Harden the young plants off and plant them where they will grow. Initially, they make untidy mats, but after a while there will be enough growth for you to be able to clip them into neat dome-like shapes after flowering.

SAGE (*Salvia officinalis*) is ridiculously easy to germinate from its large, easy-to-handle seed at around 15°C/60°F. Prick out the seedlings into individual pots or cells and grow them on into small plants. Nip out growing tips to make them branch and harden them off before planting out. Like thyme, sage is evergreen and the silvery mounds of foliage are welcome during winter.

LAVENDER (*Lavandula angustifolia* cvs) and **HYSSOP** (*Hyssopus officinalis*) For low hedges and edges, lavender or hyssop make good choices and both are straightforward to grow from seed.

CHIVES (*Allium schoenoprasum*), **FENNEL** (*Foeniculum vulgare*), **MARJORAM** (*Origanum majorana*) and **SUMMER SAVORY** (*Satureja hortensis*) are easy to germinate under glass and grow on for the garden.

PARSLEY (*Petroselinum crispum*) can be temperamental. I usually sow seed thinly over the surface of a filled, prepared seed tray and leave the tray out on the staging. Parsley seed responds to varying temperatures and the fluctuations between warm days when sun is intensified through glass and cool nights usually do the trick. I prick the seedlings out into seed trays, harden them off and then plant them out. Being able to gather huge bunches of super-fresh parsley is a real luxury.

Herbs from cuttings

After the spring rush, when you have planted outside most of the flowers and vegetables raised for the garden and the greenhouse is set up for summer, it is a good time to take cuttings of a wide range of plants including herbs.

There will be plenty of tempting shoots on sages and thymes and at this time of the year they root speedily and well. Following the instructions on page 24, take semi-ripe cuttings of bay (*Laurus nobilis*),

Cuttings of bright-leaved bay are inserted into gritty compost

lavender (*Lavandula angustifolia* cultivars), rosemary (*Rosmarinus officinalis*) and myrtle (*Myrtus communis*) during summer, remembering to keep them good and short. You can use a propagating case, but make sure that it is well shaded and kept cool. I find that cuttings struck into pots, covered with polythene and kept out of the sun seem to root well. Evergreens such as bay and myrtle usually take longer to root, so be prepared to leave the cuttings undisturbed through winter, and take plenty to allow for losses. With sage, thyme and lavender, the best cuttings material arises after the plants have been trimmed back following the first flush of flowering.

GREENHOUSE CROPS

4

Even if you do nothing more adventurous than grow a few tomatoes, you'll find that home-grown fruit allowed to ripen on the plant and in its own time will amaze you with its flavour. There are many exciting tomato varieties to try, but do find room as well for cucumbers, peppers, aubergines, physalis and more. A greenhouse opens up all sorts of fruitful possibilities and you could grow peaches, melons, grapes and citrus. These are surprisingly easy to grow and need not take up too much space. You can also use the greenhouse to raise winter lettuce and to force tender stems of rhubarb or sea kale.

Rich pickings from the greenhouse

A VARIETY OF CROPS TO TRY

A seedling of cucumber 'Birgit' thrives in the warmth

Owning a greenhouse opens up exciting opportunities to grow crops that need a longer, warmer growing season than that available out of doors. Even with minimal heating, a greenhouse extends the season because glass intensifies the heat of the sun and the crop plants are protected from frost, wind and rain.

Plan what to grow carefully. Permanently planted long-lived crop plants such as grapevines, figs, peaches or fruit salad bush will lock up a lot of space in a greenhouse border. Even though they'll yield better if given a generous root run, growing them in large pots is usually a better alternative, as pots allow you to move them about and even place them outside for part of the year.

Seasonal plants such as tomatoes, melons and cucumbers have a specific slot in the year, taking up their growing positions during spring and finishing in the autumn, when you can take their dying haulms out of the greenhouse and compost them prior to a good clean-up. These make large plants and you often have to secure their growth to the greenhouse roof, which makes them difficult to move. It is a good idea to draw a rough plan of your greenhouse and work out exactly how you are going to use it during the coming growing season. This way, there will be no wasted space or money. When I fill out my seed orders, at the same time I plan where the tall crops will grow, and whether they will be in beds, growing bags or large containers. Smaller potted crop plants such as aubergines, peppers and physalis are more mobile and slot in around the others on the floor or staging.

Winter-hardy lettuce and other vegetables

By winter, my greenhouse is crammed full of plants sheltering from the weather and there is little room for winter-hardy lettuce. If you've space, though, it is satisfying to raise some under glass for fresh, early pickings in spring. Perhaps the easiest way to grow lettuce is to leave once-used growing bags where they are in the autumn. Pull out the thickest root masses of old tomato and cucumber plants and loosen the compost with a hand fork before soaking several times to thoroughly moisten it and adding fertilizer. Cut the plastic to make a larger growing space in the top of the bag and then either sow or plant. I find it easier to sow into pots, prick the seedlings out into small pots or cells and then transplant into the top of the growing bag 15–20cm/6–8in apart. Choose varieties suitable for greenhouse cultivation such as 'Fristina' and 'Rosetta'. Three sowings, made in early, mid and late autumn should give a useful succession in spring.

Other candidates for growing bag tops or borders are late-winter sowings of radish and carrot, especially stump-rooted types. Experiment in spring with early sowings of French beans.

With all greenhouse crops growing during winter and early spring, keep the air around them as dry as possible by practising good ventilation and watering during fine mornings. Feed weekly and watch out for aphids attracted to the soft tissue.

Potatoes

The greenhouse is a useful place to raise potatoes to eat out of season for a special treat. Outdoors, the planting of quick-growing early varieties is usually timed so that growth appears above ground when frosts are no longer likely, though some gardeners push the boundaries and cover the tops with fleece. Under glass, plant during late winter, setting chitted (sprouted) seed potatoes two per pot. Containers need to be at least 30cm/12in wide; virtually anything will do, including old dustbins and buckets with drainage holes in the base – even an old compost sack or bin liner with holes in the base and a rolled-down top will save on large pots. Use potting compost, good garden soil or a mixture of the two, and place a 12cm/5in layer in the base. Stand the potatoes on top and cover so that they are buried by 10–15cm/4–6in of compost. When the shoots are 15cm/6in tall, cover them with more compost so that the leaf tips are just showing. Continue adding compost, or 'earthing up', in this way until there is no more room in the container. For the best crops, water and feed well. Try both early and second early varieties. Seed potatoes become available again in summer and plantings made then will crop in winter.

Forced crops

Rhubarb crowns lifted during autumn, left loose on the ground to feel the frost (this breaks dormancy) and then potted, covered and set under the staging in the greenhouse will send up long pale early stems for harvesting during early and mid spring. The covering could be a large pot with holes blocked, or even a thick black polythene bag.

Pot-grown strawberries are a treat, but they need good ventilation

Sea kale, too, can be forced in a similar way. Harvest the pale shoots and they should be crunchy and mild with no strong cabbagey taste.

Both should be discarded after cropping. Or plant them back into the garden and rest for a year before harvesting again.

Early strawberries

Root a few runners in pots during summer, pot them on into larger pots when they are ready and leave the plants outdoors until early winter. Bring them under glass, pot them on again if necessary, and keep them frost free but extremely well ventilated with plenty of space around them. Where heat is available, 10°C/50°F is an ideal temperature for gently forcing strawberries on during late winter and early spring, but they will still produce early fruit with the minimum of protection. When they show signs of growth, feed them every two weeks and as the early flowers open, hand pollinate them with a soft brush, transferring pollen from flower to flower, to ensure a good set of tasty berries.

TOMATOES

The tomato (*Lycopersicon esculentum*) belongs to the potato family, *Solanaceae,* and has a long history of cultivation in Mexico and Peru by the Incas, Mayas and Aztecs. Soon after the conquest of Mexico, seeds found their way to Spain and under the name of love apple the tomato eventually reached France and then Britain around 1596, where it was viewed with suspicion, as some thought it poisonous, while others were under the illusion that it might be an aphrodisiac. British colonists carried tomatoes to North America, where many varieties have been named and recognized over the years.

Home-grown tomatoes are one of the easy pleasures available to anyone with a greenhouse. As they need space between spring and autumn, even a small, unheated or frost-free greenhouse is suitable. The flavour of home-grown tomatoes surpasses anything to be found in a shop and even the most humble variety will be transformed by having been allowed the time to ripen properly on the plant. Watching the plants develop, tending them and experiencing the distinctive smell on your yellow-stained fingers is deeply satisfying.

Growing tomatoes under glass

The three most popular ways to grow tomatoes are in soil beds, in growing bags and in large pots of 30cm/12in diameter. There is much to be said for soil beds, as the plants will enjoy a greater root run and will not need watering so often as those restricted to bags and pots. But when the same soil is used year after year pests and diseases build up. Dig the border over carefully, adding plenty of well-rotted garden compost or other soil conditioner but nothing as strong as manure, or else the plants will grow fast and leggy. Ideally, let the soil settle for a few weeks before planting. If you grow the plants cordon-style, as one main stem with the side shoots removed, they will need to be set 45cm/18in apart and a good 17cm/7in away from the glass or wall. I would carry on growing them like this from year to year, perhaps resting the bed periodically by switching to cucumbers or putting the tomatoes in growing bags. Should the plants show signs of losing vigour or succumbing to disease, either change the soil or place them in growing bags on top.

In my greenhouse, staging runs down one long side and there is a soil bed across the bottom end. This is too shaded for tomatoes, but ideal for four cucumbers and three melons. This leaves the other long side free for four growing bags and for four large pots in which I grow my tomatoes. I fill smaller gaps with potted aubergines and marigolds grown to repel whitefly.

Those short of time can whizz down to the garden centre in spring and pick up tomato seedlings or young plants ready for planting out, or send off for them, but I like to raise mine from seed, choosing as many as six different types (see page 70). This is an indulgence, but the different shapes, sizes and colours of the fruits look so wonderful together. I don't grow more than three plants of each, so there will be seed left over. You can reduce the cost of doing this by sharing with friends or storing surplus seed in a dry, cool place for the following year.

It is often said that cucumbers and tomatoes do not grow well in the same greenhouse but, though they prefer slightly different growing conditions, they can be made to compromise.

Growing from seed

Tomato seeds germinate readily in a temperature of 21°C/70°F, easily achievable in a heated propagating case. But timing is all if the resulting plants are to receive the warmth and light necessary to grow on. Gardeners with a greenhouse heated to a minimum of

HOW TO GROW TOMATOES

If gardeners do nothing else with their greenhouses, most will grow tomatoes, as they are so easy and worthwhile. The protection of glass means earlier fruit and less chance of blight.

1 Sprinkle seeds thinly and evenly over prepared compost, cover lightly and germinate in warmth. Remove from the propagating case and as soon as the seedlings reach this stage, prick them out into individual 9cm/3½in pots and grow on.

2 When the roots are well established, plant into a growing bag, soil border or larger pot. For growing bags, the best method of training is to coil some nylon string under the root ball and fix it to a wire above, and then wind the stem around the string.

3 Tomatoes are mostly grown as cordons, which means restricting the plant to one main stem. To do this, remove all the side shoots formed in the gap between leaf and stem. Don't remove flower buds by mistake.

prick out four seedlings into separate 9cm/3½in pots when their true leaves (shaped ones) start to show. When these pots are full of roots and the plants 10–15cm/4–6in high, they are just the right size for planting into growing bags. But if they are intended for borders or larger pots, pot them on to 12cm/5in pots. Give each a cane as support and remove any side shoots produced between stem and leaves with finger and thumb. Give away or swap any surplus plants.

Training and tying

Where several plants are growing in close proximity, the cordon method (in which you remove all side shoots to create a single stem) is the best way to get maximum crops in the shortest space of time. However, this should not stop the curious from experimenting – perhaps setting one plant in the middle of a growing bag and training out two side shoots from the base of the plant, one on either side, to form three upright fruiting stems (you then remove their side shoots). Do this by fixing three upright canes, one in each planting hole. Tie a cane horizontally between them at the base and tie the developing side shoots to the canes so that they grow along at first, and then upwards. Those on a tight budget can buy one plant and make more of it this way, and the plant will benefit from having the whole growing bag to itself. Another wheeze is to root long side shoots as cuttings. Bush varieties of tomato have been bred to produce fruit with no need for supports or side shoot removal. They take up more space, but save time for busy people.

Providing support is easy whatever growing method you are using. For plants in growing bags, make the planting hole, coil one end of a length of nylon string (natural fibres will rot) in the base, plant on top of this, then wind the string around the stem of the plant and secure the other end to a wire fixed 1.5–1.8m/5–6ft above, using a quick-release knot. Continue to wind the stem around the string as growth continues, loosening the string if it becomes too tight. Plants in soil borders are easy to support using canes, but these look neater and hold weight better if tied in to horizontal wires higher up. My freestanding pots have freestanding canes, as I often want to move them. Fixing canes to growing bags is only

I learned not to use natural fibre strings, as they rot

10°C/50°F can sow with confidence during late winter, but those of us whose greenhouses are either unheated or heated only to exclude frost have a juggling act to perform, and no two seasons are ever alike. I usually sow some varieties in late winter, and the rest in early spring. Tomatoes are surprisingly tough and even if those started early don't grow as fast as they should and I sometimes have to bring them into the house at night, they make it in the end and produce early fruit.

I sow the seeds thinly in a 9cm/3½in pot, cover them lightly with compost and leave the pot in the propagating case until they germinate, which takes about a week. I remove them as soon as the seed leaves (the first narrow pair) emerge and, to end up with three good plants, easy if they are standing on an earth border and the canes can be pushed down into the soil. Otherwise secure the tops to wires fixed across the glass.

Stopping

When the plants reach the greenhouse roof, nip out the growing tip a couple of leaves past the topmost fruiting truss. Unless the plants got off to an early start in a warm greenhouse, five trusses are enough anyway. More may fail to ripen and waste the plants' energy.

Care

Tomatoes are not particularly labour intensive, but they need lots of regular attention. They grow fast, so you need to remove side shoots and tie or train the main stem about every three days. As plants mature, remove old, tatty leaves towards the bottom of the plant when they turn yellow. Also, cut away odd leaves here and there to let light penetrate through and reach developing fruit trusses. Plants in containers will be thirsty and need their water requirements checking twice a day at peak growth. They'll also need a high-potash liquid fertilizer at every other watering as the first fruits begin to set. Failure to supply enough water and food causes discolouration of the foliage and encourages blossom end rot. Plants will also flounder if temperatures rise above 32°C/90°F. Adjust the vents and damp the greenhouse down three times a day in hot weather if possible. If the thermometer still registers high temperatures, apply some light shading to the south-facing side. Do not damp down when temperatures and light levels are low. Tomatoes can suffer from a range of pests, diseases and disorders but most are reversible if spotted early. Tomato blight (the same disease as potato blight) is the worst threat to a crop and starts with yellow and brown marks on both leaves and stems. This disease is not as bad under glass as it is outdoors and can be controlled by spraying with Bordeaux mixture. Most symptoms involving discoloured leaves are disorders associated with poor care (conditions may be too dry, too wet, too cold or too hot, or the plant may be starved).

TOP Pick fruits by snapping a joint just above the calyx
BOTTOM Tomato 'Red Zebra', suffering from blossom end rot

ABOVE A dark fruit of tomato 'Black Brandywine'
OPPOSITE: CLOCKWISE FROM TOP LEFT The small yellow fruit of tomato 'Ildi'; with 'Kellogg's Breakfast' it's a case of carve the tomato; 'Striped Stuffer' bears beautifully marked fruit; tomato 'Ponderosa Golden'

Fruiting

Fruits set well on their own, but tapping a plant's cane or string sets the pollen flying. Leave fruits on the plants until they are fully ripe, and then pick them by snapping the bend in the old flower stalk, so that the fruit comes off easily with calyx (spidery part) attached. There are usually a few green fruit left at the end of a season. Pick these and place them on a warm, sunny windowsill or in a drawer with a ripe apple or banana. Ethylene, a gas given off by the fruit, will speed up ripening.

My favourite tomatoes

There is now such a wide and mouth-watering choice of tomatoes that when perusing the seed catalogues during autumn it is hard to settle on just a few varieties to grow each year.

Everyone has their favourite tomato cultivar and mine is the F$_1$ variety 'Sungold'. The plants are draped with long trusses strung with cherry-sized orange fruits from early in the season right to the very end. Thin-skinned, bite-sized and the sweetest tomato I've ever tasted, they rarely make it to the kitchen as I eat most of them while watering the greenhouse. I usually grow 'Shirley' as well. This is not a particularly adventurous

choice, but you can't beat it for tasty, medium to large, round, bright red tomatoes produced in liberal quantities with no fuss. These two are my basics, leaving me free to experiment by choosing a few different types each year. I like unusual colours, and growing a wide range means a summer of impressive-looking tomato salads. I have enjoyed striped 'Tigerella' for its orange-yellow stripes on red fruits 5cm/2in across. Heritage varieties are interesting, but although I've tried a few, including massive, pink-hued 'Brandywine' and blackish 'Noire Charbonneuse', none has so far made it to the top of my list.

The smallest tomatoes are tinier than cherry types. Although they're a little fiddly to pick, the likes of 'Mexico Midget', 'Currant Gold Rush' and 'Ildi' are useful for adding whole to salads. Cherry types are an ideal size for picking easily and eating without cutting or slicing. For a long time 'Gardener's Delight' was a favourite with me, but although the fruits are tasty I prefer 'Sungold' and certainly find the latter easier to grow and more trouble free. If your greenhouse conditions are not exactly right, 'Gardener's Delight' can be prone to cracking or greenback, where an area of unripened leathery tissue spoils the fruit. 'Cherry Roma' bears 2.5cm/1in long plum-shaped fruits of good flavour.

Medium-sized tomatoes are ideal for slicing for sandwiches and as toppings to gratins. Some of the yellow kinds, such as 'Lemon Boy' and 'Limon-liana' (syn. 'Plum Lemon'), are said to have a citrusy flavour. Not all tomatoes have a round shape and some are long, like 'Sausage'. These days there is a lot of interest in the large-fruited types. The beefsteak kinds such as 'Big Boy' and 'Dombito' have been joined by a wide range of large-fruited heritage varieties, many from the USA. On the whole, the large-fruited types take longer to ripen and you should give these first priority when it comes to sowing. The names alone are worth contemplating, such as 'Halladay's Mortgage Lifter', which produces individual fruit weighing 450–900kg/1–2lb; 'Kellogg's Breakfast' bears huge, juicy, pale fruit and 'Striped Stuffer' large, attractively striped fruit. You can really show off with some of these, when it's a question of who's going to carve the tomato.

AUBERGINES

Aubergines or egg plants (*Solanum melongena*) in the tomato and potato family (*Solanaceae*) are native to Asia with a record of cultivation stretching back to fifth-century China. They have also long been popular in India and anyone familiar with Indian cuisine will recognize them by the name brinjal. As they are essentially short-lived tender perennials, we tend to treat them as one-season wonders. They are wonderfully uncomplicated to grow and all gardeners should give them a go. You can grow the large, dark purple fruits of commerce, or choose jazzy purple-flecked varieties or those with white fruits or long, narrow fruits like sausages or snakes. Their large purple flowers are showy enough to rival the ornamental solanums, and the plants are not massive and therefore easy to accommodate.

Sowing aubergines

Sow the seed during early spring, sprinkling them thinly over the surface of prepared compost and covering lightly with their own depth of compost. Germinate in the propagating case at 21°C/70°F. Although books will tell you that they need warm temperatures after germination, in my experience the seedlings can withstand cool nights as long as their compost is not too wet. Take them out of the case after germination and let them acclimatize to the greenhouse temperature before pricking them out into individual pots.

Care

Pot the young aubergine plants on as they fill their pots with roots, finishing them in a 23cm/9in pot. They can be planted into growing bags, but I prefer to leave these for larger crops like tomatoes and stand the aubergines in pots on the floor or staging wherever they will fit in.

Successful fruiting depends on restricting the number of fruits to five per individual plant. When the plant reaches 60cm/2ft tall, pinch out the growing tip and secure the main stem to a cane. When five well-spaced fruits have formed, pinch out further side shoots and any further flowers and developing fruits, so that all energy is channelled into swelling the chosen few. Failure to do this means a larger, more straggly plant with lots of small fruit struggling to reach a good size and maturity before the end of the growing season. To free up valuable space during late summer, when temperatures are reliably warm there is no reason why you shouldn't stand the attractive, fruitful plants outdoors.

Water the plants adequately, and feed them with a general-purpose fertilizer at any growing stage when the plants are established in their pots. As soon as the first fruits have set, give the plants a high-potash fertilizer weekly. Aphids, whitefly and spider mite can be a problem, but good husbandry will keep them at bay.

Types

Reliable purple-fruiting kinds include 'Money Maker No 2' and 'Purple Prince'. 'Violetta di Firenze' bears violet and whitish-pink fruits but needs a good summer to do well. 'Zebra' is striped purple and white. 'Brilliant' is a long, pale purple variety and 'Green Wonder' bears a cucumber-shaped fruit of palest green. 'Casper' is a good white with elongated fruit, while those of 'Clara' are rounded. You can buy mixtures too, which yield a variety of colours and shapes, but I like to know my plants' individual names.

CLOCKWISE FROM TOP LEFT Aubergine 'Bambino' is attractively striped; the fruits of 'Bianca Ovale' are rounded and white; for a long sausage shape, choose 'Brilliant'; the snake-like fruits of 'Tropic Long' are purple; 'Money Maker No. 2' is a traditional dark blackish purple; the long fruits of 'Thai Long Green' (syn. 'Elephant Tusk') are pale green

CAPSICUMS

Capsicums are hot and sweet peppers, members of the potato family (*Solanaceae*) originating in tropical America. Both are forms of the wild species *Capsicum annuum*. The hot chilli peppers have the longest history of cultivation, especially in ancient Mexico. They were discovered by Christopher Columbus and found their way into Europe during the fifteenth and sixteenth centuries.

Sweet peppers, also known as bell peppers or pimentos, produce the largest fruit, starting off green when immature but ripening to green, red, orange, yellow, brown and even near-black. Chilli peppers have smaller fruits and vary in the fieriness of their taste. The heat of chillis is a serious business and measured in Scoville units. Some are very mild, but others – notably 'Orosco', 'Scotch Bonnet' and 'Thai Hot Dragon' – could blow your head off. It is the oil in the seeds that provides the most intense heat, so de-seeding a chilli pepper helps defuse it somewhat. The oil will taint your fingers, so wash well after handling them and avoid touching eyes or delicate skin. Some chilli peppers have been bred mainly for ornamental purposes, with compact size and a profusion of small fruit.

Peppers are slower to mature than tomatoes and the plants are smaller. I usually grow mine in large pots, constantly moving them around to where there is space. With their colourful fruits, they are as ornamental as they are productive. In a cool greenhouse not blessed with heat for an early start, crops will mature towards late summer. I like to grow a selection, including a large-fruited sweet pepper good for stuffing and one or two chillis of different strengths.

CLOCKWISE FROM TOP LEFT Paprika sweet pepper 'Albaregia'; long, narrow, crispy sweet pepper 'Big Banana'; chilli 'Galkunda Miris'; ornamental purple-red chilli 'Masquerade'; the famous and prolific hot chilli 'Jalapeño'; chilli 'Calypso Dkbona'

Sowing peppers

In early spring, sprinkle a few of the flat, rounded seeds into a small pot of seed compost and place the pot in a heated propagating case at 15°C/60°F. After germination, harden the slender seedlings off in the general atmosphere of the greenhouse and when they are large enough prick them out into single pots or cells. As they fill their containers, move them on to larger pots, finishing them in anything from 17cm/7in to 25cm/10in depending on the scale of the plant. Some of the more ornamental types of chilli pepper whose fruits tend to be small, prolific and stingingly hot on small bushy plants may be suited to pots of 10–17cm/4–7in diameter, whereas the larger sweet peppers will benefit from a greater root run.

Care

Make sure that the plants have the space they need to develop and feed them with a high-potash fertilizer when the first fruits start to set. Pollination should occur naturally, but a humid environment will help it along. A light spray up under the foliage when the flowers are open is a good idea, especially when the atmosphere is hot and dry.

As a tribe, capsicum plants vary in height and shape, so treat them according to type. Peppers with long stems and heavy fruit need a stake; the shorter more compact varieties can do without. Sweet pepper varieties like 'Cherrytime' produce lots of small fruits and can be left to their own devices. Those with fewer, larger fruits such as 'Lany' may need thinning to push the plant's energy into a few good-sized fruits.

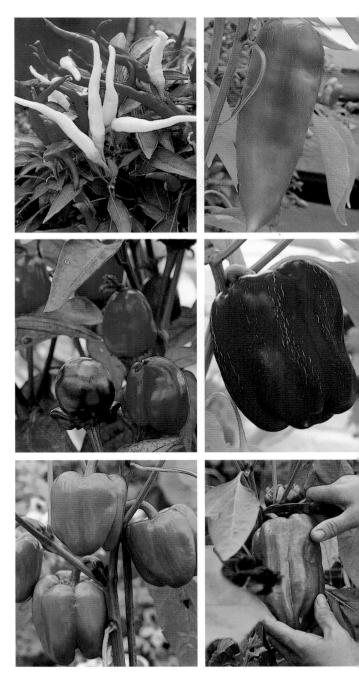

CLOCKWISE FROM TOP LEFT Hot, ornamental and compact chilli 'Medusa'; attractive but fiery hot chilli 'Orosco'; large sweet pepper 'Titanic' is ideal for stuffing; sweet pepper 'Lany' also reaches a good size; sweet pepper 'Cherrytime' produces many smaller fruit; the medium hot chilli 'Peruvian Purple'

PHYSALIS

TOP LEFT Young plants of the Cape gooseberry *Physalis peruviana*
TOP RIGHT The attractive Cape gooseberry flower
ABOVE Fruits grow in lantern-like calyces
OPPOSITE When the calyx turns papery, the fruit will be ripe

The Cape gooseberry (*Physalis peruviana*) belongs to the potato family (*Solanaceae*) and, as the botanical name suggests, has its origins in South America. Best described as a short-lived tender perennial, it is easy and rewarding to grow, yielding a crop of tasty orange fruit enclosed within papery calyces towards the end of summer and well into the autumn. These last well even after being picked and if stored at cool temperatures will still be edible at Christmas time. Although the plants are usually kept for just one growing season, they can be overwintered for earlier crops the following year.

These are tall plants, reaching up to 1.8m/6ft, but there is another tasty and fruitful species, *Physalis*

pruinosa, known as goldenberry, which is shorter and bushier, growing to about 60cm/2ft. This North American annual yields a generous crop of smaller fruits. As temperatures cool, production stops and the plants die back. Closely related *P. alkekengi*, better known as Chinese lantern, is grown for its showy orange 'lanterns' but bears unpalatable fruit.

Sowing physalis

Sow seeds in early spring, spacing them out over the surface of prepared seed compost in a pot and covering lightly with a sprinkling of compost. Place them in a heated propagating case to germinate at 18–21°C/65–70°F. When the seed leaves have opened out, move the pot to the staging and leave for a few days before pricking the seedlings out into individual 9cm/3½in pots or, if space is at a premium, into cells to pot on later. As the robust plants develop and fill their pots with roots, move them on into larger pots until they reach a large container of 23–30cm/9–12in diameter. Once they are cropping, you can stand the plants outdoors when the weather is hot and dry, but bring them in when temperatures start to cool.

Care

When physalis are established in their pots, feed them weekly with a general-purpose fertilizer, changing to a high-potash one when the fruits begin to set. With their pretty yellow and dark maroon flowers and dark-veined calyces, these plants are decorative, so use them well between other plants in the greenhouse display.

The taller types may need staking to keep their long stems upright. After fruiting in winter, keep the plants frost free and put up with as much top growth as possible until spring, because winter pruning tends to result in dieback. Prune hard as growth resumes and the plants will sprout back into growth, flowering and fruiting earlier than fresh plants raised from seed.

CUCUMBERS

ABOVE LEFT A spring seedling of cucumber 'Palermo'
ABOVE RIGHT 'Palermo' produces abundant crops in summer

The cucumber (*Cucumis sativus*) in the family *Cucurbitaceae* originates from southern Asia and, despite the fruits being bitter, it was widely grown by ancient Greeks and Romans. Fortunately for us, modern breeding has given us crisp, all-female varieties without a trace of bitterness.

Slice a cucumber fresh from the plant and it is so full of moisture that you can see beads of it glistening on the cut surface. It is possible to grow cucumbers outdoors, but they are a different type, with their own charm. If you want the long, straight, smooth-skinned fruits of commerce, but better, grow cucumbers in a greenhouse to harvest from midsummer to autumn. Self-sufficiency in both tomatoes and cucumbers for one quarter of the year is well within the reach of anyone with a greenhouse.

Sowing cucumbers

Where seed is cheap and plentiful, sow two per 9cm/3½in pot and if both germinate, pull the weaker out, leaving the strongest to grow on with no root disturbance. F$_1$ seed is expensive; my favourite variety 'Palermo' currently costs about £3 for only five seeds. Sow these singly, on edge rather than flat, in 8cm/3in pots, placed in a warm propagating case (21°C/70°F is ideal).

As with all tender crops, timing is important because young plants must be able to tolerate prevailing night temperatures soon after germination. You can wean them gently by putting them on the open staging by day, but replacing them in the propagating case for the night. For a frost-free greenhouse a mid-spring sowing is about right, especially if the plants are destined for a border where the soil needs to warm up. Avoid planting young cucumbers into cold, damp soil and, if necessary, buy time by potting plants on into 13cm/5in pots and keeping them up on the staging until the soil in the border warms up. A useful tactic is to plant into a slight mound raised above the general level of the bed.

Planting

In the border, an ideal spacing for cucumbers is 60cm/24in apart, but mine have to put up with paired plantings 30cm/12in apart, although there is more space around the pair before reaching the melons next door. The soil will have been forked over and nourished with well-rotted garden compost and some general fertilizer, then left to settle for a few weeks.

Cucumbers thrive in growing bags; two per bag is more sensible than three in such a restricted space. Alternatively you could grow one cucumber in a large (minimum diameter 35cm/14in) pot, but pot on gradually to this size.

Training

The simplest way to grow cucumbers is on a cordon or single stem, rather like tomatoes. Once a plant has established and begun to grow, tie a string to the base of the plant, wind the string around it and secure the string to a wire fixed as high as possible above. Continue to wind the main stem around the string as it grows. Side shoots will grow out from the main stem and produce flowers, which in most cultivars will all be female and have an immature cucumber developing behind the flower. Should male flowers be produced, nip them off, as fertilization can result in bitter-tasting fruit. When you have a small cucumber growing, nip out the growing tip of its side shoot two leaves after the fruit. If you do this to all the side shoots, the plant will stay under control. When the main stem reaches the top wire, you have to be creative and tie another piece of string to the wire and fix the other end to a point higher up in the eaves, thus creating an extension. Cucumbers will keep forming along the stem for as long as the plants are fed and watered, until cooler autumnal weather halts production.

Care

Feed cucumbers in borders every two weeks with a high-potash fertilizer and those in pots and growing bags weekly, starting as the first fruits form. I usually mulch the roots of established plants in borders, as watering gradually exposes surface roots: a mixture of 50:50 good topsoil or potting compost and well-rotted garden compost spread 5cm/2in deep over the surface makes a difference. Cucumbers like a warm, humid environment and I spray up under the foliage on hot days to cool the plants and help prevent spider mite. Tall marigolds (*Tagetes*) here and there help repel whitefly. Powdery mildew is almost inevitable on older leaves, but controlling growth as described above and providing maximum ventilation for good air movement

Cucumber 'Petita' makes a good crop of chubby fruits

helps moderate this disease. Strong plants will outperform the mildew, succumbing only towards the end of the season when plants are finished anyway. Pick the fruit regularly when it is slim, fresh and succulent, so as to keep more coming.

MELONS

Sowing melons

There is no doubt that you will enjoy the best melon plants and crops from greenhouses warmed up by generous heating (ideally to 15°C/60°F) early in the year. This enables an early start, and consequently more fruit will ripen. To grow plenty of melons, you need space, as even under ideal conditions each plant is likely to yield only four or five fruits. With the joint advantages of warmth and space, you can make two or three sowings, starting in late winter and finishing in mid to late spring, to give a succession of fruit to be cropped sixteen to twenty weeks after sowing. Thus harvesting will be finished in time for an autumn clear-up, followed by an influx of tender plants. Sow as for cucumbers, setting two seeds per pot and thinning down to one after germination – unless the seed is expensive, in which case every one counts. The plants are smaller than cucumbers and slower to grow.

Planting and training

After young plants have produced five leaves, plant them into borders or growing bags. Melons grown in a large, heated greenhouse, where there is room to train stems properly and support fruit with net hammocks in the traditional way, are a joy to behold. In a small greenhouse maybe the answer is to eschew other crops for a year and just grow a whole side full of melons really well. The ideal is to fix taut horizontal wires 30cm/12in apart up the inside of the wall and roof. Tie the main stem to the wires as it grows. After planting some 90cm/3ft apart, equip each young melon with an upright cane to take the main stem. When this reaches the top wire (the height of this will be dictated by the size of the greenhouse), nip out the growing tip to stop the stem. Meanwhile, stop side stems (laterals) by pinching the growing tip out after

five leaves. Male and female flowers develop on secondary side shoots close to the main stem. Once you can see that fruits are set and growing, and to prevent rampant growth, stop any other shoots made after one leaf, as these will be superfluous.

An awful compromise

In my medium-sized, barely heated, general-purpose greenhouse I grow my three melon plants a year squeezed between two sets of cucumbers in a less than ideal fashion. I don't have the patience to position wires across the glass and neither do I have time to net the fruit. I attach a string to the base of each plant, as with cucumbers, twine the string around the plant and fix it above the plant. Each plant produces only three melons per season and these reach only a moderate size and therefore the plant seems to be able to support them naturally. I know I could do better, but this compromise still yields six home-grown melons we really look forward to and enjoy.

Pollination

Female flowers are obvious because they have a small fruit behind the bloom. For a reliable set of fruit, hand pollination will be needed. Remove a male flower while the greenhouse is warm at midday and the sun is shining, pull the petals back to expose as much pollen as possible and brush the stamens lightly in the centre of all the female flowers open.

Types

There are plenty of tempting varieties described in the seed catalogues and few will disappoint. If, like me, you are running a cold greenhouse, look for varieties especially suited to low temperatures. Cantaloupe types include 'Bastion' with smooth golden skin and sweet orange flesh, 'Sweetheart' with grey-green skin

HOW
TO
GROW
MELONS

In my greenhouse, heated only to exclude frost, there is a long wait for the soil bed to warm up in spring. On a visit to a range of renovated Victorian greenhouses, I picked up the idea of sowing and raising young melon plants in terracotta tubes. This way, the roots are not disturbed or suddenly surrounded by cold, wet soil. The method would work just as well for cucumbers.

1 I stand my three terracotta tubes on a short length of plywood and fill them with compost, firming gently as the compost settles into the tubes. Brush away any excess and then sow two seeds per tube. Water in gently and transfer the lot into a heated propagating case for germination at 18°C/65°F. Once the seedlings have grown, move them out on to the staging and thin down to one per tube.

2 When the roots have penetrated to the bottom of the tubes, slide one tube at a time from the plywood and into position on the moist, prepared soil bed or growing bag. Make sure it is secure by twisting down slightly into the soil or compost. The roots will grow down into the soil unhampered. I usually space three melon plants 45cm/18in apart along the back of the border, and then train them up strings fixed to a horizontal wire higher up.

3 As the plants grow and produce flowers, pollinate them by hand and restrict growth by stopping the side stems after five leaves. Stop further shoots after one leaf. Allow three well-spaced fruits to develop on each plant and remove any others. Water the plants, damp down regularly and feed weekly. You'll smell the ripe melons when they are ready to pick.

and light orange flesh, and the French heirloom variety 'Petit Gris de Rennes' with tasty orange flesh.

Care

Cultivation of melons is straightforward. Problems arise, though, when temperatures are still low during spring and providing the sort of heating they should have is too expensive. When planting straight into the soil border of a greenhouse, I would let the young plants fill 13cm/5in pots with their roots first. Set the rootball slightly higher in the soil than is normally recommended, but pull some soil up to cover the roots, creating a slight hill. This raises the stem base above soil level and prevents it from rotting.

Several weeks prior to planting, the bed should have been prepared with additions of well-rotted manure or compost to ensure healthy growth and development. There should be a good layer of loamy soil on top of any manure, again to protect the stem and roots from cold, wet conditions early on.

Water in the mornings, using tepid water, especially when temperatures are cooler than you would like. Melons enjoy growing conditions similar to those preferred by cucumbers, particularly when it comes to warmth and humidity in the early stages. Later, when the fruits have set, a drier atmosphere is better. In my greenhouse, where I grow such a mixture of plants, I am afraid melons have to endure a drier, well-ventilated atmosphere, although I do spray water up under their leaves regularly.

Feed weekly with a high-potash fertilizer when the fruits reach 8cm/3in across. Melons take their time to ripen and should not be cut until they are ready to eat. Mine always let me know when this is by emitting a sweet fragrance.

LEFT The weighty fruit of melon 'Oregon Delicious' is well supported
RIGHT Melon 'Bastion' is ideal for a barely heated greenhouse

CITRUS

ABOVE Citrus seedlings are beautiful, but plants raised from seed rarely crop well.
OPPOSITE Calamondin (x *Citrofortunella microcarpa*) bears many small fruits.

Citrus trees such as oranges, lemons, limes and kumquats (*Fortunella*), from the *Rutaceae* family, originate from south-east Asia and islands of the eastern Pacific, but long cultivation has spread them to almost every corner of the globe. In warmer countries, they are grown outdoors as crop plants, and in colder climes they are cherished in house, conservatory or greenhouse for their evergreen, aromatic foliage, scented blossom and fruit. Owners of greenhouses heated only to exclude frost will probably end up shunting their citrus plants between greenhouse, house and garden during the year, but with a little effort, healthy fruitful plants are within reach.

Position

Finding the best place for your plants to grow might require some juggling but will keep them active, healthy and showing as much flower and fruit as possible. Citrus can tolerate temperatures down to freezing, but although plants will remain alive in a cold or cool greenhouse, they will drop fruit and take some time to wake up in spring. At temperatures below 12°C/54°F citrus stop growing and while their roots are inactive they can't make good use of any fertilizer you are giving them. So those expensive winter feeds will just accumulate in the pot unless the plant is warm enough to use them. They won't set fruit below 11°C/52°F. The best bet is to move your plant to a warm conservatory or bright room in the house for the winter, but even here there are pitfalls. The room needs to be cool, ideally 12–15°C/54–60°F, without the dry air and fluctuations in temperature usually experienced when temperatures soar higher. Ideally, citrus should feel only a slight variation between night and day temperatures.

Once the greenhouse has warmed up in spring, citrus plants can be moved into it to benefit from the extra light available, but they will need shading as light intensifies. In summer, stand citrus plants outdoors in a lightly shaded spot among other plants so that they can benefit from the humidity given off from pots and from leaves. As temperatures drop in autumn, move them first into the greenhouse and then to their indoor winter quarters.

Potting

Citrus cultivars (the named varieties of orange, lemon and so forth) rarely grow on their own roots and have usually been grafted on to stock plants. The stock can often be lime intolerant, so unless you know otherwise, it is safest to assume that citrus are lime-hating plants. They need a pH of 6.5 and tend to find proprietary ericaceous composts too acid. Therefore, it is best to make your own. Take three parts of John Innes No. 2 compost and mix it with one part of either lime-free grit or potting-grade bark.

Potting on generally needs to be done every two to three years, when the plant is pot bound. Do this in spring, carefully teasing out a few roots and choosing a pot just large enough to fit a finger around the outside of the rootball in order to push the new compost into the gap. Citrus will grow perfectly well in plastic pots but clay ones look better and are heavier, and therefore more stable and porous, allowing the roots to breathe better in winter.

Care

Citrus need soft water and rain water is the best choice when it is available. If it is not and your water is hard or alkaline, the best bet is to boil the water and let it cool before using it. But if push comes to shove, it is better to give them tap water than let them suffer extreme dryness at the roots. Water when the surface has dried out, making sure that you give enough to those in large pots to penetrate to all the roots. Where citrus spend winter at cold temperatures, let the top few centimetres of soil dry out between waterings.

Citrus are hungry feeders whose leaves will turn yellow at the drop of a hat if they are starved or kept so cold that they cannot use the food they are given. I feed them weekly when they are showing signs of active growth and fortnightly at other times. At low temperatures, it is best not to feed them at all. There are specific citrus liquid fertilizers on the market, but you can use a high-nitrogen feed with added trace elements in summer, changing to a well-balanced feed during winter.

Pruning

Regular pruning won't be needed, and correcting the shape of a plant by snipping out the odd shoot here and there during spring is about as much attention as a citrus needs. Should you need to prune hard for any reason (to be rid of pests or tired, yellow foliage, for instance), plants will respond astonishingly well from cuts made into thick, woody stems.

Propagation

Although growing citrus from pips found in commercial fruit is fun, this can't be viewed as a serious method of propagation leading to fruitful plants. The pips usually germinate readily, especially those of Seville orange, but could take twenty years to flower and fruit. Those of lemon and lime are usually the best bet, and being less highly bred they are more likely to resemble the parent.

Cuttings of named cultivars root with moderate ease but also take their time to fruit. This is why most plants are grafted commercially. Experiment with seed and cuttings, but invest in a couple of good named citrus so that you can enjoy their flowers and fruit during the wait.

Types to try

Although growing plump, juicy oranges sounds tempting, unless you have the space for plants to grow large, the fruit may look out of scale on short plants pruned to fit inside a small greenhouse. Better choices, if you want smaller orange-type fruit, would be satsuma (*Citrus unshiu*), mandarin (*C. reticulata*) or willow-leaved tangerine (*C.* x *nobilis*). Most gardeners start off with lemons. For years, Meyer's lemon (*C.* x *meyeri* 'Meyer') – strictly a lemon and lime cross – was the most widely recommended and grown. Most specialists now say that *C.* 'La Valette' is a better choice, being more robust and fruitful. Limes are fun and you might harvest enough key lime fruit (*C. aurantiifolia*) for a pie. An alternative would be sweet, pipless Tahiti lime (*C. latifolia*). The leaves of Djeruk lime (*C. amblycarpa*) can be used to flavour food and this small citrus is usefully windowsill-sized.

The kumquat *Fortunella* 'Fukushu' is an extremely attractive small plant, rarely without both flowers and fruit. But I don't find the oval fruits particularly tempting to eat. I'd say the same for the limequat hybrid known as Calamondin orange (x *Citrofortunella microcarpa*, or x *C. mitis*, to use its old name). Maybe the best idea is to harvest the fruit green and use it like a lime. You can try growing grapefruit (*C.* x *paradisi*) if you have space, and there are curiosities such as Buddha's hand (*C. medica* var. *digitata*).

CLOCKWISE FROM TOP LEFT *Citrus aurantiifolia*, otherwise known as key lime; the shapely lemon *C. limon* 'Garey's Eureka'; *C. sinensis* 'Malta Blood' has deep crimson juice and flesh; Buddha's hand (*C. medica* var. *digitata*) is strangely finger-shaped and used to scent rooms; *C. maxima* or shaddock produces large fruit good for marmalade; *C. limon* 'Variegata' is both attractive and edible

DESSERT GRAPES

TOP A standard-trained vine looks bare after winter pruning
ABOVE LEFT New growth on standard-trained 'Madresfield Court'
ABOVE RIGHT Remove tendrils as they are produced

The domestic grape (*Vitis vinifera*), from the *Vitaceae* family, has enjoyed such a long history of cultivation that its origins are hard to pinpoint, but it is thought to have come from the Mediterranean and Black Sea coasts.

Grapevines are tendril climbers and under glass they have the potential to take up a lot of space. The classic method of training is to plant the roots in a bed outside the greenhouse and run the stem inside (through a hole made large enough to allow for expansion of the stem). A rod or rods (the main stems) are then trained vertically under the glass of the roof. Or you can give the roots the run of a specially constructed greenhouse bed. Horizontal wires are fixed to the sides and roof to support the side shoots, from which bunches of grapes hang downwards. The proper care of a grapevine is time consuming and in the spring it needs regular attention by way of tying in and pinching back to restrict and restrain growth. The leaves make a shady canopy during summer but fall during autumn to let light through for winter.

An alternative approach is to grow grapevines in pots, and I think this method suits small to medium-sized greenhouses given over to mixed collections of plants better. You can still enjoy the fresh young vine leaves, bunches of grapes and autumn colours from a couple of vine varieties without them dominating half the greenhouse.

Growing grapes the traditional way

The first job is to create a wide, rich bed of soil to sustain the roots of your vine. Dig the border as best you can, incorporating plenty of well-rotted manure. An old-fashioned border would be about 1.5m/5ft wide, but most of us will have to compromise here. A 75cm/30in width would be all I could offer in my greenhouse.

The job of fixing horizontal wires 25–30cm/10–12in apart and preferably a good 25cm/10in, or at least 15cm/6in, away from the glass is not an easy one. In a wooden greenhouse, vine eyes fixed to the main supports can support taut wires. They must be strained tight, as baggy wires look dreadful. You can buy various gizmos for fixing wires to aluminium greenhouses. Getting the wire a sufficient distance from the glass is difficult but it is important for air circulation around the foliage.

Planting, training and pruning

Usually, only one vertical rod is trained per vine. Start by planting a two-year-old vine when dormant, preferably in the autumn. If there is space for more than one, set the vines 90cm–1.2m/3–4ft apart. Next – and although this seems a vicious thing to do to a young plant it is essential – you must cut it back immediately to two buds. This encourages vigorous growths, one of which will be the main stem or rod attached to the wires as it grows. The other can be rubbed out with your fingers.

While the vine is reaching its ultimate height, you should stop the leader each winter. In its first winter after planting, remove half to two-thirds of the growth it made in the previous season, cutting into ripened rather than soft wood. Again, this seems harsh, but it helps establish strong laterals. During the second and subsequent winters, prune back one-third to half of the new growth made in the previous growing season until the main rod reaches its ultimate height. If you have the glass space to train two or three main rods, but want to accommodate only one lot of roots, you can train more than one rod from a single plant, but make sure that they run vertically and remain at least 90cm/3ft apart from each other. Remove fruit during the first two years.

In spring, secure the laterals or side shoots growing from the main rod to the horizontal wires on alternate sides and nip back any superfluous side shoots to one leaf. The chosen side shoots don't sprout horizontally by nature and are easily snapped, so tie these down gradually by tightening the string a little every day. They should produce flowers, in which case stop them two leaves after the flower. If they don't, stop them after five leaves. Stop further shoots made after one leaf. Regular pruning takes place every winter soon after the leaves have fallen and removes almost all the growth made during the previous summer, by cutting back the lateral shoots to two buds. This regular pruning builds up stumpy spurs along the main rod. One of the buds will become next season's fruiting lateral. The other is security in case the first is broken. Remove the spare shoot once the first and main lateral is growing well. Avoid cutting into older wood, except when the leaves are off in winter, because at other times, especially late winter and early spring, the cuts will bleed sap.

Care

In late winter, loosen the rods from their ties and allow them to drop down to a lower, more horizontal position rather than following the roof. Then, when they are ready to grow, the sap flow will be even, encouraging equally strong shoots from the bottom spurs as the top. Once they have sprouted, tie the rods back to their original position and begin training. During this surge of new growth, damp both rods and floor when temperatures are warm, to create humidity. Moisten the roots well too; this might take several soakings after a dryish winter rest. During winter, vines are best kept unheated, so that they can lose their leaves and become dormant. Should you need to keep the greenhouse frost free for other plants, you will just about get away with this. With mature vines, while they are dormant, you can peel the top layer of bark away from the rods. This important though not essential winter task removes overwintering pest eggs or disease spores and is satisfying to do. Every winter, top dress the bed with a mulch of two parts of good potting compost and one part of well-rotted manure.

Fruit

When the flowers have opened, hasten pollination along by gently stroking the flower cluster in one hand, then passing on and doing the same to the next. Do this at midday with the sun on the flowers, and then damp down to create the humidity necessary for pollination.

LEFT The grape 'Mrs Pearson' is a Muscat needing heat to mature
RIGHT Muscat 'Hamburg' is good for a pot and needs warmth
OPPOSITE 'Mrs Pince's Black Muscat' bears fruit of superb flavour

Thinning will be needed, both in terms of bunches and individual grapes within the bunch. In the first proper growing season, allow only two or three bunches to form, gradually allowing more until the vine has reached its full size. Then you can allow a bunch roughly every 30cm/12in. To thin the grapes properly, without damage, you need a stick with a small fork at the tip and a pair of long, narrow vine scissors. The first thinning takes place when the small grapes are pea-sized and you'll need to do it a couple more times before the grapes ripen. Failing to thin means crowded, splitting and possibly mildew-infected fruit struggling to swell.

Grapes in pots

For the majority of greenhouse owners, growing grapevines in pots is ideal. You can stand tubs of grapes outdoors for the summer, making an extension of the greenhouse. Their foliage looks very Mediterranean and each potted vine can be expected to yield six bunches of grapes when mature. I train mine as standards,

encouraging a long stem with a tree-like head of growth. To do this, let the main stem reach 1.2m/4ft, pinching out side shoots but leaving three shoots at the top from which to create the head. During winter, prune these shoots back to two buds. In spring, let five well-spaced shoots develop and, as for traditionally trained vines, stop growth two leaves past the flower cluster, or after five leaves if no flowers develop. Stop subsequent shoots after one leaf. Support the main stem with a stout cane, prune back to spurs during winter and pot your vine on every year until it is in a container 45cm/18in across. Thereafter, top dress with fresh compost.

Types

Unless you can provide a burst of extra heat early in the season (minimum 10–13°C/50–55°F) to push dormant vines into growth and bring flowering on early, it is best to choose grape varieties suited to cold or cool greenhouses. I have struggled in vain to grow a decent grape on my 'Madresfield Court' and have finally faced the fact that I've persisted with the wrong type of grape for my barely heated, just frost-free greenhouse. Although this is established in a pot and I'll miss its fabulous autumn leaf colours, I shall replace it with a Sweetwater type: 'Schiava Grossa' (syn. 'Black Hamburgh') perhaps, or amber-fruited 'Buckland Sweetwater'. White grapes 'Foster's Seedling' and 'Royal Muscadine' should also do well and are excellent in pots.

Pests and diseases

The biggest concern of vine growers is usually mildew. This can be prevented or alleviated by increasing ventilation. When training rods against the glass, make sure that they are far enough away. If your greenhouse lacks adequate ventilation, replace some ordinary panes with louvres to increase air circulation. Scrupulous pinching back will curb rampant growth, increasing air movement between the leaves.

Mealy bug like to colonize the rough bark and regular winter stripping (see above) will rid the vine of bad infestations. Control spider mite by introducing predatory mites (see page 186).

PEACHES

Fan-trained peach 'Hale's Early' gives early, juicy fruit

The peach (*Prunus persica*) belongs to the rose family (*Rosaceae*) and originates from China, where there are records of cultivation stretching back to the tenth century BC. Their spread to Europe was surprisingly slow for such a tasty fruit, possibly because they were tried first in warmer countries where, deprived of their winter dormancy, the trees would have been disappointingly barren. Peaches finally reached Britain in the mid-sixteenth century.

Peaches are small hardy deciduous trees by nature, but their flowers come early in the year and late frosts frequently jeopardize pollination. They are also prone to the fungal disease peach leaf curl, whose spores arrive in wind and in rain. The protection of glass means that plants kept under cover early in the year usually remain unblemished. Birds are prevented from eating the fruit too. These are three good reasons for growing peaches under glass. Nectarines are smooth-skinned peaches needing the same training and care.

Training

As with grapes, a traditionally trained glasshouse peach or nectarine will take up a lot of space. Should you be lucky enough to have a lean-to greenhouse with a soil bed against a generous back wall with a height of, say, 2.5m/8ft, you could devote this space to a beautiful and productive fan-trained specimen. Training and pruning is exactly the same as for fans grown outdoors.

Begin by setting horizontal wires against the wall about 30cm/12in apart and 13cm/5in away from the wall. You can start with a young or maiden tree, pruning it back within about 60cm/2ft of the ground in its first late winter and training in two lower laterals, one on each side. From these, train the side shoots in to fill the spaces on each side so that the whole plant makes the shape of a fan. Alternatively, buy older plants whose training has already been started.

Eventually, regular pruning consists of letting shoots develop and tying these in to fruit. Then, after harvesting, cut out the fruited shoots and tie in replacement side shoots. These side shoots are the result of pinching out in spring and summer. Alongside the fruiting stem, others will develop. From these, earmark a likely replacement for each fruiting stem and select a reserve side shoot as well. Reduce all others to two leaves. Stop the replacement and reserve stems when they reach 45cm/18in. The fruit-bearing stems should be stopped after six leaves. After fruiting, cut out the fruited shoots, tie in the replacements and cut back the reserves. This pruning can be carried out year after year almost indefinitely and gets easier the more you do it.

Small potted peaches

Fortunately for those of us with small greenhouses, genetically dwarfed cultivars, such as peach 'Bonanza' or nectarine 'Nectarella', grow well in pots, remain compact and need hardly any pruning. Pot-grown dwarf peaches are a delight. I move mine under glass during early winter, enjoying the display of fine blossom in early spring.

Care

To give permanently planted peaches the dormant period they need the greenhouse should be unheated or, at the most, frost free during winter. Add a good general-purpose fertilizer to the bed in spring and mulch soil beds with well-rotted compost. Keep the trees well watered during summer and spray up under the foliage to ward off spider mite. Move dwarf trees in pots under glass during winter and shade from harsh sun in spring. In summer, put them back outdoors, so as to alleviate the pressure of space in the greenhouse and minimize the likelihood of spider mite infestation. Make sure that the trees are well watered and pot them on as and when they need it, using a 50:50 mix of John Innes No. 2 and a soil-less compost. When they reach the largest pot you can accommodate, make do with a yearly top dressing and give a high-potash liquid fertilizer from late spring through to cropping. In colder areas, protect the rootballs while the trees are standing outdoors in late autumn and early winter by wrapping the pot with insulating layers of hessian or bubble plastic.

Pollination and fruiting

When the flowers are open, go round them at midday with a fine paintbrush, tickling the pollen and moving it from one flower to another. A good set usually follows, but when the fruits are still small you should thin them. On fans they should be at least 15cm/5in apart and evenly spaced. On dwarf cultivars, leave one fruit per cluster and don't expect a mature tree to carry more than ten to a dozen large, juicy fruit.

TOP LEFT The early blossom of peach 'Bonanza'
TOP RIGHT A prolific set of fruit will need thinning
BOTTOM Fruits of peach 'Bonanza' reaching maturity

THE SHOWHOUSE

5

By making a succession of attractive displays throughout the year you can elevate the greenhouse from a utility for overwintering, propagation and crop production to its rightful place as a decorative part of the garden. As important as any shrub or flower bed, it not only offers a different growing environment for a wide range of plants but should be so beautiful that everyone is drawn inside to admire the show. This chapter is all about the ornamental plants of the greenhouse and how to display them. Even for an unheated or barely heated greenhouse, there are plants to flower during every month. Rearranging the display regularly to keep it looking fresh and making artful combinations of flowers and foliage both above and below the staging are some of the joys of greenhouse gardening, and help make it a place that is inviting and great to work in at any time of the year.

The unusual spotted leaf of *Farfugium japonicum* 'Aureomaculatum'

LOOKING GOOD
ALL YEAR

The greenhouse in early spring with bulbs and young plants

There are many beautiful plants able to benefit from the shelter of a frost-free or cool greenhouse and all have different roles to play. Out in the garden, plants break themselves down into a permanent framework of trees and shrubs, with smaller shrubs and perennials filling gaps and exciting additions of bulbs and bedding plants providing quick, easy colour, and it is helpful to think of the greenhouse similarly. Here, you can have permanent plants that you will come to cherish over the years, looking forward to their annual display and the challenge of keeping them healthy for a long period. Raising a variety of shorter-lived plants every year brings a wonderful opportunity to ring the changes. Against this backdrop, there is also room for collections, of carnivorous plants, fuchsias, showy chrysanths or bulbs.

Although this chapter is about plants grown entirely because they are attractive and interesting, do mix them up with productive plants and those passing through the greenhouse on their way to other parts of the garden.

To help you envisage how plants can be used decoratively, I'd like to take you through the seasons in my own greenhouse, where work takes place against a backdrop of fascinating crops and an eclectic collection of ornamentals.

Spring

As light levels and natural temperatures rise, plants in the greenhouse wake up. I make an early start with seed sowing and bulb planting (of summer-flowering kinds), as I need to pace myself for the heavy workload of late spring and early summer. I plug in propagation cases and erect temporary extra staging, and the greenhouse becomes an attractive jumble of plants in pots, artfully positioned with an eye for shape and colour.

Spring bulbs are in full swing, with pots of crocus, narcissus and fragrant hyacinths arranged along one side of the staging, mixed with pots of ferns. Further along, where long-term residents such as the variegated New Zealand Christmas tree (Metrosideros kermadecensis), succulents and pelargoniums dominate, the unusual South African bulbs Lachenalia and Veltheimia are in full bloom. On the floor at the far end, large tubs of bird of paradise (Strelitzia reginae) are producing flower buds, while their leaves make firm paddle shapes against the glass. One year there might be the ferny, tree-like Acacia baileyana, full of fragrant yellow blooms; another, I might make room for a fruity-scented Canary Island broom (Genista x spachiana). In the midst of all this, the potting bench is in constant use and the extra staging is filling steadily with young plants.

By late spring, my greenhouse is bursting at the seams and I long to give everything more space. The most difficult time is when I must take out the extra staging in order to set up four growing bags for tomatoes. I lose space at the bottom end too, when I plant out cucumbers and melons in the small bed. This is when a cold frame or small standing out area comes into its own, as you can place tender bedding plants and crops destined for the garden outside, protecting them from late frosts with a glass lid or fleece.

Inside, the birds of paradise are in full bloom, the yesterday and tomorrow (*Brunfelsia pauciflora*) fills the air with scent from its deep blue flowers, and pelargoniums are flowering around large pots of fast-growing aubergines and sweet peppers. To avoid mayhem I tinker with the display every couple of weeks, and visitors marvel at the energy and productivity.

Summer

The greenhouse almost sighs with relief as I move the last summer plant outdoors to be hardened off and planted. Summer is when you can really enjoy staging a fabulous display of plants, giving each the room it needs to grow, with short-term plants growing alongside long-term ones to give extra summer colour. Mix flowers, foliage and crops in an attractive melange according to height and colour. My porch is shadier than the greenhouse, so as the sun strengthens I transfer plants that prefer those conditions – begonias, streptocarpus, sinningia, ferns and lilies – from the greenhouse to the staging in there. From the porch, I move large pots of South African *Haemanthus*, whose leaves are dying back, to the greenhouse, where they live out the summer dormant and as dry as a bone, on a strip of portable staging in front of the tomatoes.

Autumn

As summer switches to autumn, suddenly, there is a change in the air. The sun is lower in the sky, the nights are cooler and plant growth slows down. There are major changes in the greenhouse as temporary, summer-flowering ornamentals come to an end and tomatoes and other tender crops finish, and I strip them out of their growing bags, pots or borders. This is the cue for a good wash down inside and out in preparation for a sudden

Tall *Antirrhinum majus* 'Royal Bride' adds to the summer display

influx of plants from the garden. Tender subjects, like Egyptian paper rush (*Cyperus papyrus*), candle senna (*Senna didymobotrya*) and acacias which might have spent high summer standing out around the outside of the greenhouse need to come back in and I amalgamate them with inmates still flowering or coming freshly into bloom, such as Chinese foxglove (*Rehmannia elata*) and the newly awakened blood lilies (*Haemanthus coccineus*).

Winter

Winter is not the dour season one might imagine, for the greenhouse in winter is a great place. By choosing carefully, one can be arranging and displaying interesting subjects such as *Pelargonium* 'Copthorne', camellias, *Correa* 'Mannii', *Daphne odora*, South African heathers and *Primula malacoides*. It's not long before the earliest spring bulbs begin to flower and soon, stunning snowdrops such as 'Dionysus', winter aconites and early crocus are fooling us that spring is on the way.

ARRANGING YOUR PLANTS

LEFT Use large and small plants to make attractive displays
RIGHT Aubergines make a great backdrop for scarlet blood lilies

Arranging potted plants on the staging so as to set off each to its best advantage is one of my favourite greenhouse jobs. Taking the time to do this makes all the difference to how the plants look and also gives them the space they need to grow. Handling plants regularly is also a good discipline, because it gives you the chance to remove dead leaves and flowers and to spot pests and diseases before they become a nuisance.

I shield shade-loving plants from the sun during the hottest part of the day by placing them under the canopies of larger plants. Ferns, Cape primrose (*Streptocarpus*) and *Begonia sutherlandii* benefit from this kind of protection.

Height is important if the staging is to look full, and climbing plants have a role to play. Some, such as star jasmine (*Trachelospermum jasminoides*) or passion flowers (*Passiflora*), will last from year to year and pruning will keep their size down for smaller

greenhouses. Either train the climbers to free-standing structures or place their pots under the struts of the greenhouse and encourage their shoots to scramble up and overhead. Short-lived climbers such as cup and saucer vine (*Cobaea scandens*) and Spanish flag (*Ipomoea lobata*) are great fun for this. Sometimes they make such profuse growth that their flowering shoots drip down and entering the greenhouse feels as though you are pushing your way through a lush forest.

You will need other taller plants, so don't be afraid of allowing some of your plants to grow into fine, large specimens. Bushy plants like olives, jade trees and pelargoniums will make the greenhouse look bigger, whereas lots of small plants in tiny pots create a muddled, cluttered feeling. For tiny greenhouses, it is especially important to have a few larger plants to lend some drama to the staging. Inevitably, there will be dormant plants and those that have just been pruned or are sickly. I usually put these together in a separate area, as they tend to have different watering needs as well.

Once you have spaced the larger plants along the staging, including crop plants like aubergines and peppers, use medium-sized plants to fill the middle ground, mixing flowers and foliage for the best effect. Although plenty of colour is marvellous, flowers often look better set against a backdrop of contrasting foliage so that you can really see individual shapes and colours. Use young plants to fill the front of the staging, spacing them out informally around the larger ones. All stages of every plant are interesting and beautiful.

Some of my plants are so tall that they have to stand on the floor. I arrange these in small groups so that I can move around them for watering and to open vents. A bird of paradise (*Strelitzia reginae*) and *Canna* 'Panache' might be joined by an Egyptian paper reed (*Cyperus papyrus*) with some smaller ferns at their feet. Nowhere else in the garden can you create so many changing scenes with quick-growing and developing plants.

HOW
TO
STAGE

Staging is an enjoyable task and, if carried out regularly, doubles as a cleaning exercise. At the end of a session, every plant should be shown off to best advantage, with enough room for growth and air circulation. In the process, dead leaves and flowers are removed and surfaces swept.

1 I usually start by taking most of the plants off the staging and sweeping down the wooden slats. I put back the largest, most imposing plants first, such as this *Scadoxus puniceus*, climbing *Cobaea scandens* and *Metrosideros kermadecensis* 'Variegata', standing them along the back and giving each plenty of space.

2 The next informal row consists of slightly smaller plants such as this tree-shaped, succulent *Crassula ovata* 'Hummel's Sunset'. Stand the plants in the gaps created by the back row, so that they are not quite touching – otherwise they will looked packed in and will suffer for want of light and air.

3 The idea is to achieve a tiered effect from high at the back to short at the front. Some plants, like this *Lotus maculatus*, will be too short for the position you need them for, so raise them on upturned pots to gain height.

4 Low-growing plants like this squirrel's foot fern (*Davallia mariesii*) whose growth flows over the edge of their pots are invaluable for the front of the display. Try growing smaller plants in shallow pans rather than pots, especially for decorating the edge.

5 The finished effect should be an exciting tumble of plants from back to front, with a few surprises between. Use interesting foliage shape and colour and add groups of flowering plants such as the *Viola hederacea*, or young plants growing on.

UNDER THE STAGING

TOP LEFT *Viola hederacea* thrives in light shade
TOP RIGHT A davallia fern enjoys humid shade under the staging
ABOVE *Farfugium japonicum* 'Aureomaculatum' needs refuge from harsh sun
OPPOSITE An attractive fringe of maidenhair ferns beneath staging

To get the most from a greenhouse means using all the available space, and this includes the gap between the floor and staging. This space might seem inhospitable, but it makes a lovely shady, damp home for plants like ferns, piggyback plant (*Tolmiea menziesii*), *Viola hederacea* and other shade-lovers. In turn, their leaves give off moisture and help keep temperatures down during summer.

If you have a soil bed, you can create a marvellous fringe of tradescantia or silvery aluminium plant (*Pilea*

cadierei) during the course of one summer, even though temperatures might be too cold during winter for these plants to thrive year round. The trick is to keep a generous potful as a house plant, strike plenty of cuttings during spring and plant these out under the staging as temperatures warm up naturally during late spring.

My favourite display plants for this shady spot are both hardy and frost-tender ferns. These are cheap to buy as youngsters in spring and, if potted on as soon as their roots fill their pots, they soon grow into beautiful specimens. Grow a mixture of evergreen and deciduous types, because the evergreens will keep the display going throughout winter. Smaller potted ferns can come up on to the top of the staging during spring, the better for you to enjoy their unfurling fronds. They make an excellent foil to pots of spring bulbs. Somewhat tender ferns such as evergreen *Asplenium bulbiferum* do better with warmer temperatures (minimum 7°C/45°F). The delicate fronds of this plant bend down nicely and are usually well furnished with tiny plantlets.

For a mass of large, evergreen leaves burgeoning from under the staging, try hardy *Farfugium japonicum* 'Aureomaculatum'. This humorous plant bears bright green leaves liberally splashed with yellow spots, and although I've never enjoyed it when it is planted out in a garden, I do like it in pots, either as a house plant or poking out from under the greenhouse staging. Repetition is as strong a tool here as it is out in the garden, and I like to see three or more spaced out under the length of my staging, interspersed with ferns.

In an unheated greenhouse, experiment with hardy winter-flowering shrubs such as some of the shorter Christmas box (*Sarcococca humilis* or *S. ruscifolia*). Kept in pots, they can decorate the space under the staging from autumn to spring and delight everyone with their scented winter flowers. After flowering, stand them back outdoors so that they can escape the heat of summer.

LONG-LIVED PLANTS FOR GREENHOUSE DISPLAY

Prostanthera rotundifolia produces pretty pink flowers year after year

Many plants pass in and out of a busy greenhouse, but there can also be a core of long-lived residents that stay put from year to year. They will repay your care by creating a backbone of display plants around which the less permanent plants can revolve.

What to grow

There are many more permanent plants available than the favourites I describe below, and you'd need a pretty big greenhouse to grow even all of these at once. Deciding what to grow for ornamental display depends on your character and discipline. You could collect plants in a totally random fashion as I do – a visitor once raised her eyebrows at my exciting jumble of plants and pronounced them 'an eclectic mix'. The alternative would be to concentrate on certain types or trends of plants. An Australian collection would be totally appropriate because they enjoy good light and many are slightly tender but able to thrive in a frost-free greenhouse. Or you could forego winter heating and grow hardy winter- and spring-flowering plants such as camellias, perhaps with Christmas rose (*Helleborus niger*). Then you could put all these out in the garden for summer to make room for bedding plant or tender crop production.

A collection of South African heaths, Mediterranean garden favourites like olives, oleanders and bougainvilleas, or tender rhododendrons would be satisfying to build and grow.

My favourite permanent greenhouse residents represent all kinds of different types of plant. Some would be trees in the wild, yet are kept small by restriction to a pot and by pruning, so they are almost like bonsai. Many would be shrubs, whose woody stems persist for years and are amenable to pruning. Clump-forming perennials are a useful group of non-woody plants, usually long-lived and amenable to being divided up. Some are evergreen but others are herbaceous, meaning that they die back, usually in winter, to grow again in spring.

Long-term care

The secret of caring for your plants lies in reading the clues in front of you and stepping in at just the right moment before the plant deteriorates. The skills outlined in the other chapters are fairly easy to pick up, but the trick lies in knowing what to do and when to do it.

A shrubby plant restricted to a pot for many years may suddenly lose its vigour, becoming small-leaved and making few flowers. When a plant has made a complete wall of roots in the pot, it then finds it difficult to take up water and nutrients. Feeding roots are forced to the outside where, up against the sides of the pot, they are prone to drying out and dying off. If I have the space in my greenhouse, I will always pot on, because I love to grow impressively large specimens. Top dressing (see page 28) is an option, but the ultimate solution might be to take cuttings with the intention of replacing the plant.

Sometimes loss of vigour is simply down to a bad or inefficient feeding routine (see page 179). Most permanent plants need a dose of well-balanced liquid fertilizer every week to encourage growth in that crucial growing period between spring, when temperatures rise, and the end of summer. Feeding can slow down into autumn and stops when plants almost stop growing in winter.

Mature, clump-forming plants eventually stop flowering when their growth becomes too congested. You can either pot the lot on to a larger pot, or if that is impossible, divide the crowns of growth and pot separately.

Climbers will need tying and staking.

Pruning

Shrubby plants benefit from regular pruning to keep their shape compact and attractive. In most cases, flowering performance will be improved too. Most amateur gardeners prune too lightly. Remember that in most cases the plant will sprout new growth from just under the point where you make your cut. So if you want to get rid of straggly old stems, you must cut them back hard, leaving short spurs of one or two leaves. Always cut just above a node, the position where a leaf grows or where a mark or ridge on the stem indicates that a leaf once grew. Generally, the best time to prune is in late winter or early spring, just as a plant starts back into growth. Some plants will tolerate pruning right back into hard, old wood (citrus, oleanders and brugmansias) but with others, this is taking a risk and it's best to leave as many pegs of younger wood behind as there are on the plant. These younger, greener pegs are much more likely to sprout. I don't prune all my plants every year, but tend to be guided by appearance. Sometimes it's good to let them gain some height and maturity, in which case a biennial pruning makes sense. I allow some, olives for instance, to run up on a short bare stem and develop a head of growth at the top, like a small tree.

TOP An unpruned and rather straggly potted olive
BOTTOM The same olive, pruned and sprouting sturdy new shoots

LONG-LIVED PLANTS FOR DISPLAY

PLANT

Acacia baileyana
Cootamundra wattle, mimosa

H 1.8m/6ft S 1.2m/4ft in a pot

Anigozanthos flavidus
Albany kangaroo paw

H 1.5m/5ft S 45cm/18in

DESCRIPTION

With its manageable size, fern-like, silvery foliage and abundant yellow blossom from late winter to spring, this member of the *Mimosaceae* family is ideal for a medium-sized greenhouse. Although plants make small evergreen trees in their native western Australia, size can be restricted by pruning. I've kept my plant going for about ten years now and its growing cycle fits in well with the way I use the greenhouse. I prune it hard directly after flowering, stand the plant outdoors from spring until autumn and bring it under glass during winter to protect it from frost and wind damage. Look out for the handsome purple-leaved *Acacia baileyana* 'Purpurea'.

I'm a great fan of the Australian kangaroo paws, as they produce such unusual flowers. These are evergreen perennials in the *Haemodoraceae* family, and when not in bloom, their grassy, evergreen foliage takes up little space. *Anigozanthos flavidus*, the Albany kangaroo paw, is a variable treat with furry, paw-like flowers of green, yellow or red. You can buy plants of flowering size, but raising them from seed is easy and they should flower after a couple of years. I'm also fond of *A. rufus*, whose flowers are purplish red. Alternatively, buy seed of mixed species, raise a whole bunch of plants and keep those that flower in your favourite colours.

HOW TO GROW

As soon as an acacia has bloomed, prune back the flowered stems to within a node or two of the older wood. You should be left with a long stem topped by short, truncated branches. These will soon sprout new shoots. Water and feed the plant regularly and well throughout the growing season and stand it outdoors during summer. Pot it on during spring or summer while it is in full growth. When it reaches a final pot size, top dress the surface. To raise new plants, sow seed in spring. It withstands temperatures to 0°C/32°F.

Sow seed into pots or shallow pans during spring or summer, germinating at 13–18°C/55–65°F. Prick the seedlings out into individual pots and pot on during spring or summer until they reach flowering size. Feed established plants monthly while they are in active growth. Keep kangaroo paws frost free in winter and on the dry side, letting the top half of the compost dry out between waterings. But give them a good soak when they need it, choosing a warm, bright morning. They don't mind standing outside for summer. Mature plants are easily split into sections during spring and summer while the plants are in active growth. Separate the crowns by cutting through the rhizomes (underground stems) and pulling them gently apart. After potting, water extremely carefully.

Asparagus densiflorus 'Myersii'
Foxtail fern
H 60cm/24in S 75cm/30in

Billbergia nutans
Queen's tears, friendship plant

H 50cm/20in S 45cm/18in

Brugmansia sanguinea
Red angel's trumpet, datura

H 1.8–3m/6–10ft S 1–2m/3–6ft in a pot

Although fern-like, asparagus plants are evergreen perennials, belonging to the family *Asparagaceae*. With tough, succulent, water-storing roots, they can withstand dry conditions far better than ferns, making a useful alternative. The leaf-like stems of foxtail fern are clumped together into characteristic, tapering tails of growth making it the most structural and interesting of the group. *A.d.* Sprengeri Group has a looser habit than 'Myersii' and twining *A. setaceus*, the true asparagus fern, is undeniably dainty, but watch out for those thorns. These South African plants produce tiny white flowers, which are sometimes followed by berries.

This tough bromeliad (a plant in the pineapple or *Bromeliaceae* family) from South America is ideal for a cool greenhouse, as it can withstand temperatures down to and even a little below freezing, is of moderate size and is not too prickly. A dense colony of individual narrow green rosettes of leaves will soon expand to fill a 17cm/7in pot. Mature rosettes each produce a flower spike in late spring and early summer. A spear of pink bracts appears first; then as the spike elongates, beautiful flowers of blue and green dangle downwards. At this point, I move my plant into a central position, raised on a pot for added height.

The South American angel's trumpets are spectacular evergreen shrubs in the potato family (*Solanaceae*), which grow large unless pruned regularly. *Brugmansia sanguinea* produces 15–25cm/6–10in long, tuberous yellow-orange flowers from spring right through to autumn, and though unscented, these make a splendid show. For the heady brugmansia perfume, grow night-scented, white-flowered *B. suaveolens* (though there are pink and yellow forms too), *B. x candida* (among whose ranks are apricot-hued 'Grand Marnier' and double hose-in-hose-flowered 'Knightii', where one flower appears to sit inside another) or *B. arborea*.

Asparagus need frost-free conditions to thrive, and though they are tough, the biggest problem lies in dealing with their outrageous root growth. Once they are established, feed them regularly to keep the foliage deep green, and divide congested plants during spring or summer, using a sharp bread knife or saw to cut through the root. Luckily, asparagus are easy to raise from seed sown in spring or summer at 15°C/60°F, though they may take one to three months to germinate.

Queen's tears could not be easier to care for: I even left a plant outdoors for a couple of years and it survived. But to ensure that plants give of their best, apply a liquid feed monthly while they are in active growth. Once a clump has expanded to fill its pot, rejuvenate it after flowering either by potting on or making more plants by dividing it into smaller sections. Fresh potting compost (use three parts soil-less potting compost to one part large-grade perlite) and extra space allows the individual plants to expand to fuller size and flower more spectacularly.

Brugmansias respond well to hard pruning. Although the usual recommendation is to do this in spring, I always find myself cutting back in autumn. This avoids overwintering the old summer stem and foliage, often with attendant bugs (notably whitefly and spider mite). I cut my daturas down almost to the base, or reduce the head of stems to short stumps atop a trunk of main stem. Keep plants frost free during winter and they will leap back into growth during spring. Should they need re-potting, do so after the new stems have grown a little. Top dress once they have reached their final pot and take shoot cuttings in spring or summer. Feed established plants monthly while they are in growth and water them well. All parts are poisonous. Raise new plants from seeds sown at 15°C/60°F in spring.

LONG-LIVED PLANTS FOR DISPLAY

PLANT

Brunfelsia pauciflora
Yesterday, today and tomorrow

H 75cm/30in S 60cm/24in in a pot

Camellia japonica
'Adelina Patti'

H 90cm–1.2m/3–4ft in a pot
S 60–90cm/2–3ft

DESCRIPTION

This shrubby evergreen or semi-evergreen in the potato family (*Solanaceae*) with its origins in Brazil makes a fine, scented addition to the greenhouse display. The plants bud up in spring, eventually producing flowers of intense mauve-blue that fade to pale blue and then white over a period of three days – hence the common name. There is a larger-flowered form, *Brunfelsia pauciflora* 'Macrantha', but its flowers are unscented. After a summer rest, plants bloom again in autumn.

Camellias are aristocratic, woodland-type shrubs or small trees in the tea family (*Theaceae*), growing in acid soils from north India and the Himalayas to China and Japan. Although they are normally planted outdoors, as autumn turns to winter potted specimens react well to being brought under well-ventilated glass, where their flower buds can open unimpeded by frost, wind or rain. Put them back outdoors for summer. All camellias are lovely, but pink, white-edged semi-double *C. japonica* 'Adelina Patti' and speckled, double red on pink 'Kick-off' are especially good. With their late winter to early spring flowers, camellias are good for filling unheated greenhouses during winter.

HOW TO GROW

Although brunfelsias would probably prefer slightly warmer winter temperatures, I have kept them going in a very chilly greenhouse where the temperatures hovered around freezing point. The plants dropped some leaves, but they came back into leaf and flowered spectacularly the following spring. As with all overwintering plants, the secret is to keep the compost and roots as dry as you dare during cold snaps and water thoroughly on bright mornings during milder spells. Feed fortnightly during spring and summer when the plants have woken up and are growing actively. Pot on every two years or when necessary, but when they reach their final pot size (30cm/12in or the biggest you can accommodate), top dress instead. Propagate by taking shoot cuttings in spring or summer to replace stock.

Regular watering and feeding is important; otherwise the leaves may turn yellow. Camellias do best in an ericaceous compost and should be watered with rain water. Once they are established, a liquid feed formulated for acid-loving plants given every three to four weeks will keep them healthy; or apply a slow-release fertilizer to the surface of the pots in spring to last for the entire season. Prune after flowering if necessary. Provide light shading as the sun intensifies in spring. Stand them outdoors in a semi-shaded position for summer, preferably surrounded by other plants. Propagate by taking semi-hardwood cuttings during late summer.

Canna 'Panache'
Indian shot

H 90cm–1.2m/3–4ft S 60cm/2ft

Coronilla valentina subsp. glauca 'Citrina'

H and S 75cm/30in

Correa 'Dusky Bells'
Australian fuchsia
H and S 30–90cm/1–3ft

Cannas are rhizomatous herbaceous perennials in their own family (*Cannaceae*), originating from Asia and tropical North and South America. Widely used as large summer bedding plants (see page 48), they also make good greenhouse specimens. Here, they can be examined close to and seem to stand out more as individuals. I choose carefully for the greenhouse, bypassing cannas with huge leaves and blowsy flowers. My favourite is the refined cultivar 'Panache', whose habit is slender and small flowers a subtle apricot, shading to warm pink at the centre.

Although this delightful small evergreen shrub will stay outside for winter in all but the coldest regions, it also makes a first-class specimen for an unheated greenhouse. You really can't ask much more of a plant that provides a long succession of sweetly scented, lemon-yellow, pea-like flowers over blue-green foliage in the depths of winter. One or two of this native of Portugal and Spain from the pea family (*Papilionaceae*, formerly *Leguminosae*) could transform your greenhouse staging in winter.

Despite the common name, correas bear only a superficial resemblance to fuchsias and are not even related, belonging in the rue and citrus family (*Rutaceae*). These diminutive evergreen Australian shrubs make great greenhouse plants because of their small scale and ability to withstand cold temperatures down to freezing, though not much lower. A tendency to flower during winter brings colour when most needed. This cultivar bears a profusion of small, bell-shaped pinkish-red flowers but there are several others from which to choose, including *Correa backhouseana*, whose cream flowers contrast beautifully with its neat oval leaves.

Cannas are easy to grow in the greenhouse. New growth starts in late winter and accelerates through spring – a good time to pot on to a larger pot. When a congested plant has reached the largest pot size you can accommodate, split it into two or three pieces and pot each separately. Spares are ideal for the garden. Feed them fortnightly throughout summer and water regularly. By late autumn, the plants will stop flowering and look tired. Ease up on watering, keeping the rhizomes ticking over by just giving them the occasional drink on nice winter days. Soak the large, hard canna seed for twenty-four hours in warm water before sowing at 21°C/70°F in spring, but named cultivars like 'Panache' will not come true from seed.

Coronilla has a tendency to become straggly, but this is easily cured by a good pruning and shaping directly after the first flush of flowers is over. Though plants sometimes keep going for a surprisingly long time and often carry on flowering almost year round, I prune them back hard in spring, just prior to standing them outside for the summer. Pot on when necessary, as soon as the plants have made growth in early summer. Bring them back under glass in mid- to late autumn, or when convenient, giving them maximum light and ventilation. Water them carefully, and feed the plants monthly while they are in active growth. Should the plants become too large, you can always plant them out. Propagate by rooting cuttings during summer.

Correas dislike lime and prefer rain water where tap water is hard. When re-potting in spring or summer, use an ericaceous compost. You can stand plants that have flowered in winter outside for the summer, so freeing up space in the greenhouse as well as giving the plants a cooler environment. Feed established plants monthly while they are in active growth. Water them carefully during winter, making sure that the surface of the compost has dried out before watering again, but don't let them go too dry while they are flowering. Ventilate the greenhouse as much as possible to avoid dank air. You can take semi-ripe cuttings in summer, but they may be slow to root.

LONG- LIVED PLANTS FOR DISPLAY

PLANT

Cycas revoluta
Japanese sago palm

H and S 1–2m/3–6ft

Erica canaliculata
South African heath, channelled heath
H 90cm/3ft S 60cm/2ft in a pot

DESCRIPTION

Although this cycad, a member of the *Cycadaceae* family, may seem rather large for the greenhouse, smaller youngsters are both available and affordable. Even when they've grown on for a few years, the stiff leaves arch up and over, umbrella style, leaving room beneath for smaller plants to grow and benefit from the shade. Of great character, this ancient type of plant grows erratically, suddenly sending up a whole set of new leaves following a period of apparent inactivity. Plants are either male or female, producing cone-like flowers when mature enough.

Shrubby, evergreen South African heaths in the heather and rhododendron family (*Ericaceae*) bring welcome colour to the greenhouse in winter and early spring. There are a number to try, and this fine species is a personal favourite, for its masses of white flowers marked with contrasting black anthers. In a border it would reach 1.8m/6ft. Look out for the fire heath (*Erica cerinthoides*), whose long stems of narrow, softly hairy leaves are tipped by clusters of tubular, salmon-pink flowers. The smaller, compact garden hybrid *E.* x *hiemalis* is often seen in florists', tempting gardeners with its large white flowers marked with pink.

HOW TO GROW

Although sago palms are sometimes left outdoors in mild regions, or kept as house plants, I think it is advisable to stand plants under lightly shaded glass while the new leaves are unfurling, as they are soft and vulnerable in their early stages, and liable to be damaged by uneven light (which rules out most house rooms), rain and wind. After the leaves have emerged and toughened up, you can stand them outside during summer. They withstand a little frost, but their condition and appearance will deteriorate if you do not protect them. Cycads can inhabit the same pot for many years, but eventually will need potting on in spring or summer. Reduce watering in winter. Start new plants from the large seeds, sown at 15–21°C/60–70°F in spring. Large plants produce offsets.

The Cape heaths are not the easiest plants to grow, being susceptible to overwatering, underwatering and lack of ventilation. Pot them into ericaceous compost mixed three parts to one with sharp sand or grit and water thoughtfully using rain water. Be guided by the compost surface, waiting until it starts to dry out before watering well to reach all the roots. Keep the plants frost free during winter, when the intervals between waterings will be wider apart. While they are in active growth, feed them monthly. They do not usually need regular pruning, but if plants become too large, cut out any unwanted stems after flowering. To propagate, take semi-ripe cuttings in summer, preferably with a heel.

Gardenia jasminoides
(syn. G. augusta)
Cape jasmine, gardenia
H and S 75cm/30in in a pot

Gerbera jamesonii
Barberton daisy

H 30–45cm/12–18in S 25cm/10in

Hedychium gardnerianum
Kahili ginger

H 1.8m/6ft S 90cm/3ft

Originating in China, Japan and Taiwan and belonging to the coffee family (*Rubiaceae*), gardenias must be some of the most beautiful and desirable of flowering perennial house plants. Their deliciously fragrant, double white flowers are set off by glossy, dark green foliage and age delicately, through cream to yellow. Yet it is difficult to keep these shrubby plants healthy in a house. Fluctuating temperatures, dry air and gloomy corners play havoc with their well-being and plants forced unseasonably into bloom often drop their flowers and turn yellow. Keeping them in a greenhouse is a better option.

Prized as cut flowers, South African gerberas from the daisy family (*Compositae*) make great pot plants too. Easy to raise from seed, these evergreen perennials form a low rosette of leaves and produce a succession of large, brightly coloured daisy-like flowers over a long period from spring to autumn. Garden hybrids, including short-growing types like 'Dwarf Pandora Mixed', are common in seed catalogues and might be good for windowsills, but for greenhouse bench display I prefer longer-stemmed flowers. From a good mixture, expect blooms of apricot, red, yellow, orange and pink.

This ginger lily from India and the Himalayas is a spectacular plant for frost-free conditions under glass. Although it belongs to the same family as edible ginger (*Zingiberaceae*), its aromatic, rhizomatous roots cannot be eaten. I have four plants, each in a 35cm/14in pot, which flower every year in my porch as summer turns to autumn. Together, they create a spectacular forest of tall stems bearing lush leaves and topped by generous candles of fragrant yellow flowers with striking red stamens.

Gardenias are lime-hating plants and like soft water and an ericaceous compost. They are often sold three or four plants to a pot, in which case it often pays to separate one away from the cluster and grow it separately for a longer life. Stand in a shaded spot in the greenhouse and when established feed monthly. Although gardenias prefer a minimum temperature of 10°C/50°F, they can tolerate colder but frost-free temperatures. Once you have these requirements under control, the biggest enemy is spider mite. Keep the air humid and at the first signs of it, introduce biological control in the form of predatory mites (see page 186).

Gerberas need a minimum winter temperature of 4°C/40°F and should be kept very much on the dry side during winter: water only on fine, bright days when the top half of the compost has dried out. In summer water plentifully and feed them every two to four weeks to keep a good succession of flowers coming. Deadhead when each flower has finished. When a plant seems tired and old, divide it in spring into separate crowns of growth, potting each separately, or raise more from seed. Sow seed in spring at 18°C/65°F and prick the seedlings out into individual cells or pots. Pot them on when they are ready, finishing them in 13cm/5in pots.

After flowering, cut away the dead flowers at the top of each stem but leave the rest of the stem and leaves in place, because they will persist for most of the winter, gradually turning brown when new growth pushes up from the rhizomes in late spring. During winter water only when the top half of the compost has dried out, but water more frequently as growth accelerates in spring and summer, as well as giving a monthly feed. I don't need to shade the glass of my north-west-facing porch, but shading would be necessary in a bright greenhouse. New plants are sometimes acquired as chunks of rhizome. Plant these horizontally into a pot in spring, with the top of the rhizome just visible at the surface, and keep warm. Divide mature rhizomes in spring, cutting through the rhizomes with secateurs.

LONG-LIVED PLANTS FOR DISPLAY

PLANT

Helleborus niger
Christmas rose

H and S 30cm/12in

Lotus 'Gold Flash'
Parrot's beak

H and S 70cm/3ft

DESCRIPTION

This tough little European hellebore is a hardy perennial in the buttercup family (*Ranunculaceae*) and although it does not need greenhouse protection, there are compelling reasons for providing an unheated or frost-free greenhouse during the winter. Apart from those of the more upward-looking cultivar 'Potter's Wheel', *H. niger* flowers tend to nod, and because they grow close to the ground, one can hardly see them, let alone their beautiful white interiors and stamens. They also often become damaged by winter weather. On the greenhouse staging, their flowers open without damage or soil splash and can be admired at eye level. The purity of the white flowers sets off early displays of spring bulbs a treat.

Trailing plants are valuable for tumbling over the sides of the greenhouse staging and I would display this delightful perennial on an upturned pot for greater impact. Its trailing stems of evergreen, needle-like silvery leaves are joined, in spring and early summer, by claw-like orange-tipped yellow flowers. This hybrid is a cross between the red-flowered coral gem (*Lotus berthelotii*) and the more yellow-flowered *L. maculatus*, which both originate from the Canary Islands and belong to the pea family (*Papilionaceae*, formerly *Leguminosae*).

HOW TO GROW

Bring potted plants inside during winter, just as their buds are plumping up, and water them when the surface of the compost starts to feel dry. Give them as much ventilation as is practical and enjoy their blooms. After flowering, you can stand the plants outdoors again and leave them there in a holding area until the following winter. Water them regularly and pot them on when necessary. Should watering be a problem, plant them into the ground and lift and pot them up again in autumn. To propagate, divide large plants after flowering in spring and pot them separately.

Parrot's beaks are sold among the vast range of tender perennials displayed by garden centres in tiny pots during late winter and early spring. You can snap them up cheaply and grow them on in a frost-free greenhouse. Pot on into a three parts potting compost, one part grit or sharp sand mix. Plants are easy to grow as long as you take care with the watering: the compost surface must dry out in between waterings. Feed them monthly while they are in active growth and provide a winter minimum of 3°C/38°F coupled with good ventilation. Prune unruly plants after flowering and propagate by taking shoot-tip cuttings in summer.

Metrosideros kermadecensis 'Variegata' Variegated New Zealand Christmas tree
H 90cm/1m S 75cm/30in in a pot

Plain-leaved New Zealand Christmas trees grow to 20m/70ft in their native country, but this variegated evergreen shrub remains compact, and it grows well in a frost-free greenhouse. When it erupts into bloom during summer, you can see why it belongs to the myrtle family (*Myrtaceae*). The flowers, 2cm/¾in long, are all red stamens with yellow anthers and make large clusters against the creamy yellow-edged leaves. These have an attractive silvery reverse. The plain-leaved pohutakawa (*Metrosideros excelsus*), is worth growing too, but it tends to be more vigorous.

This is an easy plant to grow, with straightforward potting, watering and feeding requirements. Restriction to pots keeps size under control to an extent, but fortunately the plant responds really well to pruning, which is best carried out in spring, just as the plant is coming back into growth. When a mature plant reaches its final pot size, perhaps a 45cm/18in tub, top dress as an alternative to potting on. Make sure that it doesn't go short of water and feed monthly. Stress shows in brown tips to the leaves. It roots readily from cuttings, which are best taken as side shoots with heels (see page 23) in summer.

Nerium oleander Oleander
H 1.2m/4ft S 90cm/3ft in a pot

Like bougainvilleas, oleanders have a knack of reminding us of holidays in warm Mediterranean or tropical countries, where both plants are great favourites in hotels and private gardens. They easily survive temperatures hovering above freezing, but in maritime climates they are sometimes slow to wake up and grow in spring. They do much better in warmer greenhouses, or in areas where the summers are longer and hotter. Native to the eastern Mediterranean, these tender evergreen shrubs are in the periwinkle family (*Apocynaceae*), a fact confirmed by the slightly overlapping petals of their windmill-like flowers. There are plenty of cultivars, offering white, red and all shades of pink, including doubles and plants with variegated foliage. All plant parts are toxic.

Pot oleanders on in spring as they wake up and start growing. Once they are established in their pots, feed them monthly. If you need the space, stand them outside for the summer. Should they grow too large, prune them back in late winter. They can take really hard pruning if necessary. Raise new plants from semi-ripe cuttings in summer. You can sow seed in spring at 15°C/60°F, but the resulting plants will be variable. Watch out for spider mite and scale insects.

Olea europaea Olive
H 60cm–1.8m/2–6ft
S 60–90cm/2–3ft in a pot

Olives, in the jasmine and lilac family *Oleaceae*, are characterful shrubs worth keeping for a long time, to enjoy watching them mature and grow. Periodically prune the head of growth back to create an attractive specimen. My plant grows on a short peg of older stem, but you can buy plants with long main stems rather like standards in shape. These taller plants don't necessarily take up more room, because you can stand one on the floor and arrange other plants around it. The neat, grey-green evergreen leaves are handsome and tiny summer flowers may be followed by fruits, though these rarely ripen in cooler climates.

An olive can grow in the same pot for many years and withstand root restriction well. But it will benefit from re-potting every four or five years, or failing that, a top dressing. Feed an established plant monthly while it is in active growth. The main drawback to growing olives under glass in less sunnier climates than their native Mediterranean countries is their tendency to lankiness. The solution lies in pruning them back in spring and then nipping back the growing tips of ensuing shoots when they reach 5cm/2in, keeping them neat and compact. Water an olive sparingly during winter and opt for a minimum winter temperature of 3°C/38°F.

LONG-
LIVED
PLANTS
FOR
DISPLAY

PLANT	***Pleione* hybrids** **Windowsill orchid** H and S 15cm/6in	***Prostanthera rotundifolia*** **Round-leaved mint bush** H 90cm/3ft S 75cm/30in in a pot

DESCRIPTION

Pleiones are the easiest orchids to grow and accommodate in an unheated or frost-free greenhouse. The leaves die back in the autumn to leave plump, dormant storage organs called pseudobulbs behind. In spring, plump flower buds appear – a sign that it is time to start watering. As a group, pleiones originate from high altitudes in a region from north India to south China and Taiwan. Both the species and their hybrids bear delightful flowers, usually pink, but some white or yellow. The leaves grow after the flowers have faded.

Mint bushes are evergreen shrubs belonging to the dead nettle family (*Lamiaceae*, formerly *Labiatae*) and this one originates from south-east Australia (including Tasmania). With its small, rounded, pleasingly aromatic leaves and profusion of small bell-shaped purple-pink flowers in spring, this shrubby plant makes a great specimen with which to create height on the staging. It tolerates temperatures just above freezing and plants seem to appreciate a cool winter.

HOW TO GROW

These are terrestrial orchids (which means that they grow in the ground, as opposed to epiphytic types found clinging to tree branches), and though they are said to need a special orchid compost made of bark chips and perlite, I have living proof of them thriving in the usual 50:50 John Innes No. 2 and soil-less compost mix, further mixed three parts to one with grit. Water them freely in summer, adding a general-purpose fertilizer every three weeks. In winter, while they are dormant, I barely water my plants at all. When the pseudobulbs and roots become congested, with lots of smaller bulbs preventing the larger ones from plumping up, it's wise to have a good sort-out just before flowering. Set about five pseudobulbs in a 10cm/4in pot. Discard the tiny bulbs, or use them as propagation material.

A mint bush will quickly fill its pot with roots and should be moved on to a new, larger one during spring or summer. When it reaches its final pot size of 30cm/12in or so, top dress and strike some cuttings, with the aim of replacing the original when it begins to deteriorate. The flower buds set during late summer and autumn, so take care not to let an established plant dry out too much and feed every two or three weeks. During winter, water it carefully, soaking the roots on fine mornings when you can open the vents generously, but letting the compost surface dry out between waterings. This way the plant ticks over well, holding on to its plentiful buds until flowering time. Prune after flowering, taking care not to cut into old, woody stems. Propagate by taking cuttings with a heel in summer.

Punica granatum var. *nana*
Miniature pomegranate

H and S 30–45cm/12–18in

Native to south-east Europe, the pomegranate is a deciduous shrub in the loosestrife family (*Lythraceae*) whose appearance sings of warmth. Growing a full-sized plant in a small greenhouse could be tricky, but the compact form is ideal and will make a small deciduous shrub of great character, resplendent with comparatively large, luscious orange-red flowers in summer. The petals are silky-looking and billowing, as though trying to escape from their calyces. They are said to produce fruit, but my plant never has. The leaves are narrow and shiny.

Come autumn, the pomegranate will put on a small but delightful show of yellow and orange autumn colours before dropping its leaves for winter. Keep it ticking over with the occasional watering, but let the surface of the compost dry out in between. Aim for a minimum temperature of 3°C/38°F, just above freezing. It will sprout back into growth during spring, when it will need watering more frequently. Once shoots have grown, pot it on if necessary. Feed an established plant every three weeks during active growth. To propagate, take short, heeled cuttings in summer.

Rhododendron veitchianum
Tender rhododendron

H and S 1–2m/3–6ft in a pot

Tender rhododendrons, especially the fragrant ones, make ideal greenhouse specimens, though most will take up a lot of space. Fortunately, they tend to flower during spring and can then be placed outside for the summer, thus freeing up space for tender crops and displays of summer flowers on the staging. Members of the heather family (*Ericaceae*), these are lime-hating plants. *R.* 'Veitchianum' is an evergreen shrub bearing trusses of delicate white trumpet-shaped blooms 8–10cm/3–4in wide with yellow throats, earning its space for its perfume as well as its beauty.

Barely hardy enough to grow outdoors, this rhododendron fares best with a minimum winter temperature of 3°C/38°F. Stand it in a lightly shaded outdoor spot for summer, watering it freely (with rain water) and feeding it monthly with a formula for acid-loving plants. Pot it on or top dress it after flowering, using an ericaceous compost. Pay particular attention to watering at summer's end, when next year's flower buds are setting. Move it back under glass well before the first frosts and, throughout winter, let the compost surface start to dry out before watering it again and ventilate well when possible. Try taking cuttings in summer, but they are slow to root.

Senna didymobotrya
Candle senna, cassia

H 1.2m/4ft S 75cm/30in in a pot

Offering colour and structure from summer right into the autumn, this tender evergreen shrub earns its place in the greenhouse, though you can stand it outside for the summer months. This plant has its origins in tropical Africa and belongs to the caesalpinia family (*Caesalpiniaceae*). I love the contrast between the bright green, pinnate leaves and the candles of flower buds, which are initially encased in blackish bracts. As the buds elongate and open, the effect is of yellow candles up to 30cm/12in long, set in a highly individual candelabra.

Regular encyclopaedias list the minimum temperature as 13°C/55°F, but I can't resist pushing the boundaries to see if it tolerates lower temperatures. So far, attempts to overwinter just above freezing have failed. I suspect a minimum of 4–7°C/40–45°F is nearer the truth. Water carefully during winter, allowing the top half of the compost to dry out between waterings. During late winter, watch for signs of growth and wait until new shoots are growing well in spring before attempting to prune back. The aim of pruning is to keep the plant compact. Once growth is under way, pot on or top dress and when it is established, feed it every two to four weeks. Raise new plants from seed sown at 18–24°C/65–75°F in spring.

LONG-LIVED PLANTS FOR DISPLAY

PLANT

Solanum pseudocapsicum
Winter cherry

H and S 30cm/12in

Strelitzia reginae
Bird of paradise

H 90cm–1.2m/3–4ft S 90cm/3ft

DESCRIPTION

This cheerful shrubby evergreen from South America is usually bought to decorate the house during winter, but treated right it makes a long-lasting greenhouse resident capable of withstanding winter temperatures almost down to freezing. Although it belongs in the potato and tomato family (*Solanaceae*), this solanum is not edible, but its show of spherical orange fruits will brighten up the staging in autumn and winter. The starry white summer flowers are not bad either.

This South African native in its own family (*Strelitziaceae*) is a must for any greenhouse. It is large, but its tough nature, willingness to tolerate temperatures just above freezing, stiff, evergreen, paddle-shaped leaves and incredibly exotic flowers should persuade even those with the tiniest of greenhouses to try one. This large evergreen perennial won't mind being stood outdoors for the summer, so as to release space inside for crops. Flower buds appear during late winter and open during spring at warmer temperatures, but in early summer at colder ones.

HOW TO GROW

Prune a straggly plant hard back in spring, though not into the oldest wood, to keep it compact. Pot it on or top dress if necessary once growth has started. Feed an established plant every two weeks to keep it green and healthy and look forward to the flowers. These are insect-pollinated and most well-ventilated greenhouses will attract a fair number of bees, flies and hoverflies to do the job. If in doubt, stand the plant outside while the fruit is setting. Water it plentifully during summer, but as temperatures drop in autumn allow the compost surface time to dry out between waterings. Raise plants from seed sown in spring and germinated at 18°C/65°F, and prick young plants out into small pots or cells to grow on. Or take summer cuttings and nip the shoot tips out of young plants to make them branch.

Pot young plants on every year in spring, until they reach at least a 35cm/14in diameter pot. They can then stay in their pots for a few years, though the best plants grow out of the largest pots. Water well during summer and feed monthly while they are in active growth, but let the top half of the compost dry out between waterings during winter. When a plant becomes so pot bound that it can no longer absorb enough water and nutrients through the mass of fleshy roots, both leaf quality and flowering will deteriorate. This is the signal to split a plant in spring. I've used a half-moon edging iron before now to cut between the sections of growth. Tidy the sections up and re-pot. Large portions should flower the following year despite this disturbance. Raise new plants from the pretty seeds germinated at 18–21°C/65–70°F.

Streptocarpus 'Paula'
Cape primrose

H 25cm/10in S 30cm/12in

From the same family as African violets (*Gesneriaceae*), streptocarpus are tender evergreen perennials, native, mainly, to South Africa. The plants we grow are usually not species but colourful hybrids. Those from seed mixtures are a more random bunch, but there are plenty of strong named varieties to buy. With their long hairy leaves and profusion of summer flowers, I find them ideal for filling out gaps in my shady, north-facing porch. 'Paula' is one of my favourites, for its generous reddish-purple blooms with distinct yellow throats.

Streptocarpus prefer a warm minimum winter temperature of 10°C/50°F and although they can remain alive at lower temperatures, if watered sparingly, they tend to contract into miserable, wizened little plants reluctant to wake up and grow in spring. Better, then, to overwinter them in the house or discard the old plants and order fresh rooted cuttings in spring. Pot them up into 9cm/3½in pots of three parts soil-less potting compost to one part vermiculite and finish the plants in 13cm/5in pots. Keep water off their leaves, shade them from harsh sun and feed them with half-strength fertilizer fortnightly. Propagate favourites by taking leaf cuttings. Or surface sow the tiny seed in early spring, germinating it at 18°C/65°F.

Tibouchina urvilleana
Brazilian spider flower

H 1.2m/4ft S 90cm/3ft

This Brazilian shrubby evergreen in the melastoma family (*Melastomataceae*) can grow even taller, but I think 1.2m/4ft is a practical maximum height for a small greenhouse. Plants will bloom really well at 75cm/30in. The delightfully soft, hairy leaves are joined by large purple flowers 8–10cm/3–4in across in late summer and autumn. The dark stamens in the centre of each flower look like a spider lying on its back – hence the common name.

Either keep tibouchinas under glass permanently, or stand plants outdoors for summer and bring them back inside as they bud up, to avoid the cold, wind and wet of autumn. Enjoy the display, and then care for the plants thoughtfully by ventilating the greenhouse as often as possible, keeping them frost free and allowing the surface of the compost to dry out between waterings. When the plants show signs of life in early spring, prune back if necessary. They respond well to hard pruning and you can use any good shoot tips as cuttings. Pinch back the growing tips on developing plants if they show signs of lankiness. Pot on if necessary, top dress large plants in their final pots and feed established plants fortnightly. You can make further cuttings in summer to replace older stock. Seed sown at 15°C/60°F in spring germinates readily.

Tulbaghia violacea

H 60cm/2ft S 20cm/8in

A pot of South African tulbaghia will give you a show of lilac flowers through summer and into autumn. A tulbaghia is a rather elegant deciduous perennial; the clump of linear, grey-green leaves stays at a modest 20cm/8in high, while the flower stems rise above. But there is nothing elegant about the pungent odour of onions or garlic that surrounds the whole plant and is strongest when the roots are disturbed – tulbaghia is a member of the onion family (*Alliaceae*). If you want to grow a tiny tulbaghia, track down unusual, orange-flowered *T. leucantha*, which has a height and spread of 10cm/4in.

Tulbaghia violacea overwinters happily at temperatures dipping down to and just below freezing, when growth will die back and sprout again from corm-like rhizomes in spring. Once growth is under way, this is the best time to split clumps into smaller sections. You can plant spares in the garden, where they will grow happily in mild regions where frosts are light and short-lived. Feed established plants monthly during the growing season. Water well during summer, but more sparingly in winter so that the roots are almost dry while the plant is dormant.

LONG-LIVED CLIMBING PLANTS

PLANT

Ampelopsis brevipedunculata var. maximowiczii 'Elegans'
Porcelain berry
H and S 75cm/30in

Araujia sericifera
Cruel plant

H 1.8m/6ft S 90cm/3ft

DESCRIPTION

With its origins in north-east Asia, this climber in the vine family (*Vitaceae*) is far less vigorous than the plain-leaved species, and its manageable size, combined with decorative foliage, makes it an ideal greenhouse plant. The dark green leaves are mottled with cream and pink, giving the plant a delicate, dappled appearance. Its red, claw-like tendrils will grip a support, but the plant is equally happy growing into an almost trailing, mound-like shape. Insignificant flowers appear during summer, followed by pinkish-purple fruit that mature to a fabulous turquoise-blue colour. The porcelain berry is deciduous and loses its leaves in winter.

Easy to raise from seed, a cruel plant will romp to the top of its support and produce flowers by its second year. You can restrain this rampant twining climber in the hoya family (*Asclepiadaceae*) to 1.8m/6ft, but plants reach 9m/30ft in their native South American scrubland. The long stems carry pale green leaves joined, in summer and autumn, by fragrant, white, bell-shaped flowers often tinged with pink or mauve. These have sticky pollen masses to which visiting moths, on plunging their tongues into the flowers, become stuck and are held until morning – hence the name cruel plant. Pollination is usually successful and large seed pods develop. They will persist on the plant for a year before splitting to reveal seeds with long silky hairs.

HOW TO GROW

Although technically hardy, this ampelopsis grows better if given the protection of glass, but needs shading from the harshest summer light. You can stand plants outdoors for summer, but inside they repay their protection from slugs and the ravages of weather by adding a welcome lushness to the display. Pot the plants on in spring just after the new growth has started and once they are established in their pots, feed them every month. Prune untidy plants in late winter while they have no leaves. Propagate by taking summer cuttings.

Sow seed in spring at 15–18°C/60–65°F, pricking out the large seedlings into individual pots. Pot on when necessary, provide supports and feed fortnightly. Protect from below-freezing temperatures in the greenhouse. Plants can stand outdoors for the summer, but grow better in a greenhouse border than in a pot. Prune overgrown plants in early spring as they sprout into growth, being careful not to get their milky sap on your clothes.

Bomarea caldasii

H 1.5m/5ft S 60cm/2ft

Bougainvillea glabra
Paper flower

H 1.2m/4ft S 75cm/30in

Hardenbergia violacea
**Purple coral pea,
false sarsaparilla**
H 1.2m–1.8m/4–6ft S 75cm/30in

The best way to describe bomarea is like a climbing alstroemeria. Indeed this deciduous, twining climber belongs to the plant family *Alstroemeriaceae*, originating from the scrub and forest margins of an area of South America from Colombia to Ecuador. In spring, narrow shoots thrust through the soil or compost and begin to snake up their supports. Look after them well and during summer they will produce generous umbels of narrow, funnel-shaped flowers of warm, glowing orange tipped with yellow. Rich and gorgeous, they show up well against the bright green foliage.

Bougainvilleas, from the marvel of Peru family *Nyctaginaceae*, are climbers popular for their large, showy bracts and because they remind us of holidays in exotic climes. The plants we grow are hybrids of South American species, flowering mainly during summer, with bract colours of red, pink, purple, orange or white. The true flowers are small white structures at the centre of the bracts. There are hybrids with variegated foliage and double flowers. In form, some bougainvilleas are small and shrubby, while others produce long stems, which in the wild would hoist themselves aloft by using their thorns as crampons. By training them to supports and pruning regularly, you can restrict plants that in warmer countries might reach 6m/20ft.

This fabulous Australian climber from the pea family (*Papilionaceae*) produces its flowers during late winter and spring, brightening up the greenhouse when colour is most needed. The twining, wiry stems of slender leathery leaves soon scale their supports and bear dainty flowers in great profusion, varying in colour. Those of *Hardenbergia violacea* 'Happy Wanderer' are mauve-pink; 'Pink Cascade' bears pink blooms and 'White Crystal' white.

Bomarea seems to resent high temperatures, so plant it in a greenhouse bed where it will enjoy a cooler root run. Yet it also grows well in pots of three parts of ordinary potting compost to one of grit. Provide light shade and reduce temperatures by good ventilation and humidity. Train it by positioning plant or pot under a high point of the roof, fixing string near the base and tying it to the greenhouse above. The stems will weave around the string. Feed it every two to four weeks when it is in full growth and during winter keep it moist but not wet. Aim for a minimum temperature of 3°C/38°F. Propagate by carefully dividing large plants in late winter or spring.

Pot on a bougainvillea during spring and feed it monthly once it is established. Wind the stems around a tepee of canes, tying them in securely. After flowering, during autumn trim wayward stems to save space, and in late winter prune thoroughly. When you have tied in a framework of stems, prune the remaining long side shoots hard back to within a couple of growth buds of the main stems. Giving a bougainvillea a bright, warm place in the house directly after pruning will bring on new growth and speed up flowering. It will tolerate temperatures just above freezing, as long as it is not overwatered. Propagate by taking summer cuttings.

During summer, keep the plants cool by providing light shade and making sure that the roots stay moist; otherwise the leaf tips turn crisp and brown. The best plants are those given the cooler run of a greenhouse border, though this is not always possible. Feed them monthly while they are in active growth and pot them on during spring and summer when necessary. During winter, plants withstand temperatures just above freezing. Water carefully to ensure that the roots don't dry out; otherwise the tiny flower buds might die off. Propagate by taking softwood cuttings of new growth in spring, preferably pulling them away at the correct length with some older stems attached. Or germinate seed at 21°C/70°F in spring.

LONG-LIVED CLIMBING PLANTS

PLANT

Jasminum polyanthum
Pink jasmine, Chinese jasmine

H and S 1.8m/6ft

Passiflora 'Eden'
Passion flower

H and S 3m/10ft

DESCRIPTION

Chinese jasmine, in the olive and lilac family *Oleaceae*, is one of the easiest climbers to grow under glass, where it thrives far better than it does in the house. Relishing the extra light and a cool winter, it soon romps away and begins flowering in late winter, continuing into spring. The leaves, each made up of five to seven leaflets, make a lush mass during summer and elegantly pointed, pink-tinged buds appear during winter, opening into white, sweetly scented flowers.

Passion flowers (*Passifloraceae*) are tendril climbers with a wide distrubution in tropical countries, flowering during summer and autumn. This recent cultivar bears dainty whitish-green petals edged with a narrow rim of purple. Like the hardy, common blue passion flower (*Passiflora caerulea*), it suits an unheated greenhouse (minimum temperature of −5°C/23°F). The frost-hardy maypops (*P. incarnata*) is easily raised from seed and dies back like a herbaceous perennial at low temperatures. Dainty lilac and white flowers bear delightfully speckled filaments and may set fruit. If you have more heat, try showy, red-purple *P. x caeruleoracemosa* or *P. 'Amethyst'* (minimum temperature of 5°C/41°F).

HOW TO GROW

Frost protection during winter and cool during summer will keep your jasmine healthy. Provide light shade, good ventilation and humidity. Plants given the root run of a border will soon outperform those in pots. An established plant needs a thorough pruning after flowering every year to prevent it from becoming a tangle of alive and dead wood. Cut old and weak stems back to a healthy bud or node lower down on the stem. Shorten stems that have just flowered, leaving behind short spurs of one or two nodes. The stems that grow will have flowers the following spring. Feed established plants every two to four weeks. Propagate by taking summer cuttings.

Feed established passion flowers fortnightly and train them carefully or else they will run amok, gripping other plants with their tendrils. Pot them on when necessary, finishing them in generous pots 45cm/18in across. Most are large plants and should be pruned back to restrict their size. Trim in autumn if necessary, but leave the main pruning until spring, always leaving spurs of young wood behind. Many passifloras set fruit, but hand pollination is sometimes needed: using a soft brush, move pollen from one flower to the stigma of another. Propagate species by seed, or take cuttings in summer. Watch out for spider mite and whitefly.

Plumbago auriculata
Cape leadwort

H and S 1.2m/4ft

Although this fabulous flowering shrub in the leadwort family (*Plumbaginaceae*) might reach heights up to 6m/20ft in its native South Africa, a small pot will restrict its growth and plants can flower well even at only 90cm/3ft high. Stems neither twine nor make tendrils, but are scandent or draping. From summer to autumn, generous racemes of sky-blue flowers decorate the plants. *Plumbago auriculata* var. *alba* bears white flowers, but in my opinion it is not a patch on its blue cousin.

The best plants are those grown in greenhouse borders with their stems secured to wires. Long growths tied under the roof will provide light shade for plants beneath. Pot plants on in spring when necessary, until they are in a pot at least 20cm/8in wide, the minimum size necessary for a reasonable flower display. Provide canes or a small trellis for support. Prune in early spring, removing flowered stems by cutting them close to older stems, leaving spurs behind. Thin out large, old plants by removing some stems close to the base. Shade the plants lightly in summer and protect from frost in winter. Propagate by taking summer cuttings.

Solanum rantonnetii
Blue potato vine

H 90cm–1.2m/3–4ft S 60cm/2ft

This lax shrub originating from Argentina and Paraguay is a member of the potato family (*Solanaceae*). Similar to the hardier outdoor potato vines, this one earns its frost-free home by decorating the greenhouse with generous sprays of large rich purple flowers during summer and autumn. Centred with yellow, they resemble large potato flowers. The showiest potato vine is the Costa Rican *Solanum wendlandii*, whose longer stems hoist themselves aloft with their hooked, recurved spines. The saucer-like flowers measure 6cm/2½in across, but this plant is larger and likes a slightly warmer winter, with a minimum temperature of 7°C/45°F.

Pot on young plants in spring or summer until they end up in a container at least 30cm/12in across. Tie the stems neatly to a support, water generously during summer and feed fortnightly while the plants are in active growth. After flowering, tidy the plants up for winter and water only when the top layer of compost has dried out. Prune in late winter, by shortening any unwanted stems before the new growth is under way. Propagate by taking summer cuttings and watch out for whitefly.

Trachelospermum jasminoides
Star jasmine, Confederate jasmine

H 1.2m/4ft S 60cm/2ft

Not really a jasmine at all, this distinguished twining evergreen bearing white, scented flowers during summer belongs to the periwinkle family (*Apocynaceae*). From pointed buds tubular blooms open, flaring out to five slightly overlapping lobes. The stems are strung with leathery oval leaves that turn red as the weather grows colder in autumn. Originating from China, Korea and Japan, star jasmine is frost hardy to about –5°C/23°F, but except in the most sheltered of gardens, it thrives better under glass. Here it will take the baton from Chinese jasmine and maintain a sweet fragrance in the air through to late summer.

Pot on young plants during spring, finishing them in a pot at least 30cm/12in across, and provide support for the long stems. These are woodland plants and need light shade from the hottest sun. Feed them monthly when they are established and watch out for scale insects, who love to colonize the undersides of the shiny leaves. In the wild, plants can easily reach 9m/30ft and although root restriction curbs some of this exuberance, a trim after flowering to remove the furthest questing stems is advisable. This plant is ideal for unheated greenhouses in all but the coldest regions. Propagate by taking summer cuttings.

ANNUALS AND SHORT-LIVED TREATS

Raising small batches of colourful short-lived potted plants from seed and cuttings is fun and they make wonderful gap- fillers between larger, longer-lived plants on the greenhouse staging. Similarly, short-lived climbers (page 128) add to the display.

These transitory plants are a mixture of annuals and tender perennials. True annuals will die after flowering and even the perennials are usually thrown away after one season. Some, like the kingfisher daisies, can be maintained by replacing old plants with cuttings, but the whole point of these plants is to add excitement between permanent plants and crops, without having to care for them long term. Most of us can find room for a few each year, after bedding plants and tender crops have been planted out and while some larger permanent plants are standing outside for the summer.

Choose just a couple of types to grow every year, ringing the changes to enjoy a variety of different flowers and foliage. I usually opt for one challenge such as prairie gentian (Eustoma) and a couple of easy types such as celosia and coleus (Solenostemon). When you come to choose your seed, you will find that there are several choices within each type. Prairie gentians come in different heights and colours; celosias can be the plume type or the strange cockscomb type, whose flower spike is fascinating and has the appearance and texture of a cockerel's comb; coleus can be all the colours of the rainbow or a dark-leaved mixture like 'Palisandra'.

It is also important to restrain yourself from growing too many of each type. In a small greenhouse, five of each will be plenty. There is nothing so sad as the sight of a dozen plants crowded together in small pots, unable to reach their full potential, when fewer grown to their full size would have given so much more.

TOP LEFT *Celosia argentea* var. *cristata* (Plumosa Group) Kimono Series
TOP RIGHT *Celosia argentea* var. *cristata* (Plumosa Group) 'Fairy Fountains'
MIDDLE A pink-flowered prairie gentian cultivar (*Eustoma grandiflorum*)
BOTTOM A dazzling coleus, *Solenostemon* Rainbow Series
RIGHT Young celosias ready for potting up

Sowing and growing

For small numbers of plants, sow into pots, following the instructions on page 19; or sow two seeds per small cell, and then thin down to one after germination. The important point with annuals is to make sure that their roots are never too restricted: let them become pot bound and they will stop growing and start trying to produce flowers on miniature plants. Inspect their roots (see page 28) and pot them on when necessary. Most will be able to flower and finish comfortably in a 13–15cm/5–6in pot. Sometimes it's fun to plant three from, say, 8cm/3in pots to a much larger pot and grow them together for maximum impact.

During the growing stages, annuals need careful watering when the compost surface is just starting to dry out. Immediately after potting they are at their most vulnerable to being overwatered, especially if night temperatures are still low. Water in the mornings if possible, and in the evening only if plants are wilting, using water at greenhouse temperature and not straight from the tap. These plants need plenty of air and space, so arrange them so that they aren't quite touching, ventilate well for good air circulation and remove any dead leaves regularly.

Feeding

In their early stages of growth, annuals get all they need from fresh potting compost. If you delay potting for any reason, it is essential to give them a general-purpose liquid feed (see page 179) every week until you get round to it. Once they are settled in their final pots and starting to flower, feed the plants every week or two to keep them healthy and make sure that more shoots and flowers grow.

At the end of their season, the plants will let you know when they have finished by looking tired and not producing any more flowers. They have done their job and can be safely consigned to the compost heap.

TOP Three young plants of *Maurandya barclayana* in one pot
MIDDLE LEFT The pot stands inside a wire basket
MIDDLE RIGHT Maurandya climbs, trails and opens its purple flowers
BOTTOM A mixture of pot-grown annuals brightens up staging

Bedding plants under glass

Anyone who does not exploit the wide range of bedding plants to be flowered under glass is missing out on a really easy short-lived treat. Any of the bedding plants you might choose for growing outside in the garden will almost certainly work if kept in pots under glass too. The advantages are obvious, such as having the plants at eye level where their colours, flower shapes and perfumes are more easily admired. These protected plants will also have the edge on their outdoor cousins because they are warmer and less exposed to wind, rain and slugs.

The easiest way to obtain plants is to buy them from garden centres at any stage. They will be cheapest as seedlings and plug plants bought earlier in the year to grow on, but you can spend a bit more and buy them just as they are coming into flower during late spring. The bedding plant range includes annuals grown from seed such as petunias and zinnias and tender perennials grown from cuttings. Examples of perennials include the striking, blue-flowered kingfisher daisy (*Felicia amelloides*), dainty, white-flowered *Sutera cordata* (sometimes known as bacopa), ideal for tumbling over the edge of the staging, or perennial nemesias such as *N*. 'Aromatica Rose Pink'. At the end of the season, you can simply throw these plants away and start again the following year. Or, if you want to work harder and build up a good stock, take late-summer cuttings and overwinter young plants for the following year.

There are rewards for those wanting to raise bedding plants from seed too. You can scour the seed catalogues for really special plants like the tall snapdragon *Antirrhinum majus* 'Royal Bride'. I have a passion for white-flowered plants and the blooms of this stately, 90cm–1.2m/3–4ft tall variety are strong, shapely, greenish white and fragrant. Sow and prick out the seedlings grid fashion into a seed tray in the usual way. After they've grown on, select eight strong seedlings and transfer these to individual 9cm/3½in pots. When they have filled these out, plant three per 23cm/9in pot and grow them on (the other two are spares). Support each plant with a split cane initially and then, as the plants lengthen, put one tall cane in the centre and tie the stems into this. Spares do well outdoors.

TOP LEFT Well-spaced antirrhinum seedlings ready for pricking out
TOP RIGHT The seedlings are pricked out grid fashion into a tray
MIDDLE LEFT The plants, grown on, are placed three per pot
MIDDLE RIGHT *Antirrhinum majus* 'Royal Bride'
BOTTOM The decorative tender perennial kingfisher daisy *Felicia amelloides*

ANNUALS AND SHORTLIVED TREATS

PLANT

Catharanthus roseus
Vinca, Madagascar periwinkle

H and S 30–60cm/12–24in

Celosia argentea var. cristata (Plumosa Group) Fairy Fountains Series Cockscomb, **plumosa** H 40cm/16in S 17cm/7in

DESCRIPTION

This handsome evergreen perennial from the periwinkle family (*Apocynaceae*) has the potential to live for several years and grow to the size of a small shrub, but to do well, plants need to winter in warmer conditions than most owners of small greenhouses can provide. With space at a premium in winter, most gardeners treat the Madagascan periwinkle as an annual and replace their old plants with fresh batches raised from seed sown in spring. The shiny, deep green leaves are soon joined by shimmering pink, red or white, flat-topped flowers up to 4cm/1½in across, sometimes with contrasting eyes. Note that all parts of the plant are poisonous.

These brilliant annuals from the love-lies-bleeding family (*Amaranthaceae*) are easy to grow from seed and provide dazzling colours of yellow, orange, pink or red all summer. Of the two types, I prefer the Plumosa Group, such as Fairy Fountains Series, whose tiny blooms are held in generous feathery spikes. The first and topmost will be the largest but side shoots each produce their own smaller flower spike at the tips. Cristata Group are the true cockscombs and produce flower structures with the bizarre appearance and texture of a cockerel's comb, or perhaps a coral. I usually raise about ten plants for my greenhouse and either display them en masse or dot them around between other plants, where their height and slim shape are useful attributes.

HOW TO GROW

Sow a small potful of seed in mid-spring, to germinate in a warm 18°C/65°F. Prick the seedlings out into individual cells or pots and grow them on from there, finishing in a 10cm/4in pot. Progress may be slow at first, but as the summer warms up, growth accelerates and by late summer the plants will be flowering and look great arranged around larger plants on the staging. An ideal minimum winter temperature is 10°C/50°F and plants can be carried over in a warm conservatory or as a house plant.

Sow seed in spring at 18°C/65°F. The germination rate is even and good, so I often set two per small cell and thin them down to one later. The seedlings are coloured right from the start, so you can see what kind of mixture you will end up with. Move them on to 9cm/3½in pots and then, if necessary, on again to 13cm/5in pots. Once established, these are thirsty plants and a fortnightly liquid feed will keep them flowering well into the autumn. Spare plants can be used outdoors, but perform better in pots than open soil.

Cuphea ignea
Cigar plant

H and S 30cm/12in

This small, shrubby pot plant from the loosestrife family (*Lythraceae*) is a joy for its slender tubular flowers. Reddish orange, they are tipped with yellow as though fuming, and black and white anthers protrude from the end, resembling the ash on a cigar – hence the common name. Technically, this plant is a perennial with a natural distribution from Mexico to Jamaica, but many gardeners treat it as an annual and raise fresh batches from seed each year. There are other cupheas to try. Look out for dainty *Cuphea hirtella*, whose tubular flowers are pink and yellow (see pages 2–3).

Sow seed in spring at 15°C/60°F and prick the seedlings out into small pots. They will grow on with few problems and come into bloom during summer, continuing non-stop through to the autumn in 13cm/5in pots. Should there be room in the greenhouse, do keep a couple of plants over winter, pruning them back lightly and keeping them drier than during summer at a minimum of 4°C/40°F. Prune more tightly in spring and let them break from the nodes or growing points on the slender stem stumps left behind. Nip back growing tips if they are at all long and drawn.

Eustoma grandiflorum
Prairie gentian, Texan bluebell

H 15–90cm/6–36in S 15–30cm/6–12in

These stunning North American plants in the gentian family (*Gentianaceae*) were originally known as *Lisianthus russellianus* when they first became widely available. Best known as cut flowers, they make good, if slightly tricky, pot plants for windowsill, porch and greenhouse. Personally I don't care much for the dwarf hybrids, and the tallest kinds need a lot of support. So for pots, a plant height of 30–45cm/12–18in is ideal. I would choose Double Eagle Series, mixed. Prairie gentians bear double or single flowers in a colour range including cream, pink and mauve, including bicolours. The blue-green foliage makes a good foil to the large flowers. You can keep them over winter at frost-free temperatures, but the resulting plants usually lack vigour and it is easier to raise fresh from seed.

Sow during spring into a small pot and germinate at around 15°C/60°F. I usually prick the resulting seedlings out three to a 9cm/3½in pot, or put them singly into small cells of soil-less compost. Water extremely carefully, as eustomas are prone to overwatering and a stray careless splash can finish them off. Only when the young plants have filled the pot with roots should you consider potting on. Use canes and raffia or string to support the flowering stems as they grow. Deadhead assiduously.

Exacum affine
Persian violet

H and S 15–23cm/6–9in

Although violet features in the common name, this attractive pot plant is another member of the gentian family (*Gentianaceae*), from Yemen. It is becoming increasingly difficult to track down from seed and the commonest variety available is 'Blue Midget', whose lavender-blue flowers are decorated by a mass of yellow pollen at the centre. They are said to be fragrant, but their perfume is elusive to me. The pleasing shape of the plant, liberally dotted with flowers over neat, shiny, bright green leaves, is useful for creating a hummock-like effect on the staging around larger plants. White-flowered varieties include 'White Midget' and 'White Rosette'.

Sow seeds in mid-spring at 18°C/65°F, pricking the seedlings out into small cells or closely in grid fashion in a small tray. Transfer the young plants to small pots when they are ready. These are easy plants to grow, but take care not to overwater, particularly at the early stages and when night temperatures are low. Keep water off the leaves. If plants are still going strong in autumn as night temperatures dip low, bring them indoors to last a little longer on a warm windowsill.

ANNUALS AND SHORT-LIVED TREATS

PLANT

Primula malacoides
Fairy primula

H 17–30cm/7–12in S 17cm/7in

Rehmannia elata
Chinese foxglove

H 90cm/3ft S 30cm/12in

DESCRIPTION

This pretty Chinese primula (from the family *Primulaceae*) is grown as an annual to flower during the depths of winter and into spring. First a rosette of hairy leaves forms, and then buds appear and flower stems rise up, bearing dainty blooms in shades usually of pink but also of lilac, red and white with yellow eyes. A double-flowered seed strain is available. Use fairy primulas informally around larger foliage plants on the staging, where they will make welcome splashes of colour.

As the common name implies, this delightful short-lived perennial belongs to the foxglove family (*Scrophulariaceae*). In my experience, the plants are highly individual. If you sow them one spring to produce flowers the following year, usually in early summer, out of ten plants, you might have two flowering five months after sowing, giving a splendid display during their first summer and autumn, and the rest could take a full twelve to fourteen months. Each produces a rosette of hairy leaves from which rises a stem strung with gorgeous, rosy-pink tubular flowers with spotted, yellow-streaked throats. They are tall, and I often stand mine on low staging or the floor.

HOW TO GROW

Sow the tiny seed during early summer, scattering it thinly over the surface of compost in a small pot. Cover with only a dusting of compost, so that when pressed in it is barely covered. Keep the compost moist and germinate the seeds at 15°C/60°F, being sure not to cook them in a hot propagating case. Prick the seedlings out into their own small pots and grow them on steadily, taking care not to overwater. Provide shading from scorching sun during summer by standing them in the shadow of taller plants. A minimum winter temperature just above freezing is all they need, but water them carefully, pick off dead leaves assiduously and ventilate when possible.

Sow rehmannia seed into a small pot during spring, to germinate at 15°C/60°F, pricking the seedlings out into individual pots as soon as they are large enough. I usually leave mine inside the greenhouse, but you could stand them outdoors for summer. Finish them in 15–17cm/6–7in pots, or three to a 25cm/10in pot, letting them flower when they will. Bring those yet to bloom back under glass in the autumn and keep them, well ventilated and carefully watered, at frost-free temperatures (minimum 3°C/38°F).

Salpiglossis sinuata
Bolero Group

H 60cm/2ft S 20cm/8in

There is nothing subtle about the flower of a salpiglossis. Belonging to the potato and petunia family (*Solanaceae*) and originally from Peru, it bears outrageously colourful, funnel-shaped blooms at least 5cm/2in across. It is always worth raising a few plants each year, to dot them among the display and see what zany colour combinations emerge. The base colour can be blue, purple, red, yellow or mauve, but they are patterned and veined with contrasting shades. The plants themselves are not much to write home about, being rather wispy and insubstantial. They tend to melt into the background leaving the flowers to sing.

Sow a pinch of seed into a pot, or two seeds to a cell, during spring, germinating them at a warm 21°C/70°F in a propagating case. Grow on to finish in a 13–15cm/5–6in pot. Keep the roots moist, feed the plants every two weeks and deadhead assiduously to keep them producing top-quality flowers. Should they sprawl, support them with split canes or a twiggy stick. A true annual, the salpiglossis will flower all summer and then fade away as temperatures cool and the nights draw in towards autumn.

Schizanthus pinnata
'Hit Parade'
Poor man's orchid, butterfly flower
H and S 15–30cm/6–12in

A spectacular flowering annual in the foxglove family (*Scrophulariaceae*), with its origins in Chile, the poor man's orchid produces bright green, fern-like leaves, topped by masses of close-set orchid-like flowers. The colour range includes all shades of pink, mauves and red, with contrasting marks and yellow throats. A spring sowing will bring the plants into flower during summer and autumn. But for the largest specimens, sow in late summer to enjoy flowers in late winter and spring, though this entails finding space and keeping the plants healthy throughout winter. Most seed strains result in dwarf or small plants, but hunt around and you'll find seed capable of yielding larger specimens 60–90cm/24–36in tall and wide.

I usually sow seeds into a small pot, germinate at 15–18°C/60–65°F and prick out the seedlings from there into small cells, later transferring them to pots. High-potash fertilizer every fortnight and a little support will help them along. Provide a frost-free minimum winter temperature of 4°C/40°F, ventilate freely and water carefully.

Solenostemon Rainbow Series
Coleus, flame nettle

H and S 45cm/18in

Foliage can be just as much fun as flowers and a batch of bright coleus will fill a greenhouse with colour all summer. There are numerous seed strains to try, offering a multitude of leaf colours and even wavy-edged leaves. One year I grew a stunning almost black-leaved variety, *Solenostemon* 'Palisandra', which is great for showing off other plants by creating dark pools around them. There are also named cultivars of solenostemon that can be propagated by taking cuttings.

Sow seed in spring, at a temperature of 18–21°C/65–70°F. My trick is to sow a good half trayful and prick out more seedlings than I need, setting them closely, grid fashion, in a seed tray. When they've grown on a bit, I pot up the colours I like best, thereby making the best use of my space. Sometimes I opt for the deepest reds or the most acid greens, and other times, a really good mixture. Pinch out the growing tips to make the plants branch and nip out the flower spikes as the flowers are insignificant. Pot on again if necessary and keep the roots moist. Coleus need a minimum temperature of 10°C/50°F to thrive in winter. Cuttings of favourite sorts root easily.

SHORT–LIVED CLIMBING PLANTS

PLANT	**Cobaea scandens** **Cup and saucer vine** H and S 1.5–2.5m/5–8ft	**Ipomoea lobata** **Spanish flag** H 90cm/3ft S 60cm/2ft

DESCRIPTION

From the Jacob's ladder family (*Polemoniaceae*) comes this exuberant tendril climber. It can be used outdoors after danger of frost has passed, but it flowers late in the season, often not reaching its best until autumn. The protection of glass will not only bring it into flower sooner but keep it going for longer. The fragrant flowers open cream but turn purple as they age, and each 5cm/2in long bell-shaped cup appears to sit in a saucer of pale green sepals – hence the common name. There is also a white-flowered form. Give plants plenty of space, but even under glass they won't reach the 20m/70ft possible in their native Mexican thickets.

This unusual Mexican climber in the bindweed family (*Convolvulaceae*) used to be called *Mina lobata* and although it has now been moved to the genus *Ipomoea*, its flowers are different to the saucers of morning glories. Instead, narrow, curved tubes line up in a one-sided raceme. New flowers at the top are a rich scarlet, but as they enlarge and age, they fade first to orange in the middle of the raceme, then to yellow and finally white at the bottom. The multi-coloured effect is striking throughout summer and into autumn.

HOW TO GROW

Germinate seed at 18°C/65°F in spring and grow the seedlings on, providing support and feeding monthly when they are established. I would equip the final pot with a tall tepee of canes, and then train growth up under the roof above. Although cobaea is perennial, it is best to clear away all the foliage after flowering and start again in spring. But you could cut most of the plant back after flowering, water sparingly through winter and let it grow again in spring – in which case opt for a minimum temperature of 3°C/38°F.

Sow seed in mid-spring at 18°C/65°F, pricking the large seedlings out into individual pots. When these have filled their pots, I usually put three together into a 17cm/7in pot. Once the plants are established, feed them fortnightly and if necessary pot them on again. Equip the pot with a climbing frame and tie the stems in to the base, spiral fashion, before letting them twine where they will. Watch out for spider mite. Spanish flag is a perennial, but likes a minimum temperature of 7–10°C/45–50°F during winter and tends to go into a decline anyway when light levels become low. Best, then, to throw tired plants away after flowering and raise fresh ones from seed next spring.

Maurandya barclayana

H 1.8m/6ft S 90cm/3ft

This twining perennnial climber, a Mexican native in the snapdragon family (*Scrophulariaceae*), has suffered a few name changes in recent years, and I bought seed of it as Asarina Mixed. It will excel either on a climbing frame or dangling from a hanging basket, smothering its support with bright green, ivy-shaped leaves and jewel-like flowers in purple, pink or white with pale throats. It is capable of scrambling for 3m/10ft or more in the wild, but you can keep it to 60cm/2ft if you confine the roots to a moderate pot 15cm/6in or so in diameter. Try also *Lophospermum erubescens*, a similar, soft-leaved climber with larger pink flowers.

Germinate seed at 18°C/65°F in spring, pricking the seedlings out into individual cells or pots. Feed established plants fortnightly to keep the flowers coming throughout summer and autumn. Provide light shading to protect the plants from harsh sun, especially when they are hanging near the glass roof. Although plants are easily raised from seed each spring, maurandya is perennial and you can keep plants from year to year. Maintain them just frost free and water sparingly during winter and although they die back during winter, new growth will appear in spring. Softwood cuttings root quickly in spring.

Rhodochiton atrosanguineus
Purple bell flower

H 1.2m/4ft S 45cm/18in

Yet another scrambling perennial climber from Mexico belonging to the snapdragon family (*Scrophulariaceae*), this plant makes a striking greenhouse specimen. I love the way it climbs by wrapping its leaf stalks around its support in a vice-like grip. The long stems are strung with buds right up to their tips and are extremely dainty. The summer and autumn flowers are dramatic, with dark purple, almost black tubular flowers hanging down from inside pink calyces, like long purple light bulbs from pink lampshades. I like to grow mine up a decorative metal obelisk or train it under the roof struts of the greenhouse, from where the flowers dangle effectively.

Germinate at 18°C/65°F, but be prepared for uneven results, with one seedling appearing first, another in a week and so forth. Prick them out as they become large enough, without disturbing the ungerminated seed on either side. Grow them on in small individual cells or pots, feeding them monthly when established and shading them from harsh sun. I usually plant three to a 30cm/12in pot. Purple bell flowers are perennial and will overwinter at 4°C/40°F, but are usually best raised fresh from seed each year. Watch out for whitefly.

Thunbergia alata
Black-eyed Susan

H 1.5m/5ft S 75cm/30in

This twining perennial climber from tropical Africa is a member of the acanthus family (*Acanthaceae*). In the wild it scampers up trees or swarms across the forest floor, and a reach of 2.5m/8ft is common. Under glass, from a spring sowing, plants flower young and can be kept to a modest 90cm/3ft by restriction in a small pot. The classic flower colour is the familiar orange with a dark eye at the centre, but some are wishy-washy, missing an eye and therefore less striking. Grow several from seed, let them flower and choose the best colours to keep for the summer-to-autumn flowering season. Strong reddish shades are available from mixtures like 'African Sunset' (syn. 'Blushing Susie') or can be bought as small plug plants.

Germinate seed at 18°C/65°F in spring, prick the seedlings out and grow them on individually. Finish single plants in a 15–17cm/6–7in pot, or plant three together in a 30cm/12in pot fitted with an obelisk or tepee of canes. Feed established plants fortnightly and watch out for spider mite. A perennial needing a minimum of 7°C/45°F for overwintering, black-eyed Susie is usually cleared away after flowering and raised fresh from seed each spring.

SPECIAL COLLECTIONS

6

With so many fabulous glasshouse plants to choose from, one way of channelling a collection is to focus on one or more groups of plants and collect from within them. I am often tempted to clear my greenhouse staging and start again, concentrating on tender bulbs, perhaps combined with cacti and succulents, as they would enjoy similar growing conditions. You could easily specialize in carnivorous plants, enjoying their fascinating form and flower. Some growers become obsessed with fuchsias, pelargoniums or chrysanthemums – within each of those groups there is enough variety to satisfy the fussiest collector. Or you could mix and match with a few of each, as I do. House plants are included in this chapter because if you grow a large range of these, you are likely to have some that will benefit from a spell in the greenhouse, either while they are dormant or when they are at a crucial stage in their development and need the extra light or coolness there.

Shaving brush plant (*Haemanthus albiflos*)

FUCHSIAS

Flamboyant *Fuchsia* 'Pink Marshmallow'

Fuchsias are in the evening primrose family (*Onagraceae*), originating mostly in South America. Shrubby by nature, they bear stunning flowers during summer, made up of four sepals that open to reveal short petals usually of a contrasting colour. Apart from a range of cultivars with upward-looking flowers (*F.* 'Walz Jubelteen', for example), most fuchsias have flowers that dangle, with their stamens protruding below the petals. The problem with growing potted fuchsias under glass is knowing when to stop, as there are so many lovely cultivars.

For cultivation, fuchsias are divided into two groups. There are hardy types, which can be planted outside in the garden and are able to perform well despite winter temperatures down to −15°C/5°F; and there are those needing winter frost protection. With a greenhouse at your disposal it makes sense to choose the more tender varieties, but for unheated greenhouses in colder areas, hardy fuchsias are still a good prospect. The added protection will bring them into flower earlier and you can enjoy their blooms close to.

Growing fuchsias

Having acquired young plants in spring, you can treat them in various ways. The simplest is to grow a large bushy plant with as much bloom as possible. To do this, nip the tips out of all the shoots once they have two pairs of leaves or more and the young plant will branch. After a couple of pairs of leaves have grown, pinch again. You can continue to stop in this way endlessly, but remember that it will take the fuchsia six weeks to develop flower buds after the last stop. All the shoot tips you've created will produce masses of flower buds.

Potting and feeding

As fuchsia plants grow, they need potting on. The final move, into the largest pot you'll allow (anywhere between 15 and 23cm/6 and 9in in diameter), should be into strong compost such as John Innes No. 3. Once the plants have settled in, apply a high-potash liquid feed weekly to encourage flowering. Towards the end of summer, the shoot tips might harden and stop producing flower buds. A couple of high-nitrogen feeds will bring on more soft, bud-bearing shoots.

Overwintering

When low temperatures and short days bring an end to the flowering period, cut the bush back by about half and reduce watering, so that the plant ticks over until spring. Just as the new growth starts, prune harder, leaving lots of short spurs of last season's stems behind. From these, new growth will burst forth to regenerate the plant. Nip back the shoot tips as above to make them branch. Alternatively, the new shoots will make softwood cuttings.

Where space is at a premium, overwinter your fuchsias as young plants by taking cuttings during summer. Large, space-hungry plants can then be thrown away. The heard-hearted could throw all their plants away in autumn and restock in spring. This is a

HOW TO GROW A FUCHSIA BASKET

Fat fuchsia buds and flouncy flowers hanging from the roof space of the greenhouse are a summer treat that can be yours if you plant up a hanging basket. You can raise the plants for next to nothing.

1 In early spring buy a cheap, young plant of a trailing fuchsia like 'Pink Marshmallow'. Choose one with a couple of long shoots and take these as cuttings. You'll end up with three young plants, including the parent (which will sprout new shoots). Grow them on in 9cm/3½in pots, nipping out the growing tips to make them branch.

2 An easy way to plant the basket is to remove the fuchsias from their pots and 'plant' the empty pots into the compost, spacing them evenly around the top, and wiggle the pots out so that you leave three holes just the right size for the rootballs. Slip them in, firm gently and water in. Always leave a gap at the top to take water.

3 Hang the basket from the roof and allow the plants to develop. After three to four weeks, begin feeding on a weekly basis and wait for the stems to pour down over the sides full of pale pink flowers. After the first flush, deadhead and continue to feed, and the plants should bloom all summer.

great way of exploring as many different varieties as possible. Tiny young plants at the rooted cutting stage are not particularly expensive and what I often do is buy a small fuchsia with two or three shoots, let them grow long enough to be taken as cuttings and root them. Then I have three new plants plus the parent. Do this with a trailing variety and you can easily fill a hanging basket.

Standards

Having mastered the art of fuchsia growing, you will find that it is relatively simple to train a fuchsia in the shape of a pyramid, fan or standard. Standards are popular and easy. You need a sturdy variety rather than one with weak stems. Standards made from sturdy-stemmed trailing varieties are particularly effective. Pot the plant on as it grows, supporting the main stem with a cane. Having taken cuttings, select a straight robust plant (or even two or three) and mark it with a slender cane to act as a reminder not to absentmindedly nip the growing tip out. Do the opposite, encouraging upward growth and removing side shoots until the stem reaches the desired height. Let the tip grow up 15cm/6in beyond this (or produce three sets of leaves) with the side shoots left in place and then stop it. Nip out the growing tips of the side shoots to create a rounded head, and your standard is finished.

Problems

When many fuchsias are grown together, they attract vine weevil which, in pots, can be a real problem. Look out for notches in the leaf edges made by the adults, and take steps to make sure that the larvae are not busy feeding on the roots (see page 187). Greenfly attack shoot tips and whitefly can be troublesome at any stage. Fuchsias can suffer from rust, but are sensitive to some fungicides, so always check to make sure that they can be used on these plants.

TOP LEFT Unusual, shrubby *Fuchsia* 'Rubra Grandiflora'
TOP RIGHT *Fuchsia* 'Thalia' is an upright, Triphylla type
BOTTOM *Fuchsia* 'Orient Express', upright, with deep and light pink flowers
RIGHT The classic *Fuchsia* 'Rose of Denmark' bears lilac and pink flowers

CHRYSANTHEMUMS

LEFT The single spray *Chrysanthemum* 'Klondike'
RIGHT The spider type *Chrysanthemum* 'Muxton Sable'
OPPOSITE The spray *Chrysanthemum* 'Biarritz'

Autumn-flowering chrysanths have a definite slot in the greenhouse year and add colour and that characteristic chrysanthemum smell during late autumn and winter. They are divided into groups according to flowering time, and it is the mid- and late-season kinds that need the protection of glass when the weather turns wet, damp and cold in autumn. During summer, the plants live outside in their pots, but after tomatoes and cucumbers have been cleared out of the greenhouse, and before the weather worsens, they are brought inside. You will need to ventilate the greenhouse well and use a little heat to keep frost out.

Growing and training

Young rooted cuttings are usually bought in spring and potted into 9cm/3½in pots. Having filled these with roots, they'll move on to 13cm/5in pots and should finish in 23cm/9in pots. When a young plant is 23cm/9in tall, stop the shoots by nipping out its growing tip to make it branch. Stop the shoots again in midsummer. In a small greenhouse, it might be best to squeeze two stops in by midsummer, to keep height down. Another way of moderating size is to take a second batch of cuttings in late spring and stop them in midsummer. Feed established plants weekly and after danger of frost has passed stand them outside, supported by posts and wire against wind. Cultivars grown for their large flowers should be disbudded by removing all the flower buds on a stem except the largest one at the top. Those grown to produce 'sprays' of small flowers should have their topmost, terminal flower bud removed to push energy into the smaller flowers.

Stools and cuttings

After flowering, cut all the stems back, leaving 2.5–5cm/1–2in stumps behind, shake excess compost from the roots and pack these stools into boxes of soil that will fit, later, into the propagating case. Keep them frost free and water sparingly. If you want more plants, in late winter put the stools inside a heated propagating case at about 15°C/60°F and shoots will sprout. Take cuttings and repeat the process. Watch out for whitefly, aphids and powdery mildew.

Experimenting

In the art of growing chrysanthemums under glass, there is endless opportunity for experimentation. The many cultivars respond variously to being stopped and disbudded in different ways and at different times. Spray chrysanths, grown for their stems of moderate-sized flowers, tend to be roughly 1.2m/4ft high and 60cm/2ft wide. Those grown for their single, huge blooms also tend to be tall and narrow. You could try charm type chrysanths, whose shape is naturally dome-like, smothered in small flowers, but they are greedy on space. Cascades, their lax stems bearing hundreds of small flowers, can be trained in all kinds of interesting ways.

PELARGONIUMS

They bloom mainly during spring, summer and autumn, but a few continue throughout winter. I find it hard to leaf through a pelargonium catalogue and behave decently.

Pelargoniums are a genus of some 230 species of mainly evergreen, frost-prone perennials, though it is the cultivars that we tend to grow in our gardens and greenhouses. They belong to the cranesbill family (*Geraniaceae*) and are sometimes still referred to as 'geraniums', but this can lead to confusion, because then nobody is sure whether pelargoniums are under discussion or true hardy border geraniums.

Most pelargoniums originate from South Africa and the many cultivars are split into groups. I have chosen only half a dozen favourites to describe here.

Zonal

These are the best-known pelargoniums, because they bloom from spring till autumn and are widely used as bedding plants. Derived by crossing *P. zonale* with *P. inquinans*, they are characterized by a horseshoe-shaped ring of darker colour on each of their rounded leaves. The foliage has a distinctive fragrance, neither sweet nor revolting. Plants like these have been around for a long time, the first hybrid having been made in 1714. There are several different types of Zonal pelargonium, including straightforward single-flowered and double-flowered sorts; for the greenhouse we tend to choose the compact, flamboyant and unusual cultivars.

If you have only limited space, Miniatures and Dwarfs are ideal. These are characterized by their tight branching structure and small, densely packed leaves. Miniatures rarely grow higher then 13cm/5in and include classics such as salmon-flowered, dark-leaved 'Alde', double, bright mauve 'Francis Parrett', deep lavender 'Jayne Eyre', 'Green Gold Petit Pierre', 'Millbern Engagement' and scarlet-flowered, black-leaved 'Red Black Vesuvius'. Dwarfs average 20cm/8in in height and include salmon-red, dark-leaved 'Friesdorf'.

TOP LEFT The pretty miniature Zonal *Pelargonium* 'Green Gold Petit Pierre'
TOP RIGHT Striking miniature Zonal *Pelargonium* 'Millbern Engagement'
ABOVE Miniature Zonal *Pelargonium* 'Millbern Clover'

The warm colours and leafy scents of the pelargonium tribe make these plants ideal for greenhouse display. Among their ranks are plants to climb, trail, grow into small bushy shapes or even train as standards, and they flower profusely. Most are really easy to grow; on the other hand, some of the more delicate species will present a challenge to anyone wanting to test their skills.

Fancy-leaved types are superb for brightening up the winter greenhouse. These include 'Contrast', boasting at least four colours on each leaf, where red, yellow and green overlap; single vermilion flowers complete the picture. Graceful 'Frank Headley' with cream-edged leaves and single salmon blooms is popular.

Then there are those with very particular types of flower such as the Rosebuds, whose clusters of double flowers open tightly. 'Apple Blossom Rosebud' is a well-known example. This lovely plant thrives particularly well under glass, protected from outdoor weather. Stellar types such as pale pink 'Bird Dancer' bear dainty, quilled petals that are often forked or jagged at the edges.

There are even Zonal pelargoniums with stems that are so long and lax that they can be trained in as climbers capable of reaching 1.8m/6ft in a year. Tie them in to a trellis or wires and prune back outward shoots in spring as they come into growth. A little nipping and snipping throughout the season will keep them under control. 'Antik Pink' makes masses of light, rose-pink flowers against dark, bronze-shaded foliage.

Ivy-leaved

The many cultivars of pelargonium bearing succulent leaves shaped like those of ivy on weak, mostly trailing stems derive originally from *P. peltatum*. In the greenhouse, these are useful for dangling over the edge of the staging or from hanging baskets. The long succession of flowers they bear from spring to autumn can be single or double and there are a few types with variegated foliage, notably the compact 'L'Elégante', whose pink-tinged, cream-edged leaves harmonize perfectly with single white flowers with dark maroon markings. Those with dark-coloured flowers are particularly popular.

TOP Dwarf Stellar *Pelargonium* 'Bird Dancer' bears dainty blooms
BOTTOM *Pelargonium* 'Apple Blossom Rosebud'

ABOVE The ever-popular Regal *Pelargonium* 'Lord Bute'
OPPOSITE Pretty Regal *Pelargonium* 'Parisienne'

Regals

These showy pelargoniums bred from *P. x domesticum* are known as Martha Washingtons in America. Large, frilly blooms open with great profusion in early summer, but most have a shorter flowering period than other types of pelargonium. Some Regals, notably the popular 'Lord Bute', flower on throughout summer. 'Lord Bute' has won universal favour with its deep reddish pink petals edged with brighter pink, although it has a rather lanky growing habit. The leaves are plain green, somewhat lobed and often toothed. I am partial to classy 'Parisienne', whose pale mauve flowers have white throats and a purple blotch on the upper petals. 'Bushfire' has rich, warm scarlet blooms and flowers from spring until autumn. Regals need to be pruned and propagated slightly differently from Zonal pelargoniums.

Uniques

These pelargoniums are similar to the Regals but daintier in flower and leaf, though they will build up into good-sized, bushy plants that flower from spring to autumn. Aromatic, bright-flowered 'Unique Aurore' bears red flowers with dark markings and 'Duchess of Devonshire' has flowers of soft salmon with darker markings. Treat Uniques as Regals.

Angels

These cultivars have *P. crispum* as one of their parents and bear beautifully marked flowers that float over the plants like pansy faces during spring and summer. The foliage is neat and scented on plants that grow up to 50cm/20in tall. *P.* 'Catford Belle' and *P.* 'The Kenn-Lad' are good examples. Treat Angels as Regals.

Scented-leaved

These, along with the species are, for me, the most fascinating pelargoniums. What they lack in flower power they make up for with the intense fragrance of their leaves. I find them useful fillers which provide interesting patches of foliage between flowering plants on the staging. For small spaces, *P.* 'Fragrans' makes a rounded bush to 20–25cm/8–10in high of small grey-green, pine-scented leaves smothered by tiny white flowers all summer. *P.* 'Fragrans Variegatum' has cream and white variegated leaves. *P. crispum* bears dainty leaves sweetly redolent of lemon, topped by pretty mauve flowers on an upright plant 35–45cm/14–18in high. *P. crispum* 'Variegatum' is similar, but with cream-margined leaves.

What most people mean when they say 'lemon-scented pelargonium' is *P. graveolens*, but this grows to a straggly 45–60cm/18–24in. Perhaps a better plant is the variegated 'Lady Plymouth', with touches of both lemon and peppermint on its leaves. The most intense lemon scent is undoubtedly provided by *P.* 'Mabel Grey', a large-leaved plant reaching 60cm/2ft. A peppermint scent is supplied by soft-leaved *P. tomentosum*, again a large, straggly plant that grows to 90cm/3ft, but the leaves are fabulously tactile and minty. There is 'Ardwick Cinnamon', 'Chocolate Peppermint', 'Islington Peppermint', 'Orange Fizz' and 'Apple Betty', but whether they live up to their names is a question for individual noses. My favourite is 'Copthorne'. Its leaves smell generally spicy and, although it tends to be on the gangly side, I love it for its mauve-pink flowers, which have dark purple feather markings on the upper petals. It flowers year round without the hint of a break during winter.

Care for Scented-leaved pelargoniums as for Zonals and propagate by taking cuttings as for Zonals.

The small but striking flowers of *Pelargonium* 'Ardens'

Species and species hybrids

I am very fond of these pelargoniums because they tend to be wild, wilful and a law unto themselves. The flowers are smaller than those of showy cultivars, but they are dainty and prettily marked. Some die back to tuber-like growths at the slightest provocation and need to be watched like a hawk. There are quite a few around, but some have made it to cult status. These include silver-grey-leaved *P. sidoides*. The combination of the steely leaves and the small, precise, near-black flowers is satisfying on a plant that reaches 45cm/18in. *P.* 'Ardens' has a prostrate habit of growth and in early and midsummer produces crimson-red flowers with black blotches above the grey-green leaves. Growth tends to take place from late winter, with flowering in late spring and summer, after which the plant goes dormant. Then there's *P.* 'Renate Parsley', no more than 15cm/6in high, whose wine-red upper petals contrast with pale pink lower petals over low-growing foliage. Some are mean with their propagation material and it is hard to find portions to root as cuttings. My favourite species is *P. echinatum* whose stems bear blunt spines, small grey-green leaves and plenty of beautifully marked flowers. There is a pink and a white form.

Caring for pelargoniums

As well as being gorgeous, these are easy plants for the greenhouse. Most love full light and can tolerate some dryness at the roots. What they can't put up with is wet, soggy compost, so make sure that the surface is dry between waterings during summer and that the top half of the compost is dry in winter. The air should be dry too, so in winter, water only in the mornings of bright, warm days when you can open the vents and door for a good airing. All, but especially the delicate species, need space around them. I often raise mine on upturned pots so that they can compete with other, larger plants for air and light.

During active periods of growth, usually during summer, feed pelargoniums fortnightly with a well-balanced liquid feed. Those you expect to flower profusely should have a high-potash fertilizer from when they start to bud up. However, the species will grow better given a monthly feed when well established in their pots.

Potting and composts

For most Zonal, Angel, Regal, Ivy-leaved and Scented-leaved pelargoniums, a normal potting compost (50:50 John Innes No. 2 and a soil-less compost) will suffice. For the species, mix this potting compost three parts to one with sharp sand or grit to provide the extra drainage they need.

Pot the plants on when they need it, up until high summer, because they should not go into a cold winter with too much wet compost around their roots. They should be well established and their pots full of roots.

Pruning

By the end of the growing season, your pelargoniums will have made a lot of growth. You can encourage those still flowering well to go on. But prune back those whose display is nearly over. Cut back about half their growth to tidy the plants up and reduce the amount of space they need.

If you have too many plants, it is best to throw some out and give the rest more space, as crowding creates a damp environment, encouraging weak growth and botrytis. My advice is to keep your favourites, slow-growing ones and those expensive to replace. You can always order new rooted cuttings and young plants of cheap, fast-growing types to arrive in spring.

In late winter and early spring, increased light levels mean that growth will start. Now's the time to fine-tune pruning and cut some plants back harder if necessary.

Regals (and similar) should be pruned immediately after flowering and not in late winter, as this would jeopardize their flowering.

To train a standard, use a robust, long-stemmed Zonal, P. 'Mabel Grey', or even P. crispum, and follow the same procedure as for fuchsias (see page 134).

Propagation

Ordinary Zonal pelargoniums can be raised from seed. Sow during late winter and spring, using a propagating case or warm room to ensure temperatures of at least 21°C/70°F to germinate. Remove the seedlings from this warmth into cooler temperatures and good light as soon as they germinate. From early sowings, you will have plants in bloom from late spring onwards. Seed is also available of Ivy-leaved types and some of the species. Home-collected seed usually germinates well, but only that collected from species will come true.

Named varieties will not come true from seed, but fortunately you can propagate all pelargoniums by taking cuttings of young shoots. This is done not just to increase stock but for rejuvenation, as individual plants tend to become tired and woody after a couple of seasons' worth of producing flowers, being pruned and performing again. While you can take cuttings at virtually any time of the year when there are shoots to remove, they root faster during spring and summer than in winter. There is also a rhythm to the timetable of taking cuttings, having plants in bloom and resting them during the winter months.

Cuttings of Zonal and Ivy-leaved geraniums are usually taken during summer, so that young plants are well rooted in their pots come winter. They will then go on to flower brilliantly the following year. Those short of space can take their cuttings in late summer and autumn, leaving them together in their pots until spring, when they should be potted separately. Miniatures and dwarfs take their time to build up into good-sized plants

A collection of pelargoniums, ordered by post and newly potted

and because they are slow-growing, individual plants tend to have longer lives.

Regals and those behaving like Regals are usually propagated after their main flush of late-spring blooms. They will flower as small plants the following summer, but for really splendid specimens, trim them up and then pot them on after flowering and they will reach superb proportions the following year.

How to take cuttings

Make cuttings 8cm/3in long by cutting under a leaf with a sharp knife and removing the lower leaves. Do not use hormone rooting compound on Zonal pelargoniums because they don't like it and will probably rot away. Insert the cuttings into gritty cuttings compost, setting several to a 9cm/3½in pot, and water them in, but do not cover Zonals or species with polythene or place inside a propagating case. Only cuttings of Regals, Uniques and Angels seem to root better when covered.

When sufficient roots have grown, separate the rooted cuttings and pot them individually. After a couple of weeks, and when the cuttings have begun to grow, nip out the growing tip of each one to encourage branching. If you require neat, rounded, bushy shapes, do this two or three times before letting them bud up.

CARNIVOROUS PLANTS

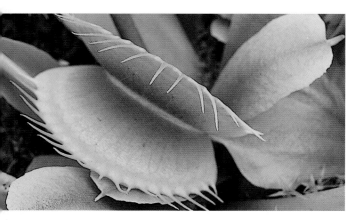

ABOVE The gaping jaws of Venus' fly trap (*Dionaea muscipula*)
OPPOSITE *Sarracenia flava* sends up sturdy pitchers

A collection of carnivorous plants is lots of fun to look after and these plants make a great year-round theme for either an unheated or frost-free greenhouse. Keep the odd Venus' fly trap or pitcher plant (*Sarracenia*) standing in a saucer of rain water amongst other plants, or have fun by filling whole or part of the staging with a miniature boggy landscape complete with tree branches and moss. The plants will love it. You will be amazed at how many insects the plants' traps catch. Smaller carnivorous plants such as butterworts (*Pinguicula*) and sundews (*Drosera*) clean up greenhouse pests such as fungus gnats and whitefly by behaving like living fly papers. Venus' fly traps are good at catching crane flies and the larger, pitcher-forming types catch many flies.

What is a carnivorous plant?

The notion of jaws clamping shut and digestive juices flowing is at odds with our perception of plants as passive. Nevertheless, carnivorous plants live in boggy, acidic soils low in nutrients and have evolved to supplement their nitrogen intake by catching, digesting and absorbing insects and other small animals. Slice open the mature leaf of a sarracenia and you'll be surprised by how many chitinous insect exoskeletons are packed into the tube-like pitcher – all that is left of the many insects the plant has consumed during a summer. The ways in which each genus of carnivorous plants attracts and traps its prey are remarkably ingenious.

General guidelines

Although it is possible to raise a wide range of carnivorous plants from seed, most people start by buying their first few plants. Each particular genus has its likes and dislikes, but most carnivorous plants will be happy to grow in a pot of well-drained compost based on peat and lime-free sand. It used to be said that they should receive no fertilizer, but a grower I know gives a tiny quantity of controlled-release fertilizer (the nutrients are made available gradually over a four-to-six-month period). This probably equates to about three granules per pot. Always give plants rain water or soft water, but if this is not available, it is better to give them tap water than let them wilt. Stand pots in wide saucers holding 1cm/½in) of water during summer. In winter, let this disappear before topping up again. On the whole, they need plenty of light, though lightly shading the glass will provide relief from the full glare of sun during late spring and high summer.

Years ago, we believed that most carnivorous plants needed frost protection and had to be kept under glass in winter. In fact, many can tolerate moderately cold weather outdoors in winter as long as they are well hardened off first. Ironically, quite a few of the commonly grown types are prone to attack from aphids. Fortunately, they can be sprayed with insecticides as long as all the usual rules are observed, including never spraying in harsh light. Alternatively, dunk your afflicted plant in a solution of horticultural soft soap. Most carnivorous plants make active growth during spring and summer, when there are plenty of insects about. They tend to die back a little and rest during winter, when there are fewer insects.

CARNIVOROUS PLANTS

PLANT

Cephalotus follicularis
Western Australian pitcher plant

H 10cm/4in S 25cm/10in

Dionaea muscipula
Venus' fly trap

H and S 15cm/6in

DESCRIPTION

These curious perennials, in their own family (*Cephalotaceae*), bear squat, almost ugly pitchers with bristled ridges and gaping, ribbed jaws. They produce a rosette of non-carnivorous leaves, present during winter at warmer temperatures or during the first part of the growing season, followed by ground-hugging pitchers. Each is held out on a stalk attached to the tops of the pitcher, so that it resembles a head on a long thin neck. From the ridges along the front, to the ribbed mouth, inward-pointing spines, slippery sides and nectar glands, everything is geared towards guiding insects in and down. They end up in a well of digestive fluid where they are broken down and absorbed.

The perennial Venus' fly trap from North and South Carolina, USA, belongs to the sundew family (*Droseraceae*). This is more of a pet than a potted plant. The leafy traps work by secreting nectar to attract insects. When one of the trigger hairs on the leaf surface has been tickled twice, or two touched in close succession, the jaws quickly move shut, clamping tightly to digest the prey. One leaf can catch and digest only about three insects in its life; therefore constantly springing the trap for fun is not a great idea, as this wastes the plant's energy. The colour of the traps varies, the plain green types being the hardiest and those flushed with red less able to tolerate cold.

HOW TO GROW

Use a compost of four parts peat to one perlite and one lime-free sand. A plant will need a good-sized pot of 15cm/6in diameter to accommodate the long roots. During winter, plants are prone to rotting away and should not be watered from below in a drip tray. Instead, water around the outside of the crown, from above, only when the surface has started to dry out a little. Keep in a frost-free greenhouse during winter. Propagate by division as the plant comes back into growth during spring. Root cuttings 1–2.5cm/½in long taken during spring should be laid flat on a compost of two parts sand to one of peat and covered with their own depth of compost. Water from below. Take leaf cuttings as for Venus' fly trap.

Grow Venus' fly traps in a compost of four parts peat to one of lime-free sand and experiment by adding a couple of grains of controlled-release fertilizer. Plants tend to pull downwards in the compost, becoming submerged by moss, so re-pot every two to three years, using on average a 10cm/4in wide pot. Remove the flower stems, because the small white blooms weaken the plant. To propagate by taking leaf cuttings in spring, lay a whole leaf flat on the surface of moist sphagnum moss and lightly cover it with torn moss. Keep the leaf moist in a propagating case and have patience, as it will take a good three months to make growth buds. Venus' fly traps tolerate a few degrees of frost.

Drosera binata
Fork-leaved sundew

H and S 30cm/12in

The Australian fork-leaved sundew bears leaves covered with tentacles, each with a drop of glistening mucilage at its tip. Glands secrete enzymes and absorb nutritious fluid into the plant. Stems of white flowers are an attractive part of this plant, which is a perennial in its own family (*Droseraceae*). The sticky fluid traps insects and their struggle stimulates more tentacles to bend around their prey, all the better to digest it.

Pinguicula grandiflora
Irish butterwort

H 15cm/6in S 10cm/4in

Also native to France, Switzerland and Spain, this Irish butterwort – a perennial in the family *Lentibulariaceae* – makes low-growing rosettes of greenish yellow leaves, covered in drops of clear mucilage held on stalked glands. The edges of the leaves curve in slightly and the plants are enhanced by a summer-long display of beautiful purple flowers. Small flies settling on the leaves are trapped by the sticky mucilage, suffocated, digested and absorbed, the leaf edges rolling in slightly to aid the process.

Sarracenia leucophylla
White trumpet pitcher

H 30–90cm/12–36in S 30cm/12in

The perennial North American trumpet pitchers, in the family *Sarraceniaceae*, are easy to grow. This one is particularly beautiful, with red veining in the white lid and throat. In spring, as growth starts, it produces tall stems, each holding a deep red flower shaped like a spaceship. At the same time, new slender pitchers push up from the perennating bud, and as they open and mature, they catch plenty of insects to feed the plant. Nectar attracts them, while downward-pointing hairs and a hooded exit encourage a downward spiral. Losing their grip and clogged by fluid, the insects end up in the bottom of the pitcher, effectively the plant's stomach.

Pot plants into four parts peat and one of lime-free sand. Some other species of drosera are hardy, but this Australian type needs frost protection. During winter, adequate ventilation is of paramount importance, in order to avoid the humidity that encourages botrytis. Should aphids appear, lift them off with a small paintbrush. Propagate by seed, but don't be dismayed when young plants produce rounded leaves at first: they need to reach a certain stage of maturity before lengthening and dividing. Take leaf cuttings as for Venus' fly trap.

This butterwort and most others die back to a resting bud during winter, for which they need cold conditions. My plants have managed to go dormant at temperatures hovering just above freezing, but any warmer and they would be better off plunged into some peat outdoors. When re-potting butterworts, bear in mind that they resent disturbance. Those that rest in winter should be potted while dormant, into a mix of four parts peat and one of lime-free sand. Half bury the dormant bud or hibernacula and it will begin growing in spring. Should the parent plant produce tiny replicas of itself, tweezer them out and grow them separately by setting them a short distance apart on moist compost.

Re-pot and divide large plants in spring or early summer while they are enjoying healthy growth, using compost of six parts peat, two parts perlite and one part lime-free sand. When plants die back in autumn, trim the pitchers back gradually from the top down, removing dead tissue but leaving the nourishment-filled bases. In all but the coldest areas, sarracenias are considered hardy when planted or plunged into lime-free soil, but they also grow well in an unheated or frost-free greenhouse.

CACTI AND
OTHER SUCCULENTS

Variable in shape, leaf, stem and flower, succulents are so fascinating that many greenhouses are filled with these alone. The plants are tough and resilient – they have to be in order to survive their natural habitats – but there is real pleasure to be gained from learning to grow them well.

Plants described as succulents are able to withstand prolonged drought by storing water in their stems, leaves or roots. Members of many different plant families can be described as succulents, including the cacti (members of the family *Cactaceae*). True cacti are succulents characterized by structures known as areoles, or pad-like buds from which shoots, spines and flowers grow. So all cacti are succulents, but not all succulents are cacti.

Succulents enjoy an intriguing range of habitats in the wild and if you have the time it is worth tracking down the origins of your plants: find the places on an atlas and try to imagine the natural landscape there. Most of us connect cacti with sandy deserts, but some grow at surprisingly high altitudes on mountainous slopes and others in humid jungles. Only a few well-adapted plants live in true deserts where less than 25cm/10in of rain falls in a year. Most inhabit arid semi-deserts, which have thin soil over rock. At higher altitudes, mists and dews make up some of their water intake and some plants have evolved ingenious methods for catching and directing moisture to their roots. Others have evolved so as to be able to deflect light or repel grazing animals.

Succulents are ideal for greenhouse cultivation because most of them enjoy good, even light and a cool, frost-free winter. These conditions are important because they allow the plants to go dormant while light levels are poor. Although these plants are adapted to withstand deprivation and harsh conditions, this is not an excuse for neglect. They will grow, look and flower better if cared for properly.

Position

For most succulents, the greenhouse must be sited in good light, or else growth will be drawn and one-sided. But despite this, some may need light shading during midsummer if they are close to south-facing glass. Otherwise, they will be marred by nasty brown scorch marks. Ventilate the greenhouse as much as possible during summer, to keep temperatures below 32°C/90°F, and in winter too, to increase air circulation and ward off botrytis. Standing plants outdoors during summer is an option, but small ones tend to be knocked over, are prone to slug damage and need light shade while acclimatizing to full sun. I prefer to keep my plants under glass permanently. If your greenhouse is unheated in winter, move succulents indoors, where they must have good light and cool temperatures. Kept dry, they will stay dormant from autumn to spring, but will grow well in the bright light afforded by the greenhouse during summer.

Watering

The key to balanced, even growth is regular watering and feeding. Watering your succulent collection shouldn't be difficult, but many people get it wrong. Generally, most cacti will be dormant during winter and need no water. Other succulents such as aeoniums may need watering occasionally to prevent shrivelling. In spring, as light and temperatures increase, succulents come to life, and giving them their first drink is always a pleasure, marking the start of their growing season. Let the compost almost dry out between waterings, but don't let them stay too dry for long. Some will go dormant in very hot weather, and when the roots are inactive water will accumulate in their pots. They are not fussy as to what kind of water you use, but keep splashes off the leaves when the sun is bright. An early-morning watering regime is best.

Echinocactus grusonii is rare in the wild, but common in captivity

TOP LEFT This *Parodia magnifica* has produced several offsets
TOP RIGHT Ease the plant from its pot, using a collar of newspaper
ABOVE Minus the offsets and potted on, the parodia is dressed with grit

Feeding

In the wild, many cacti and succulents live on a knife edge and can look pretty ropey, but in our care they should be able to flourish. You have only to look at the fabulous exhibits displayed by cactus nurseries at plant shows to see how good they can be. Special cactus fertilizers are available, or you can use a general-purpose feed with an NPK (nitrogen, phosphorus, potassium) ratio of twice as much phosphorus as there is nitrogen or potassium, plus all the trace elements, and apply this at half the strength recommended for other plants. Feed every three weeks while the plant is in active growth, which will usually be in spring and summer.

Potting on

Potting your plants on into a larger container when they are pot bound and before their shape begins to suffer is crucial. One often sees ghastly, wizened cacti whose growth has come and gone in uneven spurts. This is probably the result of uneven watering, scarce feeding and the plant having occupied the same pot for about twenty years and been subjected to extremes of heat and cold.

For my cacti and succulents I usually mix two parts of a soil-less proprietary potting compost (or a 50:50 mix of a soil-less compost and John Innes No. 2) and one of grit or sharp sand. Alternatively, you can buy special cactus potting compost. The extra grit helps water pass more quickly through the mixture rather than hanging around and potentially damaging roots. Cacti and succulents seem to be equally happy to inhabit plastic or clay pots, though the latter look better and, being more porous, they breathe better too. Choose the container carefully, opting for slightly shallow pots if the cactus shape is low in the pot. Avoid too great a leap in size, because with a lot of wet compost around them the roots could suffocate.

Smooth-bodied succulents are re-potted in the same way as any other plant, but those with spines are another matter. You need to employ special tactics in order to move them to a larger pot and push new compost around their bodies without injuring yourself or the plant.

Potting on a spiny cactus

First, loosely ball up some newspaper so that the body of the cactus and its long spines have a soft surface to lie on. Using gloves to protect your hands, lean the plant over and gently remove the pot. Long spines can snap easily on a hard surface, spoiling the plant's appearance. Try to keep the rootball intact and use the old pot as a template for the rootball. If the new pot is made of clay, crock it, put a little compost in the base and then place the old pot in the middle of the new one at the correct height and feed compost into the gap between the two, firming gently as it goes in. When you carefully slide the old pot out, the hole left should fit the rootball like a glove. Using gloves and/or a collar of newspaper, lift the cactus and slide its roots into the hole. Firm it in gently, add more compost if necessary and top dress with grit or small-grade shingle. Leave watering in for a week (or a few days if the weather is really sunny), to allow any broken roots to heal without rotting.

Propagation

Growing cacti and succulents from seed is easy and great fun, and the plants grow faster than you might think. I usually sow into a 10cm/4in clay pan or small plastic seed tray. Fill it with moist (not wet or dry) seed compost, firm it gently with a presser and sow the seed thinly and evenly over the surface. I usually cover the seed with the lightest sprinkling of compost and then a layer of fine grit, so that it is barely covered by more than its own size. Water it in by standing the container in tepid water, or by waving a can with the finest rose over the surface. Cover the tray with glass or polythene and stand it, out of full sun, in the greenhouse to germinate. Turn glass daily to get rid of condensation.

As soon as seedlings show, remove the glass or polythene. Leave pricking the individual plants out until they have reached a decent size, which may mean waiting a year. Disturb them only when they are in active growth, in spring and summer. You can then pot the tiny cacti or succulents separately or prick them out, grid fashion, into a seed tray. Lithops (pebble plants) and many barrel cacti are particularly easy to raise from seed.

The vegetative propagation of succulents is amazing, as there are so many methods to try including division, taking leaf cuttings, rooting plantlets, offsets, tubers and stem sections and even grafting one cactus on to another.

Pests and diseases

The most irritating pest is probably mealy bug. The small, pinkish brown, sap-sucking creatures cover themselves in a white, fluffy wax and seem to inhabit the most inaccessible crevices in deep stem fissures and around the base of spines; root mealy bug is even more insidious, as it infests unseen, inside the pot. For control, see page 184.

TOP Shoots formed in the head of *Aeonium* 'Zwartkop' taken as cuttings
BOTTOM LEFT Grown on in good light, the rooted plants turn dark purple
BOTTOM RIGHT A maturing rosette of *Aeonium* 'Zwartkop'

The normal range of greenhouse pests will affect cacti and succulents, including aphids, whitefly, scale insects, spider mite and slugs. Be vigilant and catch problems before they multiply, using biological control wherever possible (see page 182). Diseases such as leaf spot and corky scab are usually related to poor care. Should you ever have a bad infestation of whitefly on greenhouse tomatoes or similar, remove your cacti and succulents immediately to alternative quarters. Should sooty mould start to grow on their leaves, spikes or spines, the plants will be ruined. Some succulent leaves can be washed clean, but you will never rid hairy cacti of the mould.

CACTI AND OTHER SUCCULENTS

PLANT

Aeonium 'Zwartkop'

H 90cm/3ft S 75cm/30in

Aichryson x domesticum 'Variegatum'
Bride and groom
H 15cm/6in S 40cm/16in

DESCRIPTION

The Canary Islands aeoniums in the family *Crassulaceae* are prized for the handsome rosette formations made by their leaves. One of the most intriguing is *A. tabuliforme*, whose table-like dome forms gradually over three years, reaching a potential 30cm/12in across before rising up into a mass of yellow summer flowers. After this, it sets seed and dies. The most popular is probably *A. arboreum* and its cultivars. As the name suggests, this branches into a tree-like shape to 1.2m/4ft, and it has fine rosettes of paddle-shaped leaves at the ends of the branches. Panicles of small yellow flowers open in late spring, and the plants live on after flowering. Near-black *A.* 'Zwartkop' needs good light to keep its colour.

This pretty, long-lasting succulent from the family *Crassulaceae* originates from the Canary Islands and the Azores. The plants branch readily, each creating a wide canopy of rosettes, whose leaves are mostly green, margined with cream. Here and there the variegation varies and the creamy margins are wider, some rosettes being pure cream. The effect is delightful and the draping nature of the plant is ideal for decorating the front of the staging. Rosettes erupt into starry yellow flowers in early summer.

HOW TO GROW

When they are young, I stand my aeoniums on upturned pots, to protect them from overshadowing by other plants. Take care in winter not to overwater, which can encourage stem rot. Vine weevil larvae are partial to aeonium roots and cause sudden death. Propagate the species by sowing seed, and cultivars such as 'Zwartkop' by taking cuttings of entire rosettes. Trim each cutting to 9cm/3½in long and insert it in a pot of gritty compost to root. This technique can often be the salvation of a plant whose roots have died. Aeoniums tolerate temperatures just above freezing.

This easy plant likes full light but can also tolerate light shade in a north-facing porch. It often produces stem roots, which indicates how eagerly cuttings produce their roots. Simply trim shoot tips to 9cm/3½in and insert them in gritty compost in a small pot to root. Pot on when necessary in spring, using clay pots. Water the plant carefully during winter, when the compost has almost dried out. Although it can tolerate a minimum of 3°C/38°F, it prefers a slightly warmer 7°C/45°F to look its best in winter. It is vulnerable to vine weevil larvae.

Crassula ovata
'Hummel's Sunset'
Money tree, jade tree
H and S 90cm/3ft or more

Echinocactus grusonii
Golden barrel cactus, mother-in-law's cushion or seat
H 60cm/2ft S 75cm/30in

Echinopsis famatinensis

H 15cm/6in eventually S 5cm/2in

There are some 150 species of crassula, in their own family (*Crassulaceae*), many originating from South Africa. The best known is almost certainly the famed money or jade tree, *C. ovata*. It is said that stroking the leaves will bring good fortune. It is really easy to grow and quickly makes a small, stocky succulent tree with a woody stem and branches of stiff, succulent leaves. Those of 'Hummel's Sunset' are edged with creamy yellow and pink, the colours more pronounced in good light. A mature plant given the correct cool, dry resting period during winter and good light during summer is likely to produce masses of starry white or pinkish white flowers in autumn.

This characterful cactus of the family *Cactaceae* from central Mexico is close to extinction in the wild, originally because it has been extensively dug up and exported around the world as an ornamental garden plant but recently because of a new dam and subsequent flooding where wild populations grow. Its form is exquisite, the ribs of its barrel-like body outlined by golden spines. Even though the plant is unlikely to produce its yellow flowers until reaching a large size (thirty to forty years' worth of growth), growers are happy to enjoy the golden barrel for its structure alone. Perhaps its very desirability has been its salvation, because it is grown all over the world as a cultivated plant.

In a collection of succulents housed in a small greenhouse, there's a lot to be said for choosing tiny cacti capable of producing comparatively large flowers. The rebutias, among the first cacti to bloom each spring, and neat chaps like this echinopsis, previously *Lobivia famatinensis*, of the family *Cactaceae*, are ideal. A small species from north Argentina, it bears perhaps thirty low ribs and is warty with short, straw-coloured spines. The effect is pleasant and textural rather than sharp. Within the species, flower colour varies from yellowish white to deep red. My plant obligingly bears generous warm, orange blooms of exotic beauty from brown, furry buds every summer even though it measures just 8cm/3in high and 5cm/2in across. Having been re-potted once since I bought it, it is now at home in a 10cm/4in clay pot topped with shingle.

The plant can tolerate light shade as well as full sun, although its chances of flowering diminish in shade. Size is limited by the size of the pot. Treated to a slightly larger container every other year, this tree-like crassula has the potential to reach 1.8m/6ft, though few are given the opportunity. Fortunately, plants seem to be happy to sit in the same pot for many years, increasing in size only slightly with every growing season. Take cuttings of short shoots and root them in gritty cuttings compost.

Make sure that it receives good light and, for best results, move it to the house for winter where it can enjoy a minimum temperature of 10°C/50°F. Find a cool room with a bright windowsill and don't water it at all during winter. It tolerates temperatures down to freezing, but it is more difficult to grow the best plants at these temperatures. Propagate by sowing seed or removing and planting offsets, which are baby cacti produced around the outside of the mother plant. I often think these are best taken off anyway, as they can distort the shape of the main plant.

My dense, happy plant responds to the same treatment as all cacti, enjoying a dry, frost-free winter rest, broken by a soaking in spring and regular summer care with good light. Propagation is by seed. It does not freely produce offsets. Provide a minimum winter temperature of 3°C/38°F.

CACTI AND OTHER SUCCULENTS

PLANT

Epiphyllum oxypetalum
Orchid cactus, queen of the night

H and S 90cm/3ft

Haworthia pumila
Pearly dots

H 13cm/5in S 30cm/12in

DESCRIPTION

This plant is a jungle cactus from the family *Cactaceae*. Although a true cactus, it is unlike its desert-dwelling cousins and originates from tropical jungles in Mexico and South America, growing epiphytically from trees. This is reflected in the wayward nature of its outward-reaching succulent stems and their tendency to produce small aerial roots. The plants are no great things of beauty, but are grown for their amazing flowers. This well-known species bears huge, white, fragrant nocturnal flowers up to 30cm/12in long, flaring out to 13cm/5in wide. Their intoxicating scent is almost overpoweringly strong and the whole effect so impressive that parties are often held in their honour when the flowers are out. The lax growth habit makes it suitable for hanging baskets.

An easy and prolific succulent, this small haworthia from the aloe family (*Aloaceae*) originates from the western Cape of South Africa. The stiff, deep green leaves are almost triangular in section and marked with patterns of small silver tubercles or raised dots on both surfaces of the leaf. The generous clusters send up fine, wiry flower stems in summer. I like to grow several in matching clay pots and display them in rows or groups. Experiment with other species such as *Haworthia coarctata*, whose clasping, patterned leaves are arranged in long columns, or slow-growing *H. truncata*, whose chunky leaves resemble rock formations and are equipped with flat, opaque 'windows' to let diffused light reach the tissues beneath.

HOW TO GROW

Provide bright but filtered light as, although it tolerates low light, flower buds won't develop unless the stems receive a certain amount. Water when the surface of the compost dries out during summer and more sparingly in winter. After flowering, prune a large straggly plant by reducing the length of old, top-heavy stems, cutting them back to healthy new growth. Remove weak, damaged or diseased stems. A minimum winter temperature of 7°C/45°F is considered ideal, but it can tolerate temperatures almost down to freezing.

To get the best from your haworthias provide light shading. Keep plants frost free and dry during winter. Propagate by removing and potting offsets in spring. Leaf cuttings also root well. Pull a healthy leaf from a plant or cut away with a sharp knife. Let the cut surface dry out for a couple of days before inserting into 50:50 cactus compost and sharp sand or grit. Add a top dressing of grit for stability and keep it slightly moist. When the plantlets appear, let them grow on, then separate and pot them.

Lithops
Pebble plants, stone plants, living stones
H 2.5cm/1in S 5–15cm/2–6in

Mammillaria bocasana
Snowball cactus
H 5cm/2in S 20cm/8in or as far as the pot allows

Orbea hirsuta
Hairy starfish flower

H 10–15cm/4–6in S 30cm/12in

There are thirty-seven species of these fascinating small plants from the Livingstone daisy family (*Aizoaceae*), which successfully camouflage themselves as pebbles in the semi-desert regions of Namibia and South Africa. Above the thick underground rootstocks are stout, cone-shaped bodies consisting of a pair of fused, fleshy leaves divided by a fissure at the top. After the plants have gone through a dormant winter period, the old leaves shrivel and new ones come thrusting their way through, as do flower buds towards the end of summer. The showy, white or yellow, daisy-like blooms are often wider than the top of the plant. The flattish leaf tops are mottled or patterned to mimic their surroundings and are best displayed in a wide clay pan mulched with grit, sand and pebbles.

Give lithops good light and keep them completely dry between autumn and spring. To break dormancy in spring, soak the roots, and repeat this soaking throughout the growing season whenever the top half of the compost has dried out. Give them a half-strength cactus or general-purpose liquid fertilizer monthly during the growing season. Keep them frost free (minimum 3°C/38°F) in winter. Seed germinates readily at 18–24°C/65–75°F in spring and summer, or you can propagate by removing offsets in early summer.

The mammillarias or pincushion cacti (*Cactaceae*) are a deservedly popular group and contain some of the most attractive plants for both form and flower. *M. bombycina* is a great starter plant for the cactus grower, as it readily builds up into generous clumps of stems well furnished with dense white wool and long hooked spines, further decorated by rings of rosy-pink flowers during summer. But my favourite is another Mexican, *M. bocasana*. In no time, it produces offsets that create a dense cluster of stems smothered by white hairs and joined by cream flowers, though my form produces pale pink blooms. *M. zeilmanniana* is another handsome sort, bearing bright pink flowers.

Provide plenty of bright sunlight and make sure that winters are cool, well ventilated and dry for these beautiful cacti: aim for a minimum temperature of 4°C/40°F. Plants set plenty of their own seed, which is held in red pods. Sow the seed when it is ripe, or propagate by removing offsets to pot separately. Be vigilant against mealy bug.

I have a passion for plants in the hoya family (*Asclepiadaceae*), which includes hoya, stephanotis, ceropegia and a host of interesting succulents. The commonly grown *Orbea variegata* (previously *Stapelia variegata*) has long been a favourite, even though its tapestry-like flowers smell of rotting meat to such an extent that bluebottles, deceived by smell and appearance, often lay their eggs on the petals. I grow too the fascinatingly hairy *O. hirsuta*, also from South Africa. A clump of succulent stems rises up like fingers, sometimes tinged with pinkish red in good sun or where plants have been starved of moisture. In summer, large, smooth buds develop, popping open to reveal a fabulous purple-haired interior. Once the petals have folded outwards, the blooms are star-shaped and can reach up to 10cm/4in across on well-grown plants.

Orbeas like full sun, with perhaps a little shade from harshest light. During summer water only when the top half of the compost has dried out, and in winter give your plant one or two waterings, choosing bright mornings during mild spells to prevent the stems from shrivelling and losing condition. Aim for a minimum winter temperature of 4°C/40°F.

BULBS

Although this section is called 'Bulbs' I have used the term generally, rather than botanically, to represent plants that grow from and die back to a swollen storage organ. Some are true bulbs, but others would be more accurately described as corms, tubers or rhizomes. All share a need to escape some climatic or soil condition in their native habitat – usually drought, cold or shade.

True bulbs, including daffodils, eucomis and lilies, are made up of fleshy leaf scales bound together at the basal plate and enclosing a growing point. When you cut an onion in half, you see exactly what a bulb is. Lilies look a bit different, but only because the leaf scales are looser and don't have a papery covering. When you buy a bulb, everything is in place and waiting to grow, including an embryonic flower. After flowering, a bulb builds itself up to grow and flower again the following year and frequently produces offsets.

Corms, like those of crocus or ixia, might resemble bulbs, but they are not made up of leaf scales. They contain embryo flower shoots, but most of the corm is a modified stem and all this storage tissue is used up in one season. For the plant to continue from year to year, a new corm has to grow on top of the old one, which shrivels away. Good growing conditions are essential for cormous plants like ixia to replace themselves with a structure big enough to flower well the following year.

Tubers are swollen stems bearing growth buds either here and there or clustered in a crown at the upper surface. They normally grow gradually larger with time and are incredibly variable, from begonia and cyclamen tubers to gloriosa tubers.

Rhizomes are also modified stems, usually held below ground or at the soil surface. Growth buds are generally towards the tips. Older rhizomatous plants often have a lot of old tuber with just a few growth tips

around the outside. They need regular cutting up and re-potting to maintain them in small spaces. I have included here plants with compact rhizomes – zantedeschias, for example; others, such as cannas and ginger lilies (*Hedychium*), are to be found in other parts of the book.

The very nature of bulbs makes them robust and able to survive quite harsh conditions, and therefore easy and safe bets for the greenhouse once you understand the growing cycle of each type. They are great space savers too, because almost all have dormant periods, during which they can be tucked up in some dry corner. I exploit many types of bulb in my greenhouse, and constantly experiment with more. All have flowered consistently well, with the exception of spider lilies (*Hymenocallis*), with which I have failed dismally and consistently.

Tender bulbs generally flower year after year and are an investment for the greenhouse. They tend to increase rather than decrease, so you often get potfuls of bulbs or tubers to give away. Tuberous begonias and sinningias are compact and swell in size year on year. They are not easy to propagate, unless you are bold enough to carve the tubers up. Hardy spring bulbs grown under glass need too much maintenance to remain in small pots year after year, so I release these into the garden once they have flowered. Lilies in large pots will go on flowering brilliantly year after year.

Garden centres are a good source for bulbs of all kinds. They are usually displayed in packets, so you can see what they will grow into. But specialist mail order nurseries offer an even wider range and it is worth sending off for their catalogues.

Tigridia pavonia

TENDER BULBS

Of the many tender bulbs there are to try, all of which need frost-free conditions during winter in order to survive, I have only written in detail below about fifteen of my favourites – the easiest and most flamboyant plants I've grown from bulbs, corms, tubers and rhizomes in my greenhouse. Once you've succeeded with one or two types, you will soon realize that there is a common thread to their cultivation and I hope you will be tempted to find your own favourites.

Potting

Although I like to display most of my greenhouse plants in clay pots for aesthetic purposes, there is a practical reason too. I think that the porous nature of clay is a definite boon when it comes to bulbs, as clay pots carry less danger of waterlogging and rotting.

Choosing the best size of pot for your bulbs will be trial and error to start with. Small bulbs like ixia and tigridia make the best show when set out over the compost surface of a larger pot, close but not touching, and covered by 5–8cm/2–3in of compost. Grown like this in a comfortable 17–23cm/7–9in pot, the bulbs will relish the extra root run and perform better than fewer bulbs in a smaller, shorter pot. Larger bulbs need a deep root run but can be overwhelmed by too much wet compost while making their first few roots of the season. Choose a pot where your fingers can just fit comfortably around the outside of the bulbs to firm them in gently. You can always pot them on to a larger pot later if they seem to be drying out too fast or making disproportionate growth for the size of the pot.

As a rough guide, a 50:50 mix of John Innes No. 2 and a soil-less potting compost suits most bulbs. Combine three parts of the compost mixture with one part of grit to improve drainage for bulbs like haemanthus, gloriosa and sprekelia. Place a crock or some broken polystyrene over the drainage hole to

TOP LEFT The finger-like tubers of *Gloriosa* are potted in early spring
TOP RIGHT After a couple of months, a slender shoot appears
ABOVE Worth the wait: the fabulous glory lily

protect it from being blocked by compost, fill the pot to the level at which the bulbs will sit, test for height and then arrange the bulb or bulbs on the compost. Fill in with compost so that the bulbs are covered by the correct depth and firm gently again. Water them in, using a rose on the end of the can.

Water and feeding

Newly potted bulbs need careful watering to protect them from rotting. Make sure that the compost surface feels dry before watering again, in which case it will still be moist a few centimetres down. This way air will be able to enter the spaces between the compost particles enabling developing roots to breathe. Make sure that enough water goes in (from the top is fine) to soak down to all the roots and compost.

When growth is well advanced, add a well-balanced liquid feed to the water every two to four weeks. This not only helps promote growth and flowering during the current season but will influence how well the bulb stocks itself up for the following year.

Resting

When the leaves begin to turn yellow after flowering, stop watering and let the foliage die back. Leave the bulbs in their pots of dry compost all winter (apart from those few bulbs whose growth takes place in winter) in frost-free conditions.

Waking up

Some bulbs wake up of their own accord and the appearance of new shoots is the signal to start watering again. Otherwise, in early spring give the pots a good soak and wait for shoots to emerge. You can re-pot bulbs every year into fresh compost before they start growing in earnest, but with most types, to save time and resources, I re-pot every three years on average. Be guided by their performance.

Cape cowslips are a welcome sight in late winter

TENDER BULBS

PLANT

Achimenes
'Little Beauty'
Hot water plant
H 25cm/10in S 30cm/12in

Begonia
tuberhybrida

H 60cm/24in S 45cm/18in

DESCRIPTION

Achimenes belong to the African violet family (*Gesneriaceae*), and originate from the subtropical forests of Mexico and Central America. The unusual common name is thought to originate from their being grown in hothouses, although as a child I remember being told to water my plants by pouring hot water into the saucer (tepid water is warm enough). Each rhizome sprouts a stem bearing hairy, bright green leaves and, during summer, exotic flowers. This one bears warm pink blooms with glowing, speckled throats. There are many different cultivars, including trailing types suitable for hanging baskets.

These tuberous perennials have been bred from a number of Andean begonia species (*Begoniaceae*) and are flamboyant, easily cultivated plants. Some folk specialize in growing huge, double, prize-winning blooms, but you can enjoy pleasing results without making as much effort. The experts reduce the shoots to one for the biggest flowers and remove the two smaller female flowers flanking the larger, double male flower. This pushes energy into the best flower and avoids congestion.

HOW TO GROW

Start the small, maggot-like rhizomes into growth early in the year in a propagating case. I plant four or five to a 9cm/3½in pot, setting them 2.5cm/1in deep in three parts soil-less compost and one part vermiculite. Move them into the greenhouse when night temperatures have reached a reliable 10°C/50°F. Pot them on into a 13cm/5in pot when they are well established and provide support. Feed them fortnightly during summer, shade them from harsh light and keep water splash off the leaves. Plants die back in autumn, so stop watering then and store at 10°C/50°F (though I have kept mine at 4°C/40°F and they've survived).

Start the tubers in later winter or spring by nestling them, dished side uppermost, into some potting compost in a tray. Place them in a warm propagating case or let them sprout under polythene in a warm kitchen. Once the shoots have appeared and the greenhouse is a reliable 10°C/50°F at night, stand them out on the staging. When the shoots are about 8cm/3in tall, pot the tubers individually. When these small pots are filled with roots, pot them on to finish in a 15–20cm/6–8in size. In autumn, let the plant die back and keep the tuber almost dry at 7°C/45°F.

Cyrtanthus elatus
Scarborough lily

H 60cm/24in S 30cm/12in

The South African Scarborough lily from the amaryllis or daffodil family (*Amaryllidaceae*), which used to be known as *Vallota*, has long been a favourite greenhouse display plant. Its handsome, strap-like leaves of bright green create an emerald backdrop to umbels of up to ten impressive, scarlet-red flowers 8–10cm/3–4in across produced during late summer. Although plants stop growing during the colder, darker months of winter, they usually retain their foliage and should never be dried right out. Individual bulbs are started in small pots, but soon bulk up, making fine clumps. Try *Cyrtanthus mackenii* var. *cooperi* for its long display of sweetly fragrant yellow flowers.

Plant new bulbs in spring, setting them with their necks at soil level in pots 13–15cm/5–6in in diameter. Water them in well, allowing the surface time to dry out before watering again. Alternatively, set three or more bulbs in a larger, 17–20cm/7–8in pot. Feed them monthly when they are in strong growth, and after a few years, when the bulbs and their offsets have expanded to fill the container, pot them on while in active growth. When the plants have reached the largest pot you can accommodate, split them up into clumps and start new colonies. Provide a minimum temperature of 0°C/32°F and watch out for mealy bug.

Eucomis comosa
Pineapple bulb

H 75cm/30in S 45cm/18in

This South African bulb from the hyacinth family (*Hyacinthaceae*) makes a handsome rosette of light green leaves freckled with maroon spots towards the base. A stout, speckled flower stalk pushes its way up and by high summer has developed into a column of beautiful, waxy, long-lasting white flowers, 2.5cm/1in across. Each bears green-tipped petals, and has a dark purple ovary at the centre and a perfect crown of stamens. Their light fragrance is just about pleasant. Above the flowers sits a pineapple-like tuft of leafy bracts. *Eucomis bicolor* bears slightly shorter stems of pale green flowers, rimmed with maroon, but has an unpleasant aroma. *E. autumnalis* is daintier, with narrow spikes of greenish white, pleasantly scented flowers.

Plant the bulbs in spring, one to a 15cm/6in pot, or three to a 20cm/8in pot with the bulbs buried 2.5cm/1in below the compost. When they are actively growing, feed them monthly until the flowers have finished. When plants turn yellow in autumn, stop watering them and let them die back for winter. Keep them dry and frost free in their pots until spring and start watering when a bud appears at the top of the bulb. Re-pot them about every three years in spring.

Gloriosa superba
'Rothschildiana'
Glory lily

H 1.8m/6ft S 30cm/12in

The fabulous gloriosa is native to India and Africa and belongs to the meadow saffron family (*Colchicaceae*). I used to find gloriosas temperamental, but have now found a fail-safe method that has them springing up like exotic weeds. Gloriosas grow from curved, oddly shaped tubers the width of a chubby finger, which send up narrow shoots in spring and develop into climbers able to grip their supports using tendrils at the tips of their leaves. The plants hoist themselves aloft and produce a succession of summer flowers 10cm/4in across, each with six red, curved-back yellow-edged petals and protruding stamens.

Start plants in early spring, placing one tuber to a 17cm/7in pot, or three to a 30cm/12in pot, more or less horizontally and 8cm/3in deep. Water them in and bring them into a room of average warmth. Allow the surface of the compost time to dry out between waterings and after a couple of months, as soon as the first shoot pushes through, transfer the plants immediately to the greenhouse. Feed them fortnightly as growth accelerates and provide a tall twiggy stick for support. When the leaves turn yellow after flowering, stop watering and keep plants dry and frost free. Tubers will also grow when left in a frost-free greenhouse, but will flower later.

TENDER BULBS

PLANT

Haemanthus albiflos
Shaving brush plant

H 25cm/10in S 15cm/6in

Haemanthus coccineus
Blood lily

H 30cm/12in S 60cm/24in

DESCRIPTION

This unusual evergreen bulb from the amaryllis or daffodil family (*Amaryllidaceae*), originating from South Africa, is widely grown because it is so easy to grow and to propagate. Given frost-free conditions and the minimum of care, the bulbs produce their shaving brush flowerheads during autumn, each up to 8cm/3in across and holding as many as fifty individual flowers. These are mainly a mass of white stamens tipped with yellow pollen, held together by an outer girdle of glossy, green-veined white bracts. One bulb quickly multiplies into a domed cluster sitting on top of the compost, each producing a pair of strappy leaves.

Finding a source for this fascinating and characterful South African bulb from the amaryllis or daffodil family (*Amaryllidaceae*) is a challenge, but the bulbs are out there. This haemanthus is deciduous and has a regular pattern of growing and resting. The first signs of life begin in early autumn when it produces flowerheads. Rising on a stout, speckled stem, each head measures 10cm/4in across and may contain as many as a hundred individual flowers with prominent yellow-tipped stamens enclosed within six large red bracts. The long, broad leaves develop as the flowers fade. The plants die back in spring and remain dormant all summer.

HOW TO GROW

The bulbs can remain in the same pot for many years without coming to any harm, but eventually competition becomes intense, compromising the size of both the leaves and the flowers. To see plants reach their full potential, pot the bulbs separately, at virtually any time but ideally just as they start into growth, and they will reward you with larger flowerheads and longer leaves. Water them whenever the compost surface dries out, feed monthly during active growth and in winter water them occasionally to prevent shrivelling.

As soon as the flowers appear through the top of the dormant bulb, soak the roots. From then on, water the plants when the compost is dry at the surface and feed them monthly. Stop watering as soon as the foliage yellows and starts to die back. Blood lilies need plenty of space to give of their best, and after a few years in the same pot old bulbs begin to deteriorate and stop flowering. During growth, knock the bulbs out of their pot and separate them, burrowing between the roots to prise them apart, and pot each bulb separately so that it can reach its full potential. Provide frost-free conditions.

Ixia 'Mabel'
Corn lily

H 60cm/24in S 17cm/7in

The South African corn lilies from the iris family (*Iridaceae*) are cheap to buy and give you a pot full of colour for next to nothing. For a bold display, I plant a whole packetful in one pot and let them flower together. Tall, grassy leaves up to 45cm/18in high push through the compost and are soon joined by springy, wand-like stems of buds opening to, in this case, bright pink flowers in summer. After flowering, the foliage persists for a short time before dying back to rest.

Corms can be bought in autumn for spring flowering, but are more often sold in spring for summer flowers. Plant them close to each other but not touching in a 23cm/9in pot, covered by 5cm/2in of compost. Water them in well, place on the staging and support the slender growth, using four tall canes and string or raffia (see page 178). Water when the surface dries out. After flowering stand them outside in a resting area, continuing to water and feed until the leaves turn yellow. As the corms are cheap, you could replace them with new every year, but I stand mine outside in a sheltered spot, bringing them in as soon as growth appears in spring. In colder areas, the pot of corms would have to be more protected, as they only tolerate light frost.

Lachenalia aloides
Cape cowslip

H 20cm/8in S 13cm/5in

These South African bulbs in the hyacinth family (*Hyacinthaceae*) bring the greenhouse to life in late winter when their neat potfuls burst into flower. I love them from the moment their speckled leaves begin to sprout from the tops of the bulbs. These eventually make a strappy foil to spikes of tubular yellow flowers. Held aloft on spotted stems, each spike is suffused with a glowing red towards the developing tip. As they age, individual flowers take on a greenish tinge, so there are usually at least three colours present at once.

Plant the bulbs in late summer or early autumn, setting several to a shallow 13cm/5in pot. If you've splashed out on one unusual, more expensive type, grow it singly in a smaller pot. Cover bulbs with about 1cm/½in of compost, water them in and leave them on the staging to grow. Water again when the surface starts to dry out and keep them frost free. After flowering the foliage will turn yellow. Stop watering and keep the bulbs, in their pots, dry until the following late summer. You can re-pot them into fresh compost, but I've left bulbs in the same pot for two or three years with no ill effects.

Leucocoryne 'Andes'
Glory of the sun

H 45cm/18in S 8cm/3in

I have only recently met this fabulous Chilean bulbous plant in the onion family (*Alliaceae*). The bulbs are small and unprepossessing, and as mine came with no glossy picture, I planted them without much sense of anticipation. First some nondescript grassy leaves appeared, but they were followed by really impressive flowers. About 2.5cm/1in across, they shimmer lilac, but have glowing red-purple centres and are sweetly fragrant, enough to take away the slightly garlic aroma of the bulbs and leaves.

Although by nature these are spring-flowering plants, bulbs are usually supplied for a spring planting to bloom during summer, generally sold in fives or tens. I'd set the lot in one pot, arranging them so they are not quite touching and covering the bulbs with 5cm/2in of compost. Water them in and leave them on the staging to grow, watering again whenever the compost surface dries out. The flower stems are usually sturdy enough not to need staking. After flowering, move them to a less prominent spot and feed them monthly to keep the foliage healthy until it dies back in the autumn. Keep them dry and frost free in their pots over winter. Re-pot the bulbs in spring and water them in thoroughly to start them back into growth.

TENDER BULBS

PLANT

Sinningia 'Duke of York'
Florists' gloxinia

H 30cm/12in S 45cm/18in

Sprekelia formosissima
Jacobean lily

H 35cm/14in S 20cm/8in

DESCRIPTION

Sinningias belong to the African violet and Cape primrose family (*Gesneriaceae*), a group of about forty species of tuberous plants, mainly from Brazil. Although many of the species are beautiful, intriguing plants, especially tiny 2.5–5cm/1–2in high *S. pusilla* and the so-called Brazilian edelweiss (*S. canescens*), whose 15cm/6in long leaves are covered in silvery white, woolly hairs, it is the showy hybrids that most people grow. Cheap to buy as dormant tubers early in the year, the plants bloom in late summer, opening lavish and sumptuously coloured, trumpet-shaped flowers from fat buds.

Although the flowers are relatively short-lived, this showy Mexican bulbous plant from the amaryllis or daffodil family (*Amaryllidaceae*) is well worth growing. The narrow, strap-like leaves are modest, so when the flowers open in summer they are a lovely surprise. Each is 10cm/4in across, a deep scarlet and of exquisite shape. The upper three petals spread out and curl, while the lower three fuse to form a lip.

HOW TO GROW

Plant the tubers in trays of moist compost so that the top is at the surface and start them off in a propagating case during late winter and early spring. Once they have sprouted, acclimatize the plants to greenhouse temperatures and then pot them up. Return to the propagating case if temperatures fall below 10°C/50°F at night. Pot on again as the plants grow, feed every two weeks when established and shade from harsh sun. The earlier the start, the sooner flowers will form. After flowering, stop watering in autumn and let plants die back. Rest in their pots at 10–15°C/50–60°F, putting them in the house if necessary. Remove the tubers from the pots in spring, clean them and start again.

Plant the bulbs in spring, setting one to a 15cm/6in pot or three together in a 20cm/8in pot with the tips of their noses just poking above the surface. Water them in, and then let the top few centimetres dry out before watering again. Feed them with a high-potash fertilizer every two or three weeks while they are in active growth. When the leaves begin to turn yellow in autumn, stop watering and keep them dry throughout winter. Make sure that the pots of bulbs are safely tucked up under frost-free glass, as a combination of wet and cold will probably rot them away. In spring, begin watering when growth starts, and re-pot them every two years.

Tigridia pavonia
Tiger flower

H 90cm/3ft S 20cm/8in

Also known as peacock flower, this stunning Mexican bulbous plant in the iris family (*Iridaceae*) is often recommended for planting out in mild regions. It performs far better in pots under glass, where it is removed from competition and slugs: it grows taller and more magnificent. Long, sword-shaped leaves grow steadily to be joined, during summer, by a succession of orange, red, pink, yellow or white flowers 10–15cm/4–6in across, set horizontally atop their stems. Comprised mainly of three large petals, their centres are a kaleidoscope of patterns and markings. Being able to admire them at eye level is a real luxury.

Plant the bulbs in spring, setting a good number into a large 20–25cm/8–10in pot so that they are close yet not touching. Cover with 5cm/2in of compost and water in well. Support plants with canes and string and give them a liquid feed every two weeks. After flowering, stand the plants in a resting area outdoors, continuing to water and feed until the foliage begins to die back. Either bring them into the unheated or frost-free greenhouse to overwinter dry; or in milder areas, leave them outdoors in a sheltered spot, open to the elements, and bring them under glass in spring. They are hardy to –5°C/23°F. Re-pot every two years in spring.

Veltheimia bracteata

H 35cm/14in S 30cm/12in

Closely related to the Cape cowslip in the hyacinth family (*Hyacinthaceae*), veltheimias are larger all over than their cousins, also come from South Africa and share the same growing cycle. Wavy-edged, shiny leaves drape themselves over the pot surface and the flower spikes rise to produce pinkish red tubular flowers in late winter or spring. In full bloom they look like small red hot pokers. Look out for interesting varieties: *Veltheimia bracteata* 'Rosalba' bears flowers of a particularly strong pink; those of *V. b.* 'Lemon Flame' are a clear, pale citrusy yellow.

Plant the bulbs during late summer and early autumn, setting them one to a 13cm/5in pot, or three to a 17cm/7in pot with their tips just showing. Water them in, and leave them on the staging. Let the compost surface dry out before watering again and eventually you will be repaid by a leafy shoot at the tip of each bulb. Give them a liquid feed every three weeks or so while they are in full growth. After flowering, the leaves eventually turn yellow, and when they do, stop watering and let the bulbs dry out in their pots. Leave them dry through until late summer, when a thorough soaking should start them into growth. Re-pot them every two years and keep the bulbs frost free at all times.

Zantedeschia 'Mango'
Hybrid arum lily

H 65cm/26in S 30cm/12in

I was attracted to this showy hybrid arum lily (family *Araceae*) by the vivid colour of its spathes, the petal-like structures surrounding the spadix of tiny true flowers. Like a ripe mango, colours include orange and yellow, with an intense emerald green with red and even purple at the base. This is a hybrid of *Zantedeschia elliottiana*, a South African species bearing soft yellow flower spathes and leaves marked by silver spots and dashes, inherited nicely by 'Mango'. The plants grow from chunky rhizomes, sending up tall heart-shaped leaves which are soon joined by the flowers which persist for a long period, eventually turning green with age. There are many other zantedeschia hybrids to try, including those with white and almost black flower spathes.

Plant new rhizomes in early spring, setting them one to a 13cm/5in pot or three to a 17cm/7in pot so that they are covered by 8cm/3in of compost. Water them in and stand in a frost-free greenhouse, allowing the compost surface to dry out between waterings. When they are in full growth, keep them moist and feed them every two weeks. When in autumn the foliage starts to turn yellow, stop watering and dry the rhizomes and their compost out. Leave them to rest, dry and frost free, all winter. Every spring, turn them out of their pots, gently clean off the rhizomes and re-pot them, taking care not to damage any roots that have formed.

HARDY SPRING-FLOWERING BULBS

The double snowdrop *Galanthus* 'Dionysus' is easily admired at eye level

Although hardy spring-flowering bulbs such as narcissus, crocus, tulip and hyacinth can be grown outdoors in the garden, they make fantastic greenhouse plants too, and need no heat at all. If your greenhouse sits empty until you plant tomatoes in late spring, you are missing the opportunity to potter amongst a succession of beautiful, often scented flowers. Growing in pots on the staging and flowering at head height, they can be appreciated at their best, protected from the elements and removed from the competition of other plants in the beds and borders of the garden; you can examine every detail of them close to, and they'll bloom a little earlier. The most satisfying growing method is to buy bulbs and plant them in pots during autumn. But the cheat's way is to buy slightly forced bulbs from garden centres in late winter and early spring.

Starting bulbs off

You will need a selection of bulbs, potting compost (any kind, even once-used compost, will do) and a range of clay pots in different sizes. Don't be tempted to use bulb fibre, as this is for bulbs being forced in bowls with no drainage holes. What happens next is largely a personal choice. With smaller bulbs, I usually set plenty per pot, positioned so that they are close but not quite touching. Crock the pots and fill them with potting compost until the correct level is reached for the bulbs to be covered by the right depth. This will vary from bulb to bulb. Then set the bulbs out over the surface. When planted outdoors, bulbs are buried by twice their own depth of soil, but when planting them in a pot cover them more shallowly or else there will be insufficient space under the bulb for the roots to grow downwards. Crocus can be covered by about 2.5cm/1in, and daffodils and tulips so that their tips are just under the surface. I usually delay my bulb potting session until mid to late autumn, when temperatures have dropped and the potted bulbs can comfortably be left on the greenhouse staging.

Water them in well and make sure that each pot is labelled. The bulbs will gradually grow and come into flower when it suits them. As well as making multiple plantings, I sometimes steal the odd daffodil or tulip from a bag of bulbs destined for the garden and pot them individually. You could even lift a daffodil, scilla or chionodoxa or a clump of ipheion from the garden and pot those up. All the hardy spring-flowering bulbs are lovely, but my favourites are the snowdrop *Galanthus* 'Dionysus', yellow *Iris danfordiae*, *Crocus* 'Whitewell Purple', *Narcissus* 'February Gold' and *Tulipa* 'Apricot Beauty'.

Forcing bulbs

You can have fun with forcing too. Although forcing is more often used for bulbs destined for the house, where sudden warm temperatures bring them on really quickly, it is useful for the greenhouse too. Prepared hyacinths bought and planted towards the end of summer and beginning of autumn will flower in the depths of winter. When forcing, plant hyacinths and other bulbs so that their noses are peeking out of the compost. Stand the pots outside, ideally against a wall, and pile old compost, sand or something similar over their tops until they are buried by a good 10cm/4in or however much you think they need to protect them from frost. Here they stay until roots have grown down into the compost and green shoots have emerged to about 2.5cm/1in long. Then you can pull them out of their covering, in succession, and move them into the light and comparative warmth of the greenhouse. In cold areas they will need frost protection.

Buying potted bulbs

The range of potted bulbs available to buy seems to grow every year, starting with snowdrops, winter aconites and *Iris reticulata* before the rest of the range. You can tell that most of these have been forced because the bulbs are close to the surface and there are often traces of sand where they've been removed from their covering. The bulbs are crammed into small plastic pots, making their watering difficult, so I always pot them on into slightly larger clay pots, pushing extra compost around their roots to give them a bit more space and making a larger gap at the top to allow for watering.

Displaying spring bulbs

Arranging potted bulbs to best advantage lifts the spirits when the weather is cold and drab outside. Snug in your greenhouse, you feel ahead of the game: spring seems well on its way. I mix potted Christmas roses (*Helleborus niger*), early-flowering lungworts such as *Pulmonaria* 'Blue Ensign' and young ferns with the bulbs and create a tiered display, standing some on upturned pots.

Aftercare

When the bulbs have finished flowering I usually put them outside in a sheltered nook behind the greenhouse. They are only slightly forced and therefore able to cope with most cold weather. If you live in an extremely cold area you would need to put them in a

TOP Forced tulips thrusting their way through the compost
BOTTOM LEFT When forced hyacinth shoots are 2.5–5cm/1–2in long, bring them into the light
BOTTOM RIGHT It's easy to achieve a delightful mixture of spring bulbs

cold frame. Keep them watered so that the foliage stays alive, and when the weather has improved in mid-spring plant them out into borders, where most types will naturalize and give pleasure for years to come.

LILIES

LEFT *Lilium* 'Gran Cru' sizzles just outside the greenhouse
RIGHT Trumpet *Lilium* African Queen Group is superb under glass
OPPOSITE *Lilium longiflorum* makes a stunning addition to the staging

Although lilies will grow perfectly well outdoors in the garden, they make surprisingly good display plants for the greenhouse. In areas where lily beetle is a problem, this may well be one of the easiest ways of enjoying lilies without having them decimated by these pests.

Although individual lily bulbs bloom for only a relatively short time, by growing different varieties and staggering the planting over several weeks during spring you can enjoy flowers throughout summer. Besides which, it is not just the flowers that are attractive – and they are often highly fragrant – but the whole life of the plant, from the moment the shoots thrust their way through the compost surface.

In theory, lily bulbs are best planted in autumn, but the nursery trade is mainly geared up to supplying them in late winter and early spring. Make sure that you buy bulbs that are unblemished and have reasonably plump scales.

Planting lily bulbs

Any time during spring, I plant lilies either singly into 15cm/6in pots or three to a 25cm/10in pot. Crock clay pots and put enough potting compost (50:50 John Innes No. 2 potting compost and a soil-less mix) in the bottom so that you can arrange the bulbs with enough space to spread 8cm/3in of compost over them and still leave a gap for watering. Water them in and stand the pot inside or outside until the shoots emerge. In areas where lily beetle is rife, I would stand the pot inside.

When the lilies have made good growth, begin liquid feeding them every two weeks. Look after them well by watering carefully and feeding every fortnight even after they have bloomed, and then let them die back in autumn. To save space, I place my plants in a sheltered resting spot outside, open to the elements. But because they are planted more shallowly than normal, in colder areas where temperatures plunge lower than –5°C/23°F they will be vulnerable to frost damage and may need to be plunged or buried for added protection by digging a hole in the ground and sinking the pot. Alternatively, stand them in a cold frame and wrap the outside of the pots in bubble plastic. In spring, the lilies sprout back into growth naturally and I leave mine in the same pots until they show signs of stress. I then pot them on during spring, or split them up and re-pot them during autumn. Avoid growing lilies with tulips as they can pass viruses between them.

My personal favourites to grow under glass are the highly fragrant trumpet lily African Queen Group, a healthy, sturdy type growing to 1.2m/4ft, whose golden flowers are always welcome. The Easter lily (*L. longiflorum*) – despite the name, it flowers in summer – is another fragrant trumpet type reaching 45cm/18in with pure white flowers. The pollen can be a nuisance when it rains down upon other plants. If this is the case, nip the anthers off before they dehisce (shed pollen) using a pair of tweezers.

HOUSE PLANTS

Some house plants are beautifully adapted to growing in warm temperatures and low light. Most of the leafy sorts originate from tropical rainforests and can stay in the same indoor position year after year. But others, usually those grown for their flowers rather than leaves, prefer a brighter, cooler home. These could do with a break from the low light and warm, dry air of the house and benefit from a holiday in the greenhouse. There they can go happily dormant, or enjoy good light, cooler temperatures and a more humid atmosphere.

Plants used to the low light of the house will need shading from hot sun when they first come into the greenhouse, either under shaded glass or in the shade of other plants. Once they have adapted to the conditions, those that need it – Indian azaleas, for instance – can be potted on and encouraged to establish, ready for flowering the following autumn and winter.

Some plants brought to the greenhouse while dormant will die back – cyclamen and hippeastrum, for example. These can be dried out and should not be stood where they will catch drips from other plants. Use the greenhouse, too, as a workshop for house plants, somewhere you can clean them up and re-pot them. Remember, though, that warmth-loving kinds should be moved only during warm summer weather and shade-loving types only on dull days or else they will scorch quickly.

Returning a well-grown pot plant full of new flower buds to the house is very rewarding and house plants gain character with every year you keep them.

TOP LEFT A cyclamen returns to growth during summer after a dry rest
TOP RIGHT A healthy cyclamen with no traces of botrytis on the stems
BOTTOM LEFT Remove Indian azalea flowers once the display has finished
BOTTOM RIGHT After flowering, pot on azaleas into ericaceous compost
OPPOSITE Cyclamen make excellent winter house plants

HOUSE
PLANTS

PLANT

Cyclamen

H and S 13–30cm/5–12in

Cymbidium

H and S 45–90cm/18–36in

DESCRIPTION

Cyclamen belong to the primula family (*Primulaceae*) and cultivars used as house plants derive from frost-tender *C. persicum*, native to south-east Mediterranean regions and North Africa. There is a wealth of choice from petite, small-flowered 13cm/5in high cultivars to large-flowered types 30cm/12in high and wide. Many have a distinctive, sweet peppery fragrance.

These beautiful orchids from India, China, Japan, South East Asia and Australia produce long leaves from storage organs called pseudobulbs that sit above the compost surface. There are many hybrids, mainly flowering during winter and spring. They lend a touch of opulence to any room and for small rooms there are shorter types with smaller flowers.

HOW TO GROW

A healthy plant bought during the autumn should remain in flower until spring. When no more flower buds are forming, move the plant to the greenhouse, stop watering it, and it will die back to the tuber. I find that the larger cultivars with bigger tubers are happy to remain in full sun while dormant, but tiny plants with small tubers need shade, or else they shrivel away to nothing. After two to three months, by mid- to late summer, growth starts and the tuber will need a thorough soaking to bring the plant back into growth. Provide it with shade from full sun and re-pot every other year. Transfer it to the house when the flower buds appear, choosing a cool, bright position. You can water it from above, but keep the tuber dry. Add a liquid fertilizer every two weeks. Kept this way, cyclamen are potentially long-lived – indeed there are cases of individuals lasting for forty years or more.

After flowering, move your cymbidium to the greenhouse. Temperatures should be at least 4°C/40°F. Water carefully, testing the weight of the pot to see if it needs more and using rain water if possible. You can leave cymbidiums outdoors during summer, but in the greenhouse you have more control over watering. Apply light roof shading and a half-strength general liquid fertilizer at every other watering. Cool autumn temperatures help the orchid set flower buds before you bring it back indoors, where good light and a temperature of 10–15°C/50–60°F will keep it happy. Pot, if necessary, in spring when there are signs of growth, in orchid compost. You can divide plants at this stage as long as you support each growth with at least two back bulbs (leafless pseudobulbs); small pieces may not flower straight away. Remove dead roots and decayed compost before re-potting. Water in, but take great care with watering after potting.

Hippeastrum
Amaryllis

H 30–60cm/12–24in S 30cm/12in

The spectacular and almost fail-safe hippeastrums that we grow from giant, dormant bulbs belong to the daffodil family (*Amaryllidaceae*) and descend from plants found in Central and South America. Large-flowered sorts such as pale 'Apple Blossom' and scarlet 'Red Lion' are popular but there are small-flowered and double kinds too.

Buy hippeastrum bulbs from autumn to spring and have a potting session in the greenhouse. I like good-sized clay pots for the job, just large enough to fit a finger's width around the outside of the bulb. Pot so that the bulb's shoulders are clear of the compost. Water in and place the pot on a warm, bright windowsill in the house. Water again whenever the compost surface has dried out and after a while the flower bud will emerge, followed by foliage. Give it a well-balanced liquid fertilizer every two weeks and leave it in place for the foliage to flourish. In late summer, bring the potted bulb to the greenhouse and stop watering. Keep it dry and frost free for two to three months, before soaking the compost and returning it to the house. Re-pot every two to three years, either just before it starts back into growth or while the leaves are growing strongly in spring.

Rhododendron indicum
hybrids

H and S 60cm/24in

The Indian or Indica rhododendron hybrids are commonly called indoor azaleas. Small, shrubby and evergreen, they are sold throughout autumn and winter to flower in the house. There is a wide range of flower colours and types to choose from. Enjoy keeping them from year to year and watching their character change.

Indoor azaleas are a challenge to keep healthy. If you feel that your plant is drying out too fast, consider potting it on into a slightly larger pot with more moist compost around its roots. Use ericaceous compost and water using rain water, as these are acid-loving plants. After flowering, move your plant to the greenhouse and clean off all the dead blooms. Water when necessary, and as growth starts in spring, apply a general-purpose or acid-loving-plant fertilizer every two weeks. When light levels increase, shade lightly or place the azalea under the staging where the atmosphere is cool, humid and shaded. Some gardeners put their plants outdoors for the summer, but I find mine gets better care under glass, where I can keep an eye on it. By autumn, the plant will have budded up and can be returned to the house. Plants that stay under glass in winter will need frost-free temperatures.

Hydrangea macrophylla
cultivars
H 30–75cm/12–30in
S 30–90cm/12–36in

Hydrangeas are often sold as house plants, usually in spring, whereas these woodland plants from China and Japan (in their own family, *Hydrangeaceae*), usually bloom in late summer outside. There are plenty of different cultivars to choose from. Hortensias are mop-headed, with numerous sterile florets arranged in slightly domed heads. Lacecaps have flat heads consisting of small inner fertile flowers surrounded by showier infertile florets. The main colour palette is white, pink, mauve and blue.

Place your potted hydrangea in good but not direct light and away from radiators and other heaters indoors. As long as they are kept moist, they will still be healthy after flowering and can be brought into the greenhouse and pruned back hard, reducing each stem by half to two thirds. Let them sprout new shoots, then pot on to a slightly larger pot. Stand outside for the rest of the summer and allow the leaves to fall off in autumn. Then bring the plant into the frost-free greenhouse until it grows and buds up again. In the second year, without being forced too hard, this will probably be during late spring or early summer. Display in the house for its second year, prune back as before, but harden off and plant into the garden as forcing for too many years in a row will weaken the plant.

GREENHOUSE CARE

7

To me the routine tasks involved in running a greenhouse are never a chore. The morning check is a great way to start the day and pottering down there to open vents and water the plants, damp down in summer and make small alterations to the display are all a pleasure as well as vital for the well-being of the plants. During summer I'll be in and out of the greenhouse at least three times daily with plenty to do, but during winter two quick visits, to adjust vents and check on the heater, one in the morning and one at night, are enough. Knowing the right time to apply shading in spring or fix insulation in autumn is something one learns more by intuition than by rote. Success in the greenhouse depends less on technical expertise and more on regular housekeeping; and for this common sense and observation are key qualities for the greenhouse gardener, especially in respect of pests and diseases.

Healthy plants and an attractive display depend on good care

ROUTINE TASKS

The secret to running a successful and productive greenhouse full of healthy and beautiful plants is straightforward: pay attention to the routine, regular upkeep of the plants and the rest will easily fall into place. A regular daily routine is particularly important. At quiet times of the year your morning visit to the greenhouse will take no more than five minutes, but this brief contact with the plants will be valuable in order to assess what they need. Adjusting the vents early before heat builds up and watering dry plants in the morning, so that the compost can dry out a little and warm up by nightfall, are sure ways of keeping your plants on top form. A daily evening visit should not take long, and during hot summer days I usually pop my head round the door in the middle of the day as well, to make sure that temperatures have not risen too high. An ideal morning routine in summer would be to check vents and temperatures, clean the plants, rearrange those that need it and sweep up. Watering follows next and then damping down. Some regular jobs need weekly attention and others take place only once or twice a year.

Ventilation

Setting vents for the day is crucial, whatever the time of year. During late spring and summer, I like to go early to the greenhouse, savouring that warm, earthy smell as soon as the door slides back. It is important to open top and side vents before the sun climbs high in the sky and temperatures rise. Even on dull days, open the vents for air circulation. I usually leave the door open as well, but not on windy days. When wind or rain is expected, leave the vents at or below the horizontal to protect the plants inside.

During winter, ventilate on all but the coldest days. When the weather is at its worst, put 'a crack' of air on – in other words, the tiniest gap just to allow an exchange of air while not letting in too much cold and

rain. During gales, keep all vents and doors tightly shut in case wind gets in and blows the roof off.

During winter, vents should be closed at night, and I continue to do this right through spring until night temperatures reach around 10°C/50°F. Closing early is important during cold weather, because you want to trap as much heat as possible inside the greenhouse, where to an extent it is held in the structure, especially in bricks and wood.

Heat and cold

A daily assessment of maximum and minimum thermometer readings throughout the year helps avoid the wide temperature swings that most plants hate. Sickly plants failing to thrive are often subjected to freezing cold temperatures at night, then blisteringly hot air by day. Temperature checks are particularly vital during mid-winter and midsummer, and can be revealing. How else can you know how low temperatures plunged at night, or how high they rose while you were out at work? Maximum/minimum thermometers have a reset button. After checking the minimum night temperature in the morning, reset the thermometer so that the following day's maximum and night minimum will be accurately recorded.

Try what you like, but it will be hard to keep temperatures below 32°C/90°F during a summer heatwave. If it rises much higher, you need to seriously review the balance and timing of ventilation, shading and damping down. During winter, watch the minimum temperatures to make sure that your heating system is adequate to protect the plants you have chosen to grow. Some might need a minimum of −5°C/23°F and will require very little heating; others may need frost-free temperatures, and you should worry if the recording drops below 3°C/38°F. Some may need higher minimum temperatures of 4–7°C/40–45°F. In spring and autumn especially, look out for huge differences between minimum night temperatures and high maximum day temperatures. The answer is to ventilate sooner in the morning, or apply shading earlier in the year.

One very important annual job is to check your heater during autumn. Dust it down, make sure it works, buy fuel if necessary and keep it to hand. This will avoid a lot of angry stamping around on a dark, cold evening when the first frost has been forecast. Turn the heater on at night and check the thermometer in the morning to make sure that the minimum temperature was above freezing but not so warm that you were wasting money on fuel. In mild climates, you should be able to get away with turning the heater on only when you think you need it, but in cold climates you may have to put it on every night.

Cleaning and sweeping

If you have time in your morning routine, daily or perhaps weekly remove dead leaves and flowers, following this with a quick sweep-up, so as to keep the greenhouse really tidy. In the long term, this daily effort will save time, as there will be less need for a more major and time-consuming onslaught. What's more, visiting the plants inside will be more pleasant without having to skirt around debris and climb over piles of empty pots.

Rearranging

After the daily routine, find time – about once a week or when needed – to move plants around a little. During winter, when plants are barely growing, this will hardly be necessary; but during spring and summer, this could be a daily or weekly task. Sometimes larger plants have to be moved closer than necessary on a short-term basis to accommodate young plants destined for the garden. Small batches of newly potted young plants will start off with their pots close together,

A mixture of plants thrive when they are given the space they need

but after a couple of weeks rapid growth will mean that you'll have to give them slightly more space. Sometimes, a plant will need to be raised on an upturned plant pot to show it off or to save it from being swamped. These are the small shufflings that take place on a routine basis, don't take up much time, but make all the difference to a plant's health. Now and again, I spend longer rearranging almost all the plants to their best advantage – one of my favourite jobs (see page 98).

Staking and tying

Staking and tying are particularly important if plants are not to flop about in a confined space. The idea is to support plants with the minimum of fuss, so that the stakes and ties are almost invisible. When a plant starts to flop, either push a cane in the centre and draw each stem individually to the cane with one or more ties (use

TOP LEFT Raffia is a lovely natural material for tying
TOP RIGHT Soak the raffia before using it
ABOVE LEFT A pot of ixia is supported by canes and raffia
ABOVE RIGHT The raffia holds the foliage and flower stems

a neat reef knot) or push four canes around the outside of the pot and wind string around them, so confining the leaves and stems in the centre. Raffia is a lovely material to work with, but it ties better when wet, so dunk the strands in water before using it. Tall twiggy sticks make useful supports for tendril climbers like *Gloriosa superba* 'Rothschildiana'. Simply push a 1.5m/5ft stick into the pot and let the plant do the rest. For climbers, see also page 98.

Watering

Morning is the best time to water your plants, because during summer the sun is not high enough then to scorch their leaves, and in winter there will be plenty of time for the interior to dry out before night falls. Check your plants quickly but efficiently and move around the greenhouse in the same direction every time for speed. Check their requirements for the whole day, so judge whether a plant is likely to dry out by the evening and, if so, give it a good drink.

In summer, most plants need watering when their compost surface has started to dry out. During winter, you can allow the top half of the compost to dry out between waterings. Group dormant plants together so that you do not water them by accident. Ideally, water should be at the same temperature as the greenhouse, so try to leave two large cans filled and ready at all times. But during summer, when the greenhouse is packed full of plants, I use a hosepipe for speed, setting the water pressure low and watering from the blunt end, without a lance or sprinkler of any kind. Watering is more accurate this way, and I use my thumb to create a soft spray when needed. Should any plant become bone dry, stand it, pot and all, in a bucket of water for half an hour.

For batches of plants with similar watering requirements or lots of thirsty plants, you can use capillary matting or damp horticultural-quality sand. The principle with these is that roots take up moisture from the damp sand or fibre-like matting. In summer, you can soak your matting and go off to work confident that your plants won't run out of water.

In winter, unless dormant, plants overwintering under glass need careful watering to keep the roots moist but must not be allowed to stay too wet. Keep an eye on the situation and water only when the surface of the compost feels dry and the top half is only just moist. When possible, plan a watering session to coincide with a bright, warm day. Having decided to water a plant, give it enough water to soak all the roots. During the depths of winter, this process may be necessary only once a month, though some individual plants in smaller pots may need more regular watering. The buds on acacias, for instance, could become wizened if the roots are left too dry.

Damping down

Damping down – spraying floors and staging and flicking water up under the leaves of gaspingly hot plants – helps keep the temperature down and is satisfying to do. It is most effective during the hottest parts of the day, but that's when a lot of gardeners are at work. Consider installing an automatic watering device set on a timer to spray the floor and possibly water the staging three to four times a day during the hottest weather. Some systems have sensors sensitive to air humidity, to turn the sprayers on when the air is too dry.

Feeding

Feeding plants is crucial, because they will use up the fertilizer in their fresh compost within four to six weeks. Long-term plants well established in their pots need regular liquid feeding to carry on producing healthy growth and flowers. For healthy growth, plants need the major elements, nitrogen, phosphorus and potassium (NPK), which are always indicated in this order on packets and bottles, plus trace elements including magnesium and iron. Most plants will respond to a general-purpose liquid fertilizer, diluted into their water. This will have an equal ratio of NPK plus trace elements. Some plants need slightly different formulations. You might want to buy a special citrus fertilizer (high in nitrogen), cactus fertilizer (high in phosphate) and, for tomatoes and other crop plants or those needing encouragement to bloom, a high-potash fertilizer.

The rules for feeding are simple. Feeding is not needed for the first six to eight weeks after potting. Plants need to be growing actively in order to use food, so there is no point in pumping fertilizer into a dormant plant, as it will merely accumulate in the compost. Never feed a plant whose roots are very dry: water it well first, then return to feed it when the surface is just starting to dry out again. Never feed a waterlogged plant.

Plants being asked for high performance over a relatively short period, such as fuchsias, chrysanthemums and Regal pelargoniums, should be fed weekly when building up to flower, but for most other long-term plants feeding once a month is enough, or if you've time, give them a half-strength feed every two weeks. Make sure that the product is well diluted in the can and water in.

Slow-release fertilizers added at the start of the growing season are ideal if you are likely to forget to apply liquid feeds. They are especially good for shrubby plants.

Shading

There comes a time in spring when the sun has climbed high enough in the sky to make the greenhouse uncomfortable to work in. This is the moment to apply or fix up shading, both to prevent plants from scorching and curling up in the heat and to help keep spiralling temperatures under control.

Those lucky enough to have external or internal blinds can set them in the morning according to the weather forecast. The rest of us need to put our shading policy into action, where it will remain as a fixture until autumn.

You can pin or fix material such as fine net curtains, horticultural fleece or other light fabric to the inside of the greenhouse between spring and autumn. Or you can apply a shading paint to the outside of the glass. Mix the shading solution or powder with water as instructed and apply it according to your climate, the type of plants you are growing and the position of the greenhouse. If you need thick shading, apply it all over with a soft broom. Leaving thin, untreated stripes to let in more light is an option.

I always apply shading paint with a sprayer, which leaves a fine mist of tiny droplets. Should hot weather intensify, you can return later to add another layer of droplets. With one side of my greenhouse facing south-east and the other north-west, I often find that shading only the brighter south-eastern side suffices. In a maritime climate, it is not always necessary to shade a greenhouse and aesthetically it looks better without. In poor summers I don't shade and my plants benefit from the extra light. You can always pin fabric over specific plants or the propagating area when they need it, or place vulnerable plants under the staging or in the shade of tougher plants.

Washing glass

Wash off shading in autumn, cleaning the glass of dirt and algae at the same time, so as to let in plenty of light. Wet the outside with a hose, brush the shading off using a broom and hose again to rinse. Use a slim instrument like a label to clean algae from overlapping panes.

Wash down the inside of the glass whenever the opportunity arises, for instance after clearing out summer crops in the autumn and before installing them in spring. I use pure water, though various detergents are available.

Insulation

Plants overwintering under glass need a careful balance between light, ventilation and energy conservation. Heating a greenhouse to exclude frost will be expensive and therefore the inclination to save fuel by cladding the interior with insulating bubble plastic is strong. On the plus side, this makes brilliant sense and also helps the heater – if you have one – cope with sudden drops in temperature. But do think twice before rushing out to buy your rolls of bubble plastic. On the downside, putting this in place in autumn is a fiddly job, and once it is up the greenhouse will look unattractive all winter, light will be considerably reduced and the interior will take longer to dry out; and while you are working inside the greenhouse, you won't be able to see outside. In milder regions, where plants need mainly shelter rather than frost protection, consider leaving the panes bare. You can always set your thermostat low, so as to save money on heating, remove vulnerable individuals to the house or wrap them individually on the coldest nights.

In colder regions where winter sets in with a vengeance, insulation as well as heating is a must. Fix an interior skin of bubble plastic inside the glass, leaving a gap between the glass and the plastic. This will save heat loss and help your heater raise temperatures quickly inside when they are plummeting outside. Make provision for opening vents, because the interior must be aired as much as possible. Remove the insulation when temperatures warm up in spring, so as to give seedlings and young plants maximum light.

LEFT You can use a plant label to clean between glass panes
RIGHT Washing dirt and algae from glass increases light penetration

PESTS AND DISEASES

Aphids colonize a bud of *Hibiscus rosa sinensis*

Pests and diseases are a nuisance under glass, but there is always a way around the problem. Noticing infestations early means that you can deal with them before they reach plague proportions. Look out for signs of pests and disease on foliage, and in particular look out for sticky foliage, because sap-sucking pests excrete honeydew, flicking it on to the leaves below. Sooty mould usually grows on the honeydew, turning the leaf surfaces black. Use a hand lens to identify the smaller pests.

It is important to avoid introducing new plants with pests or diseases. Inspect new plants before buying them – looking under leaves for whitefly, for instance – and don't put plants into the greenhouse unless you're sure they're healthy. It pays to be circumspect about plants that are gifts, too.

Good cultivation (regular watering and feeding) prevents disorders like blossom end rot on tomatoes, which spreads from the blossom end of the fruit and is caused by calcium deficiency. Sometimes the answer to either a pest or disease attacking a specific plant is simply to stop growing that plant for a while.

There is a wide range of effective biological controls you can try, by which bugs are set against bugs. Order your predators or parasites from mail order suppliers as soon as you see the pests, when temperatures are warm enough for the biological control to live and breed. Don't use strong pesticides prior to introducing predators or parasites, as the residues left on the leaves may kill them. Gardeners frequently worry that biological control such as tiny winged wasps might fly away through the greenhouse vents. This is most unlikely as long as there are plenty of insect pests for them to lay their eggs in.

You can find insecticides and fungicides to cure most ills, though I rarely use them. Horticultural soft soap is a good cure-all, as repeated applications act to bung up the respiratory tubes of whitefly, scale insects, spider mite and aphids. Leaf hoppers, which leave tiny yellow marks on the leaves of salvias and similar plants, are best ignored, because they move on so fast you can't really do anything about them. Leaf miners are an irritation. The best control method is probably to track down the small caterpillar tunnelling between the upper and lower surface of the leaf and squash it, or its pupa. You can check the available approved pesticides for a particular problem on the Pesticide Safety Directorate's website (www.pesticides.gov.uk).

The following are some of the more regular offenders under glass.

Aphids

Commonly known as greenfly or blackfly, these sap-sucking pests attack soft tissue at any time of the year, even during winter. Look for sticky honeydew and the cast skins of nymphs. Ants like to feed on honeydew and are often seen in conjunction with aphids, whom they 'farm' by moving them around on a plant. Apart from removing sap, aphids cause sooty mould (see above) and are responsible for transmitting viruses from plant to plant via the sap. The majority of aphids are females, who reproduce at a frightening speed by giving birth asexually to live young (a process called parthenogenesis). In warm, summer temperatures, new-born aphids reach maturity within a week.

Fortunately aphids are parasitized by the tiny wasp *Aphidius colemanii*, which lays an egg inside the aphid, turning it brown and hard. After fourteen days, the new aphidius hatches out of the mummified aphid, leaving behind a husk complete with escape hole. A single aphidius can lay two hundred eggs in her lifetime and they need a minimum temperature of 12°C/54°F to work properly.

Where many aphids are concentrated in one area, aphidoletes may be a better choice of biological control. This small midge is mostly seen in its maggot-like grub stage. This larva uses a poison to paralyse the aphid and dissolve its body fluids, before sucking them up.

To get rid of sooty mould, first kill the pest, and then wipe off the mould.

Caterpillars

All kinds of butterfly and moth larvae will turn up in the greenhouse from time to time and are more of a nuisance than a threat. But the larvae of carnation tortrix moth are in a league of their own and cause serious damage to both the leaves and the flower buds of a wide range of plants. I've known particularly bad infestations on Canary Island broom (*Genista canariensis*) and New Zealand Christmas tree (*Metrosideros kermadecensis*). The first symptoms are leaves stuck together with web-like threads. Prise the leaves apart and inside you will find a small green caterpillar. On being disturbed, it will wriggle backwards and drop to the floor. These caterpillars pupate into small brown cocoons and hatch into small orange-brown, triangular-shaped moths virtually all year round.

Look out for pale, flat egg batches on leaves or hard surfaces (even glass and staging) protected by a thin mucilaginous covering and scratch them off, as by doing this you will destroy 10–200 potential caterpillars which otherwise would hatch after two to three weeks. Squashing the caterpillars by hand is the most effective method of control, but you can prevent so many being laid by putting up a pheromone trap. This contains a sticky card impregnated with the pheromone used by the female moth to attract the male. Hapless males fly to the trap and are caught on the card, effectively removing themselves from the equation.

Damping off disease

When newly germinated, seedlings are felled like trees in a miniature forest. This is caused by soil-borne fungi such as *Pythium* and *Rhizoctonia solani*, responsible for damping off disease. Look closely at the felled seedlings and you'll see lesions at the base. Antirrhinums and other early-sown bedding plants are particularly vulnerable.

As soon as the disease strikes, prick out the remaining live seedlings and water them and any other seedlings with a copper-based fungicide. The disease is caused mainly by cultural conditions, so work to improve these. Damp, warm conditions in the propagating case are largely to blame, so reduce the temperature if possible and open the vents in the top. Remove seedlings as soon as they have germinated. Water only when absolutely necessary and sow thinly, so that the seedlings have plenty of air around them. Wash seed trays and pots before use (but I confess I often just brush mine out). Use proprietary seed compost and mains water, not water butt water (this is safe for most established plants, but can contain spores that affect seedlings and cuttings).

LEFT Poor air circulation causes grey mould on pelargonium leaves
RIGHT A mealy bug infestation has made a mess of this cactus

Grey mould

The fungus *Botrytis cinerea*, whose spores are carried in the rain, water splash or air currents, causes grey mould. Symptoms are a distinctive fluffy grey powdery mould covering mainly dead plant tissue, with rotting underneath. Clouds of grey spores rise from infected tissue. Grey mould attacks living or dead plant material, entering through wounds or points of damage.

In my experience, there is no need to experience grey mould in the greenhouse, because if the atmosphere is right, this fungus won't thrive. What it likes is damp, humid, crowded conditions where dead material is brushing up against live. Not surprisingly, this is a disease mainly of the winter greenhouse. Should you insulate your greenhouse with bubble plastic and seal up the vents, and then pack too many plants in, forgetting to remove dead leaves and flowers, you are sending out an invitation card to *Botrytis cinerea*. Spores will grow on dead material and then spread to live. Ventilate the greenhouse well, give plants air and space, remove dead tissue promptly and you will not see it. The best method of control is to cut away and dispose of infected material and pay close attention to good housekeeping.

Mealy bugs

Spotting these small sap-feeding insects early is really important, because when their populations spiral out of control they infest a wide range of plants and are difficult to eradicate. Look out for white waxy powder and filaments covering groups of grey-white or pink, flattish insects young and old. Cacti, succulents, grapevines, bougainvillea and hoyas are some of their favourite hosts. Each female will lay five batches of 100–150 eggs protected by the woolly wax. In high summer temperatures they'll hatch within a few days into crawling nymphs which disperse and then settle. Some mealy bug species infiltrate the root systems of plants, where they are even more difficult to see and control.

The first steps are to mechanically remove as many mealy bugs as possible by pruning out infected wood and then use a soft soap or fatty acid spray to break up the wool. When temperatures reach an average of 15°C/60°F, introduce the predatory Australian ladybird *Cryptolaemus montrouzieri*. The fluffy larvae of this ladybird look frighteningly like giant mealy bugs, but both ladybird and larvae eat the mealy bugs. Another control is available in the form of a tiny predatory mite called *Hypoaspis*.

For root mealy bug, drench the compost or plunge in an insecticide solution (soft soap will do) and repeat after seven to ten days. Stand infested plants on their own saucers so that the mealy bugs cannot escape through the drainage hole to the staging.

Powdery mildew

There are a number of fungal powdery mildews but I have never found them particularly worrying under glass. If you grow cucumbers and melons, you will see white, powdery fungal growths on the leaf surface but this usually happens late in the season when light and temperatures are dropping, and the plants are old, have cropped well and are losing their vigour. Accept such growths as a fact of life, harvest the last few fruit, take away the debris and move on. Plants such as begonias are sometimes affected by mildew and this is usually because they are growing too close together or have been left dry for too long. It is these sorts of stresses that exacerbate the disease.

Grapevines are notorious powdery mildew sufferers, but again, control is all to do with good cultivation and keeping plants from stress. Stop, prune and thin the vines correctly to keep air flowing around their leaves and the grapes in their bunches. Install louvre vents for extra air movement.

Rust

Under glass, rust on pelargoniums and fuchsias is the most common. On pelargoniums, rust makes the leaves look a little poorly and yellow. On turning them over, you see small horseshoe-shaped patterns of dark brown rust spores. On fuchsias, patches of pale orange or deep yellow pustules develop on the lower leaf surfaces, with corresponding yellow marks on the upper surface. Chrysanthemum white rust is a fairly recent disease in Britain. Watch out for pale creamy raised pustules on the lower leaf surface, while the upper is marked with yellow pits.

Remove infected leaves promptly and destroy them, because rust overwinters on foliage either on or off the plant. Spray the plants with a fungicide, but check to make sure that it is one that is safe for use on fuchsias, as they are sensitive to many chemicals. Rusts are encouraged by moist, overcrowded growing conditions, so remember the rule of 'grow five well instead of ten badly' and give each plant more space. Water in the mornings of bright days and ventilate as much as possible. Some outdoor weeds harbour rust, so keep all weeds, especially willowherbs, under control.

Scale insects

For me, scale insects rank with mealy bugs as the worst greenhouse pests. The main culprit under glass is soft scale *Coccus hesperidum*, a flattish, oval, grey-green creature 3–5mm/1–2in long. Younger scales are paler and often yellow. Look out for them on citrus, bay and camellias along stems and under leaves on midribs and veins. All scale insects are female and the adults lay egg masses under the scales before dying. These hatch into 'crawlers' which disperse before settling down to feed.

The parasitic wasp *Metaphycus* attacks, eats and lays eggs in the young stages of soft scale, but needs high temperatures at which to operate successfully. There's also a beetle (*Chilocorus nigritus*), which needs 22°C/72°F to work. More recently, a nematode has been available. Using it is a bit fiddly, but it works. First, you must spray affected plants with soft soap solution or something similar, to reduce the stickiness of honeydew. Then spray on the nematodes, which swim

LEFT Powdery mildew affects cucumber leaves late in the season
RIGHT Soft scale settle down to feed on a citrus stem

in the moisture and penetrate the scales. For the nematodes to work, temperatures must be above 14°C/58°F and the leaves must stay moist for twelve hours, so stand the whole plant in a bin liner for the duration of the treatment. The nematodes are supplied to give three doses at twenty-one-day intervals.

Sciarid fly

Although not serious glasshouse pests, sciarids – also known as fungus flies or fungus gnats – are annoying. Small, dark, midge-like flies hover and almost seem to jump over the compost surface where the females will lay 100–300 eggs during a week. These hatch into tiny, almost see-through maggots which eat rotting compost and algae. They like warm, moist, peat-based composts. Where infestations become well established, sciarids will sometimes attack living plant material and seedlings are a prime target, though sometimes the same warm, moist conditions that encouraged the sciarids have caused a plant to go rotten and the flies are simply eating dead matter.

The best control is to alter conditions so that compost surfaces are not quite so warm and wet. Try top dressing plants with grit so that the females can't lay their eggs. Cover seeds with vermiculite instead of compost. Introduce predatory *Hypoaspis* mites to feed on the maggots. Grow carnivorous butterworts (*Pinguicula grandiflora*) and hang yellow sticky cards among infested plants to trap flies. There's also a nematode, *Steinernema feltiae*, which kills the larvae.

LEFT Snails and slugs frequently creep into the greenhouse to cause havoc
RIGHT Spider mite are tiny, but you can learn to recognize the symptoms

Slugs and snails

The odd snail might work its way into the greenhouse, but snails are easy to find and destroy. Slugs, on the other hand, are devious and come out at night to gnaw at your plants, hiding away by day. Their favourite nook in which they lurk is under the crock of a nearby clay pot. Should seedlings or a favourite plant suddenly sprout holes in the leaves or flower buds, you can be sure that a slug will be close by. Look for a silvery, slimy trail if you need evidence. Try looking under adjacent pots and trays. Or return after dark with a torch. If you don't find the slugs, at least move the plant, because the slug or slugs will return every night to carry on feasting.

The best control is to hand-pick the slugs and destroy them. I gave up using slug pellets a long time ago, as I like to keep the number of poisonous substances on my premises to a minimum. Birds and toads occasionally visit the greenhouse and these possibly pick up a few slugs.

Some gardeners are adamant that woodlice cause damage to plants and seedlings, despite the fact that their mouthparts are tiny. Damage is more likely to have been caused by a slug, although woodlice often look like the culprit when they move in afterwards to eat rotten tissue.

Spider mite

Glasshouse red spider mite (*Tetranychus urticae*) can spread like wildfire through a collection of plants, especially if the air is hot and dry. Hard to see with the naked eye, the mites move and feed on the undersides of leaves and are buff-coloured with two dots, one on each side of the body. Look for a mottled upper leaf surface and a scorched appearance. Infestations cause webbing when advanced, but should never be allowed to reach this stage. The mites take fourteen days to reach adulthood at 21°C/70°F and females lay over a hundred eggs each over a three-week period. As temperatures drop in autumn, the mites turn deep red and hide away in crevices on the greenhouse structure to hibernate.

Raising humidity during hot spells helps ward off red spider mite and a good scrub down in autumn helps too. While there are still relatively few mites around and temperatures are averaging 16°C/61°F and sometimes hitting 20°C/68°F, introduce the predatory mite *Phytoseiulus persimilis*. This slightly larger mite runs faster and eats spider mite. *Phytoseiulus* lays 50–60 eggs in three weeks and egg to adult takes twelve days at 20°C/68°F and less when temperatures are higher. I've found them to be a really efficient control.

Thrips

Sometimes known as thunderflies, these are tiny, slender, usually yellowish grey sap-sucking insects. Nymphs are wingless, but the darker adults can fly. A female will lay sixty eggs during the summer and larval stages last about ten to fourteen days, after which the larva drops to the ground and pupates below the surface, where it takes four to seven days to turn into an adult. In my experience, infestations of thrips are quite unusual and they are not such widespread pests as whitefly and red spider mite. When handling your plants, look for silvery mottled or flecked leaves and then scrutinize both the upper- and undersides of the leaves using a magnifying glass or hand lens. Western flower thrips can make a mess of flower petals on plants such as streptocarpus and spread viruses from one plant to another.

Biological control is available in the form of the small predatory mite *Amblyseius cucumeris*. This long-lived mite lays several eggs a day and both at young stages and as an adult eats thrips and young spider mites. It works best under humid conditions, so plenty of damping down and misting during hot dry spells will help.

Vine weevil

The adult vine weevil (*Otiorhynchus sulcatus*) is a small, dark, flightless beetle some 1cm/½in long with angled, elbow-shaped antennae. Chewed notches out of leaf edges are a good indication that vine weevil are about. But it is the pale, C-shaped grubs with dark heads that give gardeners nightmares. A plant suddenly collapses and on investigation you find that its roots have been eaten by a community of grubs feeding unseen inside the pot. All adults are females and nocturnal. They lay eggs near the base of the plant and can be found in warm greenhouses at virtually any time of the year. Vine weevil are particularly prevalent where many of one kind of plant are grown – for instance, in collections of fuchsias or primulas. The more eclectic your taste, the less likely your plants are to suffer.

Fortunately, there is efficient biological control in the shape of nematodes. These are tiny microscopic eelworms supplied in a carrier medium, which you mix with water and apply to the pots in a drench. There they swim through the compost seeking out vine weevil grubs and entering their bodies. The nematodes carry a bacterium in their gut which when released into the grub kills it and turns it into a mush in which the nematodes breed. As with all pests, there are also effecient pesticides available to control vine weevil.

Virus

Many plants can suffer from a virus and not be noticeably affected. Their health, growth rate and vigour might be reduced, but unless you were given a virus-free equivalent to observe, you would be none the wiser. However, some symptoms of a virus include distortion and markings. These include rust-coloured streaks, yellow mottling, flecks or ring spots. Flowers might be distorted or develop streaks of other colours. Avoiding virus infections is difficult, as they can be transmitted by sap-sucking insects or even on tools.

There is no cure for a virus, so control consists of recognizing the symptoms and getting rid of the infected plant before the virus can spread to others. Most viruses are specific to a particular type of plant, so in a mixed collection you should not suffer too many losses. To put things in perspective: over a long period of maybe ten

LEFT The larvae of vine weevil eat roots inside pots
RIGHT Whitefly are partial to all kinds of plants, including pelargoniums

years, I can remember disposing of only two *Clivia miniata* plants because they were showing distortion and rust-coloured streaking along their leaves. These were the only noticeable signs of virus on my plant collection.

Whitefly

Glasshouse whitefly (*Trialeurodes vaporariorum*) is an irritating sap-sucking pest. Small white flies about 3mm/1in long rise in clouds from your plants and on inspection you find that the undersides of the leaves are full of flies and young stages. Susceptible plants include aubergines, cucumbers, tomatoes, peppers, fuchsias and pelargoniums. Eggs hatch into the scale-like juveniles, which go through several stages before hatching out as adults. When temperatures reach 20°C/68°F, the egg to adult span is thirty days.

Growing French or African marigolds (*Tagetes*) among susceptible plants will ward off whitefly only if you have never experienced them. I kept them out of my greenhouse for years this way until one year I lapsed and whitefly took hold. Fortunately there is a really effective biological control in the shape of *Encarsia formosa*. This tiny wasp arrives in parasitized whitefly scales, which as a result are black. Adult wasps hatch from the scales and each female lays sixty eggs into young scales during her ten-to-fourteen-day life. Encarsia needs good light and warm temperatures, but it doesn't work well when whitefly numbers are high, so early in the year reduce numbers by using yellow sticky cards to trap them and horticultural soft soap on infected plants.

SEASONAL REMINDERS

SPRING

The following reminders are really just hints to start projects off at roughly the right time. Timings will depend on how much heat is available and the severity of the climate.

Dazzling sunshine one day may have you reaching for the shading, but the next few days could be cloudy and plants will need all the light they can get. Temperatures may be high by day, but could plunge below freezing at night. In the midst of this crazy weather, the greenhouse gardener is busy taking cuttings, sowing seeds and pricking out seedlings. You'll need all the staging space you can get; you may need to move temporary staging in to fill both sides, fix shelves or devise extra surfaces such as large

EARLY

· Take down insulation to increase light.
· Start sowing greenhouse crops like tomatoes, peppers, aubergines, capsicums and melons.
· Sow bedding plants like begonias and antirrhinums first, as they take the longest to grow.
· Start sowing ornamental greenhouse annuals like salpiglossis and schizanthus.
· Start taking basal cuttings of herbaceous perennials for the garden.
· Take softwood cuttings of sprouting pelargoniums and fuchsias.
· Pot up new lily bulbs to flower in pots.
· Take cuttings of dahlias and spray chrysanthemums.

MID

· Carry on sowing greenhouse crops.
· Continue with sowing and pricking out bedding plants.
· Sow seeds of short-lived greenhouse annuals and perennials, for example celosia and eustoma, including climbers such as cup and saucer vine (Cobaea scandens) and purple bell vine (Rhodochiton atrosanguineus).
· Sow herbs.
· Sow French beans and sweetcorn.
· Sow marrows, courgettes, outdoor cucumbers and pumpkins.
· Sow Savoy cabbage and kales.
· Greenhouse may need shading if the sun is strong.
· Start achimenes and sinningias into growth.
· Pot on permanent ornamental plants making new growth and citrus.
· Give cacti and succulents a good soak to wake them up after winter's rest.

LATE

· Continue to sow and prick out seedlings.
· Sow fast-growing bedding plants like tithonias and marigolds.
· Plant cucumbers into growing bags or border.
· Sow broccoli and winter cauliflower.
· Sow biennials and perennials.
· Prune Jasminum polyanthum after flowering.
· Continue potting on established permanent plants when they are growing strongly.
· Begin hardening off earlier-sown bedding plants ready to plant outside.
· Order biological controls as temperatures rise high enough for them to work effectively.

SUMMER

crates on the floor to use when the staging has overflowed. The biggest change comes at the end of the season when plants heading for the garden can be hardened off. I usually have a good clean-up first, washing down dirty glass, brushing the staging and sweeping the floor. This is also the time to work on other glass areas such as porches.

The weather is usually more reliable now and in most areas there should be no danger of frost. Gradually harden off and plant out all the bedding plants, biennials and outdoor crops. When they have gone, give full attention to permanent greenhouse plants and arrange these on the staging.

- Water pineapple bulbs (*Eucomis*) and Calla lilies (*Zantedeschia*) to start these into growth.
- Sow Brussels sprouts.
- Prune back over-wintering tender perennials such as heliotrope, fuchsias and pelargoniums.
- Sow basil
- Start into growth tubers of achimenes, begonia and sinningia.
- Prune bougainvillea, passion flowers and other summer-flowering climbers and shrubs as they start into growth.

- Sow *Primula malacoides*.
- Pot on cacti and succulents showing positive growth.
- Make a second sowing of runner beans.
- Plant out marrows, courgettes and pumpkins.

- Prune acacias after flowering.
- Buy new spray chrysanths as rooted cuttings.
- Lift, divide and pot canna rhizomes to force them quickly into growth.
- Take softwood cuttings of a wide range of plants.
- Set up growing bags and plant out tomatoes. Plant these and other crops into greenhouse borders or pot on into larger pots.
- Stand spring-flowering bulbs outside as they finish flowering.
- Sow parsley, thyme, sage and lavender.
- Water cacti and succulents.
- Sow cucumbers.

- Make a second sowing of French beans.
- Sow pericallis (*Cineraria*) and calceolaria cultivars to flower next spring.
- Root strawberry runners to grow in pots. They'll be brought under glass in winter.
- Take cuttings of Regal pelargoniums.
- Take semi-hardwood cuttings of a wide range of plants.
- Start cyclamen into growth.
- Take cuttings of herbs.

- Sow quick-growing bedding plants like rudbeckia and cleome.
- Make a second sowing of sweet corn.
- Sow runner beans.
- Sow ipomoeas.

- Sow hardy lettuce to grow through winter.
- Take cuttings of tender perennials from the garden to overwinter as young plants.
- Dry off hippeastrum bulbs.
- Pot prepared hyacinth bulbs to force for Christmas.
- Start *Lachenalia* and *Veltheimia* bulbs into growth for winter flowering.
- Bring potted camellias, hellibores and pulmonarias into a cold or frost-free greenhouse.

SEASONAL REMINDERS	AUTUMN	WINTER
	As summer crops come to an end, enjoy a massive tidy-up and wash the glass down both inside and out. This will remove any shading paint and dirt to let more light in. Space cleared inside will gradually fill up with tender plants needing to move under glass for the winter.	Although this is the quiet season for the greenhouse, you must pay attention to ventilation, cleaning off dead leaves and flowers and adjusting the heater. Carrying out small but important tasks like removing dead leaves and watering carefully in the mornings is a real pleasure on bright, sunny days. With careful planning and artful arrangements, the interior should still be attractive.
EARLY	· Make successional sowings of winter hardy lettuce for spring harvests. · Begin potting up and moving in tender plants to keep through winter.	· Bring potted strawberries under glass. · Prune vines once their leaves have dropped. · Bring camellias into a cold greenhouse.
MID	· Check the greenhouse heater to make sure it is working. · Plant winter lettuce into borders or re-used growing bags. · Bring in spray chrysanths as the weather worsens outdoors. · Pot up spring bulbs.	· Order rooted cuttings of pelargoniums and fuchsias. · Start hippeastrum bulbs into growth. · Bring under glass dwarf pot-grown peaches and nectarines.
LATE	· Fix insulation to the inside of the glass, if you are expecting low winter. temperatures. · Order seeds.	· Last reminder to order seeds, garlic and shallots. · Start dahlias into growth inside propagating case. · Sow tomatoes and melons if the greenhouse is warm enough. · Sow onions and leeks. · Sow sweet peas. · Pot up shallots and garlic. · Pot dahlia tubers to provide shoots for cuttings.

INDEX

Page numbers in *italic* refer to captions to the illustrations. Page numbers in **bold** type refer to plant species featured in the descriptive panels.